Preaching
for
the
Church

Preaching
for
the
Church

by Richard R. Caemmerer

PROFESSOR OF HOMILETICS
CONCORDIA THEOLOGICAL SEMINARY
SAINT LOUIS, MISSOURI

CONCORDIA PUBLISHING HOUSE - SAINT LOUIS

The Library of Congress has catalogued this book as follows:

Caemmerer, Richard Rudolph, 1904—
 Preaching for the church. Saint Louis, Concordia Pub.
House ₁1959₁
   353 p. 16 x 23 cm.
   Includes bibliography.

  1. Preaching.   ɪ. Title.

BV4211.2.C2   251   58-13260 ‡

Library of Congress

To
Dorothy

TABLE OF CONTENTS

FOREWORD

This book attempts to relate the many facets of Christian preaching, its preparation and delivery, to a covering theological principle, namely, that *preaching is God's Word in Christ to people.* This principle is in the forefront of contemporary Christian thought because of fresh interest in Biblical studies, concern for the theology of the church, and new insight into the meaning of the Word of God. It has these components:

1. *God has redeemed men through Christ to be His own and puts the Word of Christ on the lips of people to give men life and faith.*

The pulpit is not the only means by which preaching reaches people. But it is a respectable and useful one, attached usually to the fellowship of the Christian Church in worship.

2. *The Scriptures set forth God's plan in Christ and hence are the primary source and shape of this message.*

The ample Scripture references in this book are intended to describe not merely its teaching but the process by which the preacher makes use of it.

3. *The people who have come to faith in God through Christ are His church and need to receive and to give His Word for their life.*

This book is entitled *Preaching for the Church*, to suggest that the preacher, from and on behalf of the church, conveys the Word of God not merely to its own members but also to its world.

4. *Every stage of preparation for preaching, as well as preaching itself, requires that the preacher be equally concerned for the Word from God and for the people to whom the Word must come.*

This axiom leads to the discussion of many practical details in the construction of sermons and their delivery and in the management of the preacher's time and calling. They are not to lose their connection with the theological principle at the heart of preaching.

This book is not a documented survey of homiletics and carries no footnotes. The author is grateful to every Christian preacher and teacher whose work he has read. But unless otherwise stated, the theology and the process outlined herein are his own, hammered out through twenty years of teaching and thirty of preaching. *For Further Reading,* after the body of the book, suggests literature not for corroboration of the text but for the reader's continued study.

The book is laid out in small chapters grouped in sections in order to restate its basic presuppositions and in order to suggest special areas of concentration and study to the reader or to conferences that wish to use it.

Countless people have contributed to the thought of this book — lay parishioners, brother pastors, theological professors, speech teachers, students. A lasting debt is acknowledged to our late colleagues John H. C. Fritz, Frederick Mayer, and William Arndt. Among students a series of graduate fellows and teaching assistants were most helpful: Paul Harms, Edward Wessling, William Backus, Milton Rudnick, Harold Scheibert, and David Schuller, the latter now a colleague in the division of preaching; our co-workers Alex W. C. Guebert, George Hoyer, Arthur Vincent, John Pfitzer, have been stimulating likewise. Notable have been contacts and discussions at many preaching workshops in various parts of the country, at the meetings of the Association of Seminary Professors in the Practical Fields, and the lectures at the Luther Academy of Wartburg Seminary, the Passavant Lectures of Chicago Lutheran Seminary, and the Gullixson Lectures in Luther Seminary. The tough and frank demand of the seminary classes through the years and the combined indulgence and candor of my family stand out in memory.

In the preparation of this book the Literature Board of The Lutheran Church — Missouri Synod has been most helpful, particularly its chairmen, the Rev. Alfred Doerffler and the Rev. William H. Eifert. Dr. O. A. Dorn, manager of Concordia Publishing House, has been gracious through the years, Prof. Elmer Foelber and his staff in the Editorial Department have labored most efficiently, and the services of Miss Lillian Brune and her staff in planning layout and of Mr. J. H. John of the Editorial Department, who prepared the indexes, are appreciated. Miss Rosemary Lipka rendered service and encouragement as a secretary in the initial stages. Utterly essential for completing this book was the sabbatical quarter granted by my Seminary and Synod.

RICHARD R. CAEMMERER

Concordia Theological Seminary
St. Louis, Mo.

SECTION ONE

Preaching and God

Preaching proclaims a message. The message is from God. God wants to tell men about the life which He has for them as a gift. As men are born into the world they do not have this life. Preaching tells of God's gift of life, which He gives to men through His Son Jesus Christ, who died on the Cross and rose again that men might live.

Preaching does more than tell of this gift of life. It gives it. Through preaching God tells of His life to the world, but more: through preaching God gives Himself to the world.

Hence the preacher is God's tool to restore God's life in people. Preaching utters words. Yet when it is truly preaching, it is the Word of God to man and the power of God at work in man.

The preacher speaks God's own Word to man: "I have redeemed you, you are Mine."

Chapter One

THE PREACHING OF THE CROSS

Through the years the word *preach* has become a bit worn. "Don't preach to me" — that usually means: "Don't use that holier-than-thou attitude toward me, don't carp at my conduct." Or, "His trouble is that he preaches too much" — that may mean: "He talks with a great deal of pressure, and he doesn't make it interesting."

Yet the word "preach" should have a noble and vital ring to it. Particularly the man whom people call "the preacher" ought to be very clear in his own mind about what he is doing. For he brings a message from God. "It pleased God by the foolishness of preaching to save them that believe" (1 Cor. 1:21). These words of St. Paul suggest that preaching is God's own act of rescuing men from death. It is God's saving Word to men.

This means preaching of a very special kind. St. Paul went on to make clear what kind he meant: "We preach Christ Crucified" (1 Cor. 1:23). "I determined not to know anything among you save Jesus Christ, and Him crucified." (1 Cor. 2:2)

3

The Meaning of Preaching

The term *preaching* has worn out so badly, for the most part, because it has been made to refer to pious talk in general rather than to God's great message in particular. Look at some of the words which the Authorized Version translates "preaching." They help to sharpen the focus.

"To tell good news" is the meaning of *euangelizomai*. St. Paul uses it in 1 Corinthians 15 when he says:

> Moreover, brethren, I declare unto you the Gospel which I preached unto you, which also ye have received, and wherein ye stand; by which also ye are saved, if ye keep in memory what I preached unto you, unless ye have believed in vain. For I delivered unto you first of all that which I also received — how that Christ died for our sins according to the Scriptures, and that He was buried, and that He rose again the third day according to the Scriptures. (Vv. 1-4)

St. Luke uses the same word in a saying of Jesus: "I must preach the kingdom of God to other cities also, for therefor am I sent." (4:43)

Another word translated "preach" is *katangello*. This is quite like the previous term with the addition of the idea of "thoroughly, emphatically." It is used of the preaching of the apostles in Jerusalem — the preaching that put them in prison! (Acts 4:2) St. Paul uses it of his own preaching of Christ, "warning every man and teaching every man in all wisdom, that we may present every man perfect in Christ Jesus." (Col. 1:28)

Another word translated "preach" and used very frequently in the New Testament is *kerysso*, "proclaim as a herald." The message itself is then called the *kerygma*, a proclamation. That word is sometimes translated "preaching" (Matt. 12:41; 1 Cor. 1:21). In Matt. 9:35 Jesus is described as teaching in the synagog, "and preaching the Gospel of the Kingdom." In Rom. 10:8 St. Paul speaks of "the Word of faith, which we preach":

> that if thou shalt confess with thy mouth the Lord Jesus, and shalt believe in thine heart that God hath raised Him from the dead, thou shalt be saved. (V. 9)

This term stresses the fact that the preacher proclaims a stirring and vital message as he represents God Himself to the people.

Other words, too, are translated in the Authorized Version as "preach," but these are sufficient to stress the purpose, the energy, and the content of preaching.

The Content of Preaching

Look how the New Testament sets forth the content of preaching. In the words quoted above from 1 Cor. 15:1-4 St. Paul gives a quick summary of it. Preaching tells the story of Jesus Christ, namely, that He died for our sins as the Scriptures had foretold and that He rose from the dead according to that same predicted plan. This is another way of saying that Jesus is the Messiah and Redeemer planned by God for the release of His people and foretold in words of God through many centuries. That story is not for entertainment or simply for matching prophecy and fulfillment; its purpose is to help people "stand" and "be saved." That standing is not merely a steadfastness in belief and under adversity, but it is a standing upright, under the very judgment of God, as a forgiven sinner. And the salvation denotes that full and final release, a release from every enemy and malady, into which God's people shall enter on His Day.

A similar summary of the content of preaching in the New Testament sense is given by Jesus Himself in words spoken on the evening of His resurrection:

> Thus it is written, and thus it behooved Christ to suffer and to rise from the dead the third day; and that repentance and remission of sins should be preached in His name among all nations, beginning at Jerusalem. And ye are witnesses of these things (Luke 24:46, 47; the word for "preach" is *kerysso*).

Evidently St. Paul had this saying of Jesus in mind when he wrote 1 Cor. 15:1-4; and certainly St. Peter did as he addressed Cornelius and his company in the words of Acts 10:34-43. Jesus' words are a mandate to His disciples for all time, and they are the answer to the perennial question of the preacher: "What must I say in order to preach the Gospel?" Note the list of ingredients:

1. Jesus of Nazareth, born in Bethlehem, a teacher in Galilee and Judea, crucified in Jerusalem, is the Messiah planned by God to redeem His people.

2. According to that same plan, announced in the Old Testament Scriptures, He rose from the dead and thus still lives and rules.

3. The story of His life, death, and resurrection is a message which His followers proclaim to their world and to each other.

4. This message has turning and changing power, bringing the thrust of God's own life to bear on those who hear it.

5. It has this power because it conveys the forgiveness of sins, which is the purpose of Christ's death and resurrection.

Two other ingredients were explicit in the message already in the days of the apostles: this Christ is at once the man Jesus and the Son of the living God; and He will return in glory to reign forever.

The Foolishness of Preaching

Since the good news of Jesus' death and resurrection has such superhuman and eternal power and purpose, men should preach it with force, persuasiveness, and the impress of God's own seriousness and design. God Himself is at work in preaching. Is it, then, necessary to train preachers or to write books about preaching?

Preachers face an obstacle in their work, and God and His people stand by to help preachers face and overcome it. This obstacle is that the Gospel seems foolish and useless to many hearers. St. Paul analyzes the difficulty in the opening chapter of 1 Corinthians. To the Jewish mind, steeped in law and presuming to stand approved before God through behavior, the preaching of the Cross of Christ and the remission of sins seemed immoral. To the Greeks, who exalted the power of the human mind, the message seemed irrational. Both types of people found it hard to understand how God would plan to carry out His purpose through such a message, "the foolishness of preaching." Even Christians felt that the plan of God needed some sort of human reinforcement in the shape of human skill and eloquence.

These attitudes of hearers mirror themselves in the preacher, in a sense of insufficiency. How can mere words spoken by a human being carry out the plans of the eternal God? How can a weak human being, and one convinced of his own shortcomings and sinfulness, speak the words of the holy God? When Moses was commissioned to be God's servant to Israel, he felt his insufficiency keenly (Ex. 3:11). In his vision of the glory of God, Isaiah's first reaction was: "Woe is me, for I am undone; because I am a man of unclean lips, and I dwell in the midst of a people of unclean lips." (Is. 6:5)

The Power of God

The answer to these misgivings lies in God's plan itself, and every way by which preachers can be alerted to their place in His plan is therefore essential and helpful for their task. The preaching of Jesus Christ is in God's own plan for saving people. Suppose preaching is foolishness — "God hath chosen the foolish things of the world to confound the wise" (1 Cor. 1:27). Suppose we are weak and sinful and yet have the call placed upon us to be preachers of the Gospel of Jesus Christ —

> Such is the confidence that we have through Christ toward God, not that we are sufficient of ourselves to claim anything as coming from us; our sufficiency is from God, who has qualified us to be ministers of a new covenant, not in a written code but in the Spirit; for the written code kills, but the Spirit gives life. (2 Cor. 3:4-6, RSV)

Jeremiah protested God's call: "Behold, I cannot speak, for I am a child." But God said: "Thou shalt go to all that I shall send thee, and whatsoever I command thee thou shalt speak" (Jer. 1:6, 7). This is the preacher's power: God uses him in His high business, and He gives him His own Word to speak.

> God was in Christ, reconciling the world unto Himself, not imputing their trespasses unto them; and hath committed unto us the Word of reconciliation. Now, then, we are ambassadors for Christ, as though God did beseech you by us; we pray you in Christ's stead, be ye reconciled to God. (2 Cor. 5:19, 20)

Many things and many people stand by the preacher to help him in his ministry of preaching. But they will succeed in helping him and be God's own agents for that help as they continually

1) bring the preacher under the mandate of God to speak the Word of reconciliation to people;

2) shape him to be a speaker who gets himself and every human artifice out of the way of the Word of God in Christ;

3) refresh his insight into God's plan and message in Christ;

4) quicken him with God's own concern for the human beings who are to be rescued and, when rescued, to be built up in Christ;

5) lead him back to God for refreshment for his task through the Spirit of God, so that he thus finds the renewed will to invest himself wholly in God's business.

FOR FURTHER THOUGHT

Which of these analogies for the preacher of the Gospel seem appropriate:

The preacher is the sower sowing the seed of the Word of God.

In the atonement, God makes bare His holy arm (Isaiah 52). The preacher is God's finger tip where the Gospel of God's atonement makes contact with the human heart.

God saves men by His Word. The preacher is the Word of God.

Which of these statements is most adequate: Preaching is like a window that should cause people to say:

1. "Look, the window is cracked and dirty."

2. "Look, the window is made of stained glass."

3. "See what is going on outside."

What should people see through the window of preaching?

For further reading see pp. 297, 298.

Chapter Two

THE CALLING OF THE PREACHER

The preacher speaks the Word of the Cross. Another way of summarizing his task is to define it as a calling. This gives us the opportunity, at the outset of this book, to relate Christian preaching to the task of the Christian pastor.

When we move the pastorate into the perspective of preaching, we are apt to use the term "call" in several ways. Do we mean the same thing as the "call" that a congregation issues to its pastor when it is a church with a congregational polity? Shouldn't a pastor have an "inner call" to preach, like Isaiah hearing the voice of the Lord, "Whom shall I send, and who will go for us?" (Is. 6:6) What of the "calling" which every Christian has, whether he be a farmer or housekeeper or pastor?

To begin with, the "inner call" is hazardous. For we are looking for the true sense of mission within the preacher and the refreshment for his daily task. That task depends not on his feelings but on God. God summons not feelings only, but a life.

God Calls His People

Let us begin with the "calling" which the preacher has in common with every other Christian. It is a three-ply structure: God's call to be His own; the situation in which the Christian can launch that same call of God out to others; and the business of so calling others.

God calls His own when the Word comes to them that God has redeemed them from sin through Jesus Christ and made them His own (cf. Eph. 1:4 and 4:1). That great Word of God in Christ rings down within God's man, perhaps already in infancy, when he is baptized (Titus 3:4-6). That call keeps on coming to the Christian throughout life in the pages of the Sacred Scriptures and in the messages which carry out their purpose (2 Tim. 3:14-17). In every strain incurred by sin, in every fatigue induced by the weakness of the flesh and the fight of faith, that call keeps on sounding:

> Ho, everyone that thirsteth, come ye to the waters, and he that hath no money; come ye, buy, and eat; yea, come, buy wine and milk without money and without price. (Is. 55:1)

If the preacher is going to be a helper of God in speaking His Word, he must be hearing that call of God's Spirit to his own heart daily.

God's People Sound His Call

God calls His people, however, not simply to play the role of target. The call works changes: "God hath not called us unto uncleanness but unto holiness" (1 Thess. 4:7), being set apart for His service. His called ones are to be rifles launching His call into other human hearts. In the New Testament the word "calling" does not denote "job" or "vocation" in general, but it denotes the business of being a caller in particular. The believing wife is to remain at her calling so that her husband be sanctified by her, and this implies that she sound the call of the Gospel (1 Cor. 7:14; cf. 1 Cor. 6:11). Christians in the church are to walk worthy of their calling by doing the work of the ministry — to edify the body of Christ by speaking the truth to one another (Eph. 4:1, 12-16). God's people are called out that they might show forth the praiseworthy acts of God to their world (1 Peter 2:9). The Christian preacher shares with his brothers in Christ the calling, as a called man, to call men into the life of God in Christ.

Another word for this activity is *witness*. Above we noted Jesus' mandate to His disciples to preach His death and resurrection for the repentance and remission of sins of people throughout the world (Luke 24:44-48). A witness is a person who has himself been present in an event and who communicates the meaning of that event to other people.

We like to assert that Christians witness first of all by their behavior, and that is right. The whole man in all of his life and dealing with people displays the results which the presence of God has produced in him (Matt. 5:16; 1 Peter 2:12). Without the behavior, words of life may sound abstract or hypocritical. Yet behavior, however different or startling, or noble, is only a beginning. The witness must help the next man understand why he behaves as he does and why he so earnestly desires others to possess his power (cf. Phil. 2:14-16; 1 Peter 3:15). This means that he also talks, that he speaks of the redeeming action of God in Jesus Christ, by which he has hope in God and concern for his fellow man.

But this implies that the preacher, like every Christian, must sense the pressure and urgency of this speaking. He feels the great hand of the Lord Christ between his shoulder blades thrusting him out into the world to draw men to God and to keep them close to God (John 17:13-23). When he feels that pressure weakening, he knows that it will build up again as he hears the call in Christ anew. For Christian witness doesn't mumble to itself in a sodden way, "I suppose I ought to talk"; but it responds to the inner life which God Himself begins and preserves: "We cannot but speak the things which we have seen and heard." (Acts 3:1-4, 21)

The Calling of the Pastor

Most of the preaching discussed in this book is the business of the pastor of a congregation. In most Protestant communions he has a "call" from a group of people, directly or through the administration of the church, to minister the Word of God to them. The pastor recognizes that call as a process in which God is at work to place him in a calling of special service to people. What's special about it? Isn't he merely getting paid for what every Christian is supposed to do as a church person alongside his bread-winning occupation?

If we should grant this — that the pastorate is simply doing full time and for pay what other Christians do alongside other vocations — we would still be talking about a significant thing. For the pastor must be led to the decision that in the economy of God and with abilities and training at his disposal he is actually more useful for the program of bringing the Gospel to people as a full-time pastor and preacher than as a lay witness. This decision is difficult. God shapes it only in rare instances through visions or catastrophes. It takes intense soul searching to discover whether the would-be preacher is seeking escape from duties close at hand. God shapes the decision through the agency of much counsel and guidance of others; through genuine special endowments of speech and mind to be used as gifts of the Spirit; through trials and testings exploring the fitness for the task and the will for service to people; and through opportunities and direction from many sources.

However, there is more to the calling of the pastorate than that it is being a full-time Christian witness. The pastor is a gift of Christ to His church, a helper of the people, to train and equip them to carry out their calling to one another and to the world — the calling of speaking the truth, that is, God's redeeming plan fulfilled in Christ (Eph. 4:7-16). God's people are members of one body, the body of Christ, and the preacher is member with them — a servant to help all the rest be members to one another. To be a preacher is part of being such a helper of the people. "What we preach is not ourselves but Jesus Christ as Lord, with ourselves as your servants for Jesus' sake." (2 Cor. 4:5, RSV)

The Abilities of the Preacher-Pastor

This place of the preacher as member and helper of the Christian church implies that he must possess abilities above and beyond those of the consecrated lay witness. These abilities cluster about two foci. The one involves his guiding fellow Christians in the congregation. The New Testament terms this guidance oversight (*episkopeo*, Acts 20:28; 1 Peter 5:2), or rule (*proistemi*, 1 Tim. 5:17; or *hegeomai*, Heb. 13:7, 17), or governments (*kyberneseis*, 1 Cor. 12:28). These terms do not suggest the process of exerting personal authority, but they describe the function of the shepherd going ahead of the flock to give it the best pasture or of the helmsman of a sailing vessel directing its course so that the wind strikes the sails at best advantage. Preaching the Gospel is the means for guiding and moving Christians into their tasks of service to one another and to their world.

The other focus of the pastor's work relates even more directly to preaching. He should be "apt to teach" (1 Tim. 3:2; 2 Tim. 2:24). In the New Testament "teaching" is quite generally linked with preaching as one concept, just as "pastor and teacher" mean the same person (Eph. 4:11). For the pastor carries out his function toward his people not simply by affirming and proclaiming but by grooving the message of the Gospel, by applying it to life and superintending its yield. To that end he elicits and answers questions, makes restatements, examines for results, and guides into activities which utilize the power imparted by the Gospel. The pastor preaches the Gospel in all his teaching activities — preparing people for church membership, conducting group activities, evangelizing individuals. And in all his preaching he teaches. The parish sermon provides very few formal teaching devices, and hence it makes special demands on the pastor to achieve, right in the simple monolog from the pulpit, the sense of conversation, to enlist in personal and mutual service, to stimulate and answer questions. All the teaching activities of the parish serve to support the meaning and impact of the preaching, and vice versa.

The specialized and complex task of the pastorate therefore implies that the preacher be carefully trained and constantly refreshed for his work of setting forth the Word of life. Traditionally the pulpit demanded respect and was accorded prestige outstripping the other functions of the pastorate. Such a grading of values is an idle exercise in a ministry where the proclaiming of the Gospel is at the heart of all the pastor's tasks. In the parish sermon, however, the preacher speaks *to* the church as well as *for* the church, and he will therefore welcome it as one of his most precious and challenging opportunities for ministry.

FOR FURTHER THOUGHT

Which of these statements best reflects the understanding of the New Testament concerning the pastor and his people:

1. The pastor is the number-one representative of the people to the community; hence his sermons are first of all public relations.

2. The pastor speaks the witness of the Christian Church to the community; hence his sermons must be exclusively evangelistic.

3. The pastor equips the Christian Church for its mutual service and its witness to the community, by preaching the Gospel to the church.

Are both of these statements true, or is one more correct than the other:

1. The preacher is like a spearhead which the people thrust into their community.

2. The people are a many-pronged spear which the preacher thrusts into the community.

For further reading see pp. 297, 298.

The preacher aims at one goal:
to move people into the direction
which God wants them to go.

Chapter Three

THE GOALS OF PREACHING

If preaching speaks the Word by which God helps His people, then it will always hold three things before the hearer: a plan that God has for him, God's judgment on his progress or failure in meeting the plan, and God's grace in Christ by which he is enabled to fulfill the plan. This chapter proposes to discuss the plans or goals.

Preachers often fear that their hearers may find their message too hard to believe. Actually a more immediate problem is that they find preaching dull, nonessential to life, and aimless. We are concerned in this book chiefly with preaching directed to Christian congregations. Many churchgoers think of the sermon simply as a part of the service. It was good if it interested them; it was poor if they "got nothing out of it" or found it dull. Isn't the great aim of preaching simply to inform people about the Christian religion and the way of life in Jesus Christ? If they already know it, what can you do to keep them interested? Isn't the novelty or the beauty or the dignity of preaching more important than its purpose?

God's Goals for His People

In answer to these handicaps of aimlessness and staleness of preaching let us confront the great aim and purpose of Christian preaching. It is not, strictly speaking, to inform but to empower toward goals and ends. Preaching imparts information and teaching, certainly. But its fact and teaching is a means toward further ends. The Christian preacher should envision his goal carefully and set it forth frankly and plainly to himself and his people. But he should always be sure that it is precisely the goal which God Himself has in mind for them.

Already we have confronted the word which sums up all the goals of preaching. That word is *repentance* (cf. Luke 24:47). "Repent ye!" was the cry of John the Baptist, of the Lord Jesus, and of the apostles, to their hearers (Matt. 3:2; 4:17; Acts 2:38). That means "change, get a new mind!" Repentance signifies the turning of the old man from sin and unbelief to the newness of heart and life which is God's gift. Because of an accident of language "repentance" often signals to us chiefly the mood of sadness and contrition with which we view the state from which we are turning or desire to turn. But the Scriptures mean by that word the turning itself. God wants His people to turn His way.

St. John told his readers that God has two great "commandments" or plans for His people: That they should believe in Christ and that they should love one another (1 John 2:1-3; 3:23). The whole life of the Christian is to be a turning from unbelief or littleness of faith to faith; from hatred or selfishness to love. As men are born into the world, they are bent away from God, dead in terms of the life of God and His Spirit. God's great plan for them is that they be born again and do the works of God (John 3:1-15). Even after the dead person has become alive, the pressures of death and godlessness still surround and infect him, and he needs to keep on turning and growing. "Not as though I . . . were already perfect, but I follow after" (Phil. 3:12).

The Word of God in Christ is the power of God by which this turning begins and continues (Rom. 1:16; 1 Thess. 2:13). It is the seed by which the Holy Spirit gives new life in men, and the milk by which the newborn child of God is nurtured (1 Peter 1:23; 2:2). The preacher handles this Word of power toward its goals; he, too, is not ashamed of it. He uses it to turn men God's way, to reach toward God's goals.

The Goals of Faith

The first great goal that God has for His people is that they believe in Him as their Father who forgives their sins for the sake of Jesus Christ. This means much more than simply to assent to the fact that God is Father or that Jesus has redeemed us. It means to reach out with a living clutch to cling to God as the only Helper. The Psalms glow here with their pictures of God as Rock, Shelter, Refuge, Shade. Jesus' analogy for faith is the life-or-death look with which the people of Israel gazed on the serpent which Moses erected in the wilderness for healing (John 3:14, 15). Just as Jesus did to Nicodemus, so the preacher speaks of the Cross of Christ to the goal that his hearer "believe on Him." St. Paul told Agrippa that Jesus had made him a minister and witness to the Gentiles

> to open their eyes and to turn them from darkness to light and from the power of Satan unto God, that they may receive forgiveness of sins and inheritance among them which are sanctified by faith that is in Me. (Acts 26:16-18)

This goal continues to shape preaching, however, also after the hearer comes to faith. The Christian man lives in the midst of a conspiracy of world, flesh, and devil aiming to rob him of his faith in God and to dim his eyes to the existence of God and His will to help. Preaching to the goals of faith undertakes many objectives, each one of which is ample for the given sermon. Faith holds to the redeeming work of Jesus Christ for the purpose of forgiveness of sins and love of God right now. Faith adores God and worshipfully looks up to Him with humble trust and deep thanksgiving. Faith conquers the shock of uncertainty about God in trial and grief. Faith triumphs over the doubt that the world has about God and rejoices in peace with Him. Faith in God is a gift from God, an intense and living trust and conviction, the upward reach involved in the tremendous new life which God gives in Christ. All of these facets of faith become the goals of preaching as the pastor-preacher leads along the constant pilgrimage from littleness of faith to the strengthened grasp on God.

The Goals of Life

If repentance involves the reach up to God, it also involves the reach out to people — "fruits meet for repentance" (Matt. 3:8). God is in the business of raising fruit in men, their actions revolving about the great core of love (cf. John 15:1-17). St. Paul goes so far as to describe the entire behavior of God's man as love (Rom. 13:8). Love in the Christian sense is not to be confused with the sentiment of comradely affection or the reflex of sexual desire. Rather is it the determination of God's man and the act of his will to give himself for the man in need regardless of his claim on the loving individual. Jesus said that we most directly appear to be God's children through love (Matt. 5:43-48), and St. John echoes that our love for the brother is the mark of our spiritual life (1 John 3:14). Preaching directs to such love and empowers for it. It helps men recognize and carry out the purpose for which God has placed them into the world, in the callings of family, business, and community.

As long as the Christian lives in the world, he is continually oppressed by the forces of godlessness around him and within him. His flesh still wages war against the Spirit-filled nature (Rom. 7:15-25; Gal. 5:17). Preaching aims to aid the Christian man in this battle and to help him day by day be a better servant of God in Christ. He engages in this battle down to his dying moment. This means that he must be helped to endure in faith and life, to grow in patience and in the power to sustain burdens and conquer trials. The preacher aims to strengthen the Christian in this conflict, to keep him steadfast and watchful until the heavenly Father takes him home, and to give him courage and hope, particularly for the hour of death. (Cf. 1 Cor. 15; 1 Thess. 4:13-18; Heb. 12:1 ff.; 1 Peter 5:7-11)

Preaching to God's Goals

In later chapters we shall review psychological principles involved in preaching to goals that are simple, clear, and unified, so that the sermon becomes easier to understand and persuasive. At this point we must stress more than psychology. For the preacher works for God. God is making bare His holy arm. He is speaking His Word to people.

He is summoning them to repentance. He is life and peace to them. He proposes to do this through His servant who speaks for Him. The preacher says words; but they are to be the Word of God.

This means that when the preacher preaches, he must make clear at the outset that his purpose is high and holy, God's very own. He wants to be heard — but for God's purpose. He wants to keep his audience awake and interested — but always as God's tool for God's ends. He wants to give clear and occasionally even startling information — but for purposes higher than to inform. These purposes are God's. They involve the life of faith or the life of action of God's people, and they intend to change them for the better.

Preaching to God's goal implies that the hearers must know what the goal is. God is never concerned merely about the surface, about mere physical comfort or safety, about mere surface conformity to a code. He is concerned for the total man and the wellsprings of life that lie under the surface. Preaching is one of the few operations in the experience of the average person that explores his inner life. He has little practice in confronting it, and perhaps some skill in forgetting about it. Hence we shall attempt to describe some of the skills, important for preaching, of managing words, constructing pictures of the inner life, and gaining the good will of the listener for intruding on the privacy of his inner self. Yet in all of the preacher's promise to the hearer to help and improve him he must keep clear that he is directing the hearer God's way. As the preacher summons the concern of the hearer, it must not be simply for himself but for the will and way of God.

First and last the preacher must face the fact that he not merely describes goals but leads to them; that he not merely describes repentance or summons to repentance but is God's agent for working it. Entire traditions of religious thought and preaching assume that when the preacher has described what God wants and has urged to it, the preacher is through. But then his work has just begun. He must still speak the Word of life. He must still convey the power from God that moves the hearer in God's direction.

The hearer, however, does not listen to the helping Word automatically. If he is going to reach out for God's goals, he must have

God's own Word of help; but he needs God's own help for listening to that Word! Hence preaching involves all three processes: describing God's goals, alerting to God's judgment, speaking God's Gospel.

In the countries behind the Iron Curtain preachers get a food ration lower than that of industrial workers. How would you argue against this policy?

1. Preachers help workers in industry produce better.

2. The nation should be concerned about all facets of human life.

3. Man's inner life is as important as the outer one.

Are the goals latent in 1–3 adequate? Is there another way to approach this problem?

Below we suggest that the preacher write out the goal of a sermon before he prepares and preaches it. What do you think of this goal for a sermon on John 3:16: "I want my hearer to know that he has everlasting life by faith in Jesus, who died for him."

For further reading see pp. 297, 298.

The preacher speaks the Word of God's judgment upon man's sin, to alert men to the Gospel.

Chapter Four

PREACHING GOD'S JUDGMENT

The preacher is in an essential business. He speaks the Word of God. He is the specialist in the relation of God toward men. Grocers meet hunger, physicians meet sickness, policemen meet crime, the undertaker meets death. The preacher meets Death with a capital *D*. He confronts people in whom God is not yet alive or who are in danger of losing the life of God. The preacher speaks the Word of God to their situation. He helps with the help that God has. But he alerts to the need of that help, with a portrayal of that need employing the dimensions of God's own scrutiny and concern.

The Malady of Death

To describe the need of man to which the preacher speaks the Word of God we use language about man's physical existence. The analogy is not perfect. When the body dies, its inner impulses and processes stop and its flesh decays. When the life of God dies in a man, his physical existence may continue for a long time; he can

21

think and feel, he can go about the business of satisfying his hungers
and meeting the demands of life. Yet in God's terms he is dead, for
his inner self, the promptings of his desires, the drives of his ambitions
and moods, are of self rather than of God. This is the burden of the
story of man's first sin (Gen. 2:15-17). Jesus calls such a situation
flesh (John 3:6). The man of "flesh" does not possess the Spirit of
God, the life which God planned to be the equipment of man as contrasted with the animal (Gen. 2:7). St. Paul describes the death without the Spirit:

> And you hath He quickened, who were dead in trespasses and sins,
> wherein in time past ye walked according to the course of this world,
> according to the prince of the power of the air, the spirit that now
> worketh in the children of disobedience; among whom also we all had
> our conversation in times past in the lusts of our flesh, fulfilling the de-
> sires of the flesh and of the mind, and were by nature the children of
> wrath even as others. (Eph. 2:1-3)

The taint and decay of this death lingers on also in the man to
whom the Spirit of God is returning. Above we reviewed the paradox
of the Christian man, simultaneously driven by the dictates of his flesh
and by the Spirit of God.

Another picture used to describe the stoppage of the life of God
in the heart is *darkness.*

> This is the condemnation, that light is come into the world and men
> loved darkness rather than light because their deeds were evil.
> (John 3:19)

The way of darkness is perpetually seeking to mislead even the person
to whom the light has come. The forces latent in the inner being of
man and those in the godless world around him are co-ordinated by
the prince of darkness in an unceasing attack upon him. (Eph. 2:2)

With this darkness of the loss of God from the heart is associated
another picture of man's plight without God, that of blindness.

> Walk not as other Gentiles walk, in the vanity of their mind, having
> the understanding darkened, being alienated from the life of God
> through the ignorance that is in them because of the blindness of their
> heart. (Eph. 4:17, 18)

Man stumbles aimlessly or falteringly on the path that God sets before
him, and he fails to see God and to discern God's life within and

around him and God's purpose for him. The preacher alerts to this plight.

> Some of the Pharisees which were with him heard these words and said unto Him, Are we blind also? Jesus said unto them: If ye were blind, ye should have no sin; but now ye say, We see. Therefore your sin remaineth. (John 9:40, 41)

The Wrath of God

Bodily death is sad. People try to weaken its horror and escape from its threat. Yet death from God — and ultimately physical death is a token of this more dreadful thing — has a horror which is much more profound. "To be dead" means to be under the wrath of God. This word "wrath" denotes much more than human peevishness or anger. It is the revulsion in the heart of God from whatever runs counter to His plan. He made man in His image and for the purpose of reflecting and enacting His own kind of love to the world. God is concerned that His plan and purpose be fulfilled; His concern is "jealous," unceasing, probing (Ex. 20:5; 1 Cor. 10:22). The Old Testament is a case history of the God of the covenant setting people apart for His service (Lev. 19:2), and this covenant relation implies that He judges, ceaselessly scrutinizes the consecration of His people. Their failure incurs His wrath.

God's wrath means His withdrawal. He can have nothing to do with the evil thing. Nor is His wrath altered by human effort to appease or to placate Him. The harrowing words of the prophets sounded the warnings of God's wrath upon His people of old and their enemies alike. History stands before men with its display of God's withdrawal:

> The wrath of God is revealed from heaven against all ungodliness and unrighteousness of men, who hold the truth in unrighteousness. (Rom. 1:18)

The ultimate and everlasting judgment of God upon man's sin is His everlasting withdrawal, the "outer darkness." (Matt. 8:12)

The Word of Judgment

The peculiar horror of the state of man under the wrath of God is that he is unaware of it. He is like a man freezing to death in a snowdrift, imagining himself to be warm and safe under the downy flakes. He argues that if God is Love, as He claims to be, then He must love all people equally; or if He recognizes the good of some people, then He must acknowledge that there is a little good in each of us. The simplest way to maintain this optimism is to read God out of the scheme of things altogether; nor is it necessary to deny His existence in order to be oblivious to His judgment. Second Peter describes people who tell themselves that God did not make the world, so that they can assure themselves that He will not judge them at its end. (3:3-10)

God condemns godlessness. He recoils from sin, the will in man to live without God. Yet simultaneously — and this makes His ways higher than our ways — He seeks to restore Himself to lonely man and to make the unrighteous, the man under the judgment of His condemnation, righteous and approved (cf. Is. 55:7-9). But this means that He must help the self-righteous confront his sin and his condemnation. The human mind can reflect upon God's withdrawal and its own guilt (Rom. 1:18—2:16). And God puts His condemnation into a word that can be spoken, the necessary preface to His Word of forgiveness and self-restoration. (Rom. 2:17—3:20)

This is the Word of the Law, an essential component in the message of the Christian preacher. Scripture and theologians use the term "Law" in various ways. It is the name for the Old Testament Scriptures, particularly the books of Moses (Rom. 3:21b). It is the term for the full thrust of God upon the human heart, the life principle of God (cf. Ps. 19:7; 119:18; 37:31; Jer. 31:33). It is a statement of God's plans for His people, His goals for their lives (Rom. 13:8). At this point we are interested in the term as it is used to describe God's written and preached indictment of sin. The Law from Sinai served that purpose (cf. Gal. 3:10—4:5) and still functions in convincing that sin is under the condemnation of God and is the sign of death. (Rom. 7:5-12)

The Preaching of the Law

The preacher is God's agent for reaching people with His Word. This means that he speaks with God's own concern for man's plight and distance from God. People caught up in sin and tempted to withdraw from God see this distance and respond to God's concern with great difficulty. Hence the preacher preaches God's own indictment and warning. He preaches the Law. This is not to be confused with his outlining of God's plans and goals for his people, discussed in the previous chapter. The preaching of the Law is not simply a defining of good conduct from the negative: God wants us to be good, that is, not to be bad. The preaching of the Law is always God's saying: "You are cutting yourself off from Me, you are experimenting with death; see its signs! You need help!"

To stir the hearer to recognize his plight and be willing to listen to the remedy, the preacher will often begin with the surface symptoms of the underlying malady of withdrawal from God; he will speak of sins as surface marks of sin. Thus St. John seizes upon hatred as a mark of blindness and death (1 John 2:11; 3:15). St. Paul frequently catalogues the evils of the Gentile community as marks of the loss of God and invitations to His wrath:

> For this ye know, that no whoremonger, nor unclean person, nor covetous man, who is an idolater, hath any inheritance in the kingdom of Christ and of God. Let no man deceive you with vain words, for because of these things cometh the wrath of God upon the children of disobedience. (Eph. 5:5, 6)

The hidden deficiency has also other surface signals: the satisfaction with material things, the preoccupation with physical life, and worry (Matt. 6:19-34). The full panorama of human nature is at the disposal of the preacher for this diagnosis.

But let the preacher diagnose! He must remember that human needs and difficulties are not to be used for idle verbiage, or for winsome display of mere human sympathy, or for setting up verbal couches in a program of mass psychiatry. His discussion of human sin and weakness must always have the purpose to alert to the judgment of God. The goal to which he directs is God's own purpose for the hearer. The power that he plans to impart is God's own grace and self-giving in Christ. Hence the damage to which He alerts is ultimately to be defined in terms of the weakening of God's own life in the human heart, and His judgment.

Nor is the preacher's final purpose achieved when people begin to dissolve in sorrow over their sins or anxiety over their grief. Too many listeners are ready to imagine that there is some obscure merit in feeling sad about their own sins. This would be simply a piece of the death from which the preacher wants to rescue (2 Cor. 7:9-12). God Himself works through the preacher shaping the hearts of the hearers to receive "the preaching" — and that comes with the good news.

FOR FURTHER THOUGHT

St. Paul discusses the importance of the Law in Rom. 7:4-25; Gal. 3:1—4:11. How would he judge these statements:

1. The Law has nothing to say to the man who has come to faith.

2. Faith saves a man so that he can carry out the works of the Law.

3. The chief purpose of the Law is to show us how to behave.

4. The Law is our schoolmaster means that it tells us about how perfectly Jesus Christ kept the Law and that therefore we, too, should keep it.

What do you think of the idea of having a Sunday morning sermon preach Law exclusively and the following Sunday preach Gospel exclusively?

What is your judgment of this statement: "Law and Gospel should be distinguished, but not separated, from each other"?

For further reading see pp. 297, 298.

The preacher's Word of Christ is an act of God, rescuing men from sin, for life.

Chapter Five

PREACHING GOD'S RESCUE

The preacher works for God to lead people better to fulfill God's plans for them — that they love Him above all things and one another as themselves. He tells them that when they fall short of those plans, they reveal a tragic deficit in the life of God, from which God Himself must recoil. But he sounds this alert simply that the people might prick up their ears and stand with their hands outstretched,· saying: "Very well, preacher, tell us again how God rescues us." Then the "preaching," the telling of the good news, really begins.

God's Word, God's Work

When the preacher preaches, he says words. Words inform, describe, set up pictures in the mind, rehearse events. Hence the preacher may imagine that his words are nothing more than information, description, reminder — and the people may think so too. But his words are much more.

True, the preacher gives information. But it is information available from no source other than his, and he is enrolled by God in the enterprise of making it known for God's high purpose of rescuing men from sin. Thus St. Paul spoke of his own preaching:

> We speak the wisdom of God in a mystery, even the hidden wisdom which God ordained before the world unto our glory. . . . God hath revealed them unto us by His Spirit. (1 Cor. 2:7, 10)

"Mystery" in his language means not simply something mysterious and hidden. It describes the act of making clear a thing that is dear to the mind of God and crucial to the life of man. The pagan mystery cults sought to bring joy or power to their devotees. St. Paul said that he was disclosing God's plan of life in Christ Jesus. He said that he had become God's agent for bringing God's triumph over death in Jesus Christ into the experience of people. (2 Cor. 2:14-17)

The word which the preacher preaches as God's man in Christ is, like the Word of Christ Himself, an element in the great task which God sent Jesus into the world to do for men.

> Believest thou not that I am in the Father, and the Father in Me? The words that I speak unto you I speak not of Myself, but the Father that dwelleth in Me, He doeth the works. . . . He that believeth on Me, the works that I do shall he do also, and greater works than these shall he do because I go unto My Father. (John 14:10, 12)

When Jesus went to the cross in the act of making peace between God and man, and when He told of it, then God Himself moved into human life and vanquished its death. But that is precisely the work of the Word which Christ's preacher proclaims of His saving act. (John 17:19-23)

Modes of Gospel

When the Christian preacher tells of God's act in Christ redeeming the world, in effect he becomes the extension of God's own mighty arm and brings His power to bear on men. He has a simple task; for the goals he wishes to accomplish in his hearers are attainable through this Word of Christ's redeeming work. Hence St. Paul said:

> I, brethren, when I came to you, came not with excellency of speech or of wisdom, declaring unto you the testimony of God. For I determined not to know anything among you save Jesus Christ, and Him crucified. (1 Cor. 2:1, 2)

That Word might look like flimsy stuff, but it is the one power.

The preaching of the Cross is to them that perish foolishness, but unto us which are saved it is the power of God. (1 Cor. 1:18; cf. vv. 20-25)

The average sincere preacher of Christ is not too disturbed about the fact that the message of the Gospel appears weak to those who reject it. In his own heart and in his ministry to others he has had too many experiences of its power to question it. But he is apt to suffer from a different disease. The steady preaching of the Gospel makes it seem stereotyped. The more familiar he surmises his hearers to be with the Gospel — and most of the worshipers under his parish preaching know it — the more he fears that they will be bored by repetition.

Hence, for his own sake and the people's, the preacher should make use of the rich variety of expression provided by the Scriptures. Jesus and the apostles themselves were Gospel preachers, seeking to put the act of God in Christ into human language applied to the people before them toward goals which they were to attempt. Frequently they drew upon modes of statement already at hand in the Old Testament and thus also opened its resources for the use of today's preacher of the Gospel.

At the same time the preacher must remember, of course, that his word is kept vital and his hearer alert not merely through the variety of his expression. We have reviewed the importance of alerting the hearer to his need, a need toward God; and where that alerting has been successful, the most unadorned Gospel ceases to be commonplace. The Scriptures are remarkable for the close relation which they effect between the modes for setting forth man's predicament and the methods of articulating the Gospel answer. That is a cue for the preacher's art.

Pictures for the Task

Note the varieties which the Scriptures employ to describe the preaching of the Gospel. The preacher swings a censer at the head of the triumphal procession in which a new Lord takes over the government (2 Cor. 2:14 ff.). He is a soldier at work for Christ; he is a sharecropper for God producing faith in Christ as his yield in others and in himself (2 Tim. 2:3-8). He is a shepherd leading and feeding God's own flock (Acts 20:28). He is an ambassador representing his own Potentate by sounding the proclamation of His peace (2 Cor.

5:18-21). All of these pictures suggest not simply the preacher's task but the meaning of the message itself.

This message is the Gospel, and the very word focuses upon the proclamation of God's saving act in the death and resurrection of Jesus. It is a power of God unto salvation (Rom. 1:16), a seed by which the spiritual and inner life is conceived in the heart, and milk for the nurture of the newborn (1 Peter 1:23; 2:2), the seed by which the Kingdom comes to men and brings forth its fruit there (Luke 8:11 ff.). These figures jump into life as the preacher remembers how they apply to the very moment in which he is causing people to think about Jesus as their Lord and Savior.

Complexes of the Gospel

Even more remarkable are the points of view or "complexes" under which the Scriptures set forth the atonement. They can be described in various ways. Each is actually a cluster of pictures setting forth in human language the plan of God for man's life in Christ.

Life for Death. — Basic to man's need is that he is split off from God, that he is not alive with the presence of God and His Spirit. The good news tells how God gave His own Son that we might have everlasting life (John 3:16). Jesus describes Himself going "to the Father" in a transaction visible to human eyes, on the cross, that He might be our Way to the Father (John 14:1-7) and that He might be able to restore the Spirit to us (John 16:7). Jesus' death and rising is God's way of destroying our sin and death and sharing His life anew with us, namely, by drawing us into His death and new life (Rom. 6:1-11). Mankind lay in enmity toward God, but in Jesus Christ God reconciled the world to Himself and now through preachers sounds forth the Word of reconciliation. (2 Cor. 5:18-21)

Parallel to the problem of death is the problem of darkness. The good news says that Jesus Christ is the Light of the world and has conquered the prince of darkness. (John 3:19-21; 12:46; 2 Tim. 1:10)

Covering for Sin. — Man's predicament is that he is in sin; he prefers to be without God, in effect to be a rebel against God, to make himself and His own impulses the motive for living rather than God. Sin evokes the wrath of God. The good news says that God Himself covers man's sin, shields it, so that He does not hold it against him, and He does not turn away from him and leave him lonely but forgives him. This picture stood daily before God's people of the Old Covenant in the sin offering and annually in the Day of Atonement. "He hath made Him to be sin for us who knew no sin, that we might be made the righteousness of God in Him" (2 Cor. 5:21). Our sins separate us from God and doom us to eternal death, but Christ is a covering and "means of mercy" for our sins (Rom. 3:25; 1 John 2:1; expressions like "expiation" and "appeasement" are misleading). This great act of Jesus is called the redemption. God Himself, as it were, pays a price, the price of His own dearest and best, so that He might forgive our sins and return to us with the Word of His grace in the blood of Jesus. (Rom. 3:19-26)

The Judgment of Mercy. — The good news traverses the same ground in another complex of expression highlighting the contrast of Law and Gospel and the concept of God's judgment. God ceaselessly scrutinizes man and condemns his sin and rebellion. He publishes His judgment in the Law. But in the same outreach of God to men in which He judges their sin He seeks also to effect a "judgment" by which man is released from the burden and bondage of condemnation, vindicated against his enemies, and enabled to stand "upright" and just under the judgment of God. The term "judgment" in the Old Testament contains this concept of rescue very frequently (Ps. 103:6; Is. 49:4; Amos 5:24). True, that man should imagine his own behavior to be the source of God's benign judgment only redoubles the condemnation (Luke 18:9-14); for his righteousness before the face of God is wholly in God's mercy. The good news proclaims that mercy and thus becomes the means of arousing and preserving the confidence and faith which "justifies," that is, renders man righteous and accepted by the mercy of God. For it is the proclamation of One who undertook our condemnation and incurred our guilt. (Rom. 4:15-25; Gal. 4:4-7)

The complexes of the Gospel give the preacher the cue for his task, namely, as spokesman for God to reach into the malady of man under God and hold its misery up for man's conviction, to bring the thrust of God's own act in Christ to bear upon it, and thus fit his hearer for the goals of God, the goals of faith and love.

FOR FURTHER THOUGHT

Comment on this judgment of a contemporary British preacher:
The complexes of the Gospel in the Old and the New Testament are
ways of expressing God's help for man in terms appropriate to the
imagination of their age. Contemporary man cannot conceive of someone else working out his relation to God for him. Therefore the
preacher today must reshape the Biblical complexes to work out
a message by which modern man undertakes his own life under God
and Jesus becomes an exemplar.

Is this the preaching of the good news: "Jesus died for us on the
cross and rose again. That gives us life, provided that we believe in it.
All that we have to do is, on our part, to bring the offering of ourselves in faith"?

For further reading see pp. 297, 298.

*For a list of modes depicting the atonement, see Appendix III,
p. 330.*

SECTION TWO

Preaching and People

The preacher speaks for God. God has reached him with His Word that he might speak it to people. God wants to reach the people, and the preacher is God's tool for reaching them.

The power of the Word of God is bigger than the preacher. He cannot add to it, nor should he try.

But it is the preacher's business to get the Word to the hearer, to bring him to attention and keep him attentive so that he hears it.

It is the preacher's business to help the hearer understand what he is saying, recognize that it applies to him, and discover that it means power for his own faith and life. This means that the preacher must know both the Word and the people.

The preacher speaks so that men change and move into the direction that God wills and works.

Chapter Six

PERSUASION

Christian preaching is the Word of God. God is talking. But God is talking to people. His Word is His work. What is He trying to do to them?

As churches get old or fat, their sermons are liable to become formal, or chatty, or entertaining merely. People sit under them to while away the hour with a sense of religious merit. They are apt to complain if the sermon challenges them strenuously. This attitude is not in keeping with God's plan that His Word be "quick and powerful and sharper than any two-edged sword." (Heb. 4:12)

Since preaching employs human language and directs itself to human nature, it shares the properties of all good public address. Already the ancients discussed the art of influencing a person to action and called it persuasion. That is the psychological counterpart of what in theological terms we have been calling preaching to repentance — working a change in the hearer. Persuasive speech isn't just for entertainment. It makes a difference in people.

35

To a Goal

Persuasion works a change. To what? Like every persuasive speaker the preacher will do well first to write out the goal and purpose of his address. Sometimes he may find himself writing: "I want my hearer to understand . . ." or "I want my hearer to realize better than before the truth of the statement that. . . ." Notice that then he has not been thinking of a goal at all. He has committed the old and easy fumble of confusing goal and means.

We have already reviewed the goals of preaching (Chapter 3). As the preacher preaches, his purpose must be actually to move his hearers in the direction which God intends for them — better faith or better life. Each hearer is at a different stage of progress. The sermon is to move each hearer farther along on that path.

Persuasion is the "art of getting the hearer to think the one thing that you want him to think." As long as other thoughts and objectives compete in his mind for attention and interest, he won't move. As long as the speaker causes him to divide and dilute his attention, he has no desire to act. Hence every sermon should have one goal. The moment that the preacher tries to lead the hearer to more than one, he weakens the pressure toward any of them and dissipates persuasiveness. An ancient form of a sermon, termed a homily, expounded a text from Scripture and then derived a number of "lessons" or applications to the hearer from it. The art of the preacher was sometimes measured by the number of "lessons" he drew. This may have been apt for an audience concerned chiefly with information or composed of people less beset by persuasive demands than those of our time.

Let the preacher envision his goal clearly and make it one. This may be difficult for the preacher, but it makes it helpful for the people.

From a Malady

As the preacher moves his hearer along the path of spiritual progress toward a goal of conviction or behavior, he is at the same time helping to release him from a difficulty and deficiency, a malady.

Good preaching concerns itself with the basic needs and maladies of human beings. But the preacher's concern is not simply to explore these maladies or even to reveal his sympathy. For preaching concerns the deficit of the life and presence of God in the human heart. It speaks the Word of God to the end that this malady be remedied and the hearer changed in God's direction. Hence the first step in persuasive preaching is to help the hearer realize that it concerns a matter of life and death — his life or death. Until the hearer confronts this fact, he will listen idly, if at all, or at best only for the purpose of gaining some new information.

The preacher must avoid merely harping on people's troubles or causing them to brood over their miseries. For then a large number of them will stop listening altogether, for they have learned to escape from discomfort. Others will presume that what makes preaching good is simply its discomfort — God must be pleased when people put on the hair shirt of reflection upon their own shortcomings! A third segment will imagine that the purpose of the hour is to help people overcome a number of physical pains and weaknesses and to provide psychiatric assistance for the price of a freewill offering.

If the preacher purposes to define the maladies of his people in a way that in keeping with his calling is persuasive, he must confront them with a gap between themselves and God. Whatever the sin and weakness is by which he alerts them to themselves and to his message, it will have to be, in their minds, clearly a symptom of their missing the mark of God and of losing their grasp on the life of His presence.

Through the Word of the Cross

The preacher seeks to move his hearer to the point that he says: "You are right. I need the help of God Himself to repair my life and move it His way." When the preacher has done this, he is ready for the last great act of persuasion, the applying of the thrust of God Himself that will help the hearer to change. Here comes the thing that sets the preacher's task apart from every other type of persuasion. For now he speaks the message which actually produces the change, moves the hearer out from the clutch of his deficiency, thrusts him back into the field of God's own power again. That is the message of the Cross. We reviewed it in Chapter 5.

The preacher is liable to flinch. He is thinking of his people. If he has any pastoral experience at all, he knows their mood, their spirit, their strengths and weaknesses. He understands how the pull of their inner hungers and the tugs of the culture around them compete with whatever he will say. Should he forget how they think and operate with a message which he knows in advance is not wholly acceptable?

Yes, he has to brace himself to move his hearers with but one lever resting on one fulcrum — the power of the Spirit employing the fact and reminder of the redeeming work of Jesus Christ. He may have had to warn with St. Paul against the "rudiments of this world" and the lure of alien motivations for behavior (cp. Col. 2:20 or Gal. 4:9), for he wants action, not any kind of action at any price or for any cause but only that action which God Himself produces. He is not a practical psychologist making friends and influencing people. With St. Paul he has to forswear the artifices of the humanistic practitioner. (1 Cor. 2:1)

But this does not mean that he should bungle his task of putting the message before the people in the most persuasive way. The entire process of the sermon becomes a single unit to that end. He has to define the goal and plan that God has for His people and set it before his hearers as one that they can actually reach out for and begin to achieve with the help of God that is theirs to use. He has to define the deficiencies of his hearers, always making clear to them that he is not simply harrowing them with anxiety but yearning to help them with God's own answer for their needs. Hence when that help comes, it should confront a persuasive set that is already built. As the preacher speaks to fellow Christians, he is speaking to people who have in part already put the power of the Cross to the test. To all, Christian or not, he speaks as a man who has been trying out these wonderful guarantees of God and has found them to hold good. He is not a ranter or a medicine man covering up the fakery of his own craft with bluster. But he is a witness to Jesus Christ, who is his Lord.

This means that the Christian preacher is in the most exact sense a persuader. The proofs of his discourse, Aristotle would say, "depend upon the moral character of the speaker . . . putting the hearer into a certain frame of mind . . . the speech itself." Hence the preacher need "not be ashamed of the Gospel of Jesus Christ." But he can exert himself to the best of his innate and acquired ability to speak it persuasively.

For the Hearer's Sake

The preacher who works for God also works for the hearer. He is a craftsman — not for the purpose of having people admire his craft, or to be amazed by his craft, or to be rebuffed by his craft, but always to be changed by it into the directions of God, from unbelief to faith, from little faith to greater faith, from little love to greater love.

This does not imply that the preacher is there to make hard things easy; to make the judgment of God sweetish and palatable; to make the Gospel of God popular and sentimental. But he is there to help his hearers do the hard thing of confronting their weakness and shame before God and confessing it; of attempting the unusual and unaccustomed thing of envisioning the invisible God and facing Him as He seeks to reconcile us to Himself in Jesus Christ; of seeking to overcome the apathy and selfishness of their natural selves and attempting "greater works than these."

The preacher has the Spirit of God as His employer and ally in this task. The pastor-preacher has the resources of the Christian Church and its fellowship and the power of the sacraments to work with, and he takes account of them in his work. Nevertheless the best craftsmanship of insight into the message of God, the heart of people, and the management of persuasive language is none too good for playing his role as preacher of Christ. Of all places in the world the Christian pulpit has the least room for a babbler or windjammer. For there every second is precious, every word freighted with the destiny of human lives under God, every sentence a step in the design of God toward getting people to see the way to God through Jesus Christ.

"If I had a fulcrum, I could move the world," said Archimedes. The idea was good, but he didn't have the fulcrum. "I plead as an ambassador for Christ," says the preacher. His boast is not idle. For he is not boasting, but serving; and the Gospel of God is the power in his heart and on his speech.

FOR FURTHER THOUGHT

Good communication takes feedback; the hearer should signal his response to the speaker. Somebody has said that it would be fine if people in the pew could lift their ears or wave their hands or otherwise signal the moment at which they say: "Yes, I see that I need the Gospel; preach it to me." What can the preacher count on instead of such signals to tell when to preach the Gospel?

An address with many goals is like the charge of a shotgun; a persuasive address with one goal is like the shot of a rifle. But isn't the mind of the hearer darting around into many peripheral ideas while the preacher is talking, no matter how unified his goal is?

Shouldn't every sermon have the goal to lead the hearer to heaven?

For further reading see p. 298.

The preacher speaks so that people want to pay attention, not just to him but to God.

Chapter Seven

APPROACH

The preacher speaks words. He plans and prays that they be the Word of God. But words are no good to hearers unless they listen to them. For when they pay no attention, they actually do not hear.

Many a preacher — hearers, too, for that matter — will say: "That can't be true about sermons, about the Word of God. God's Word is always powerful. Just to speak it means that it will do its work." The result is that this preacher will concentrate on making his sermon true and correct, loud and distinct, but not necessarily interesting. These hearers will concentrate on being present, orderly and decorous, but not necessarily attentive.

Even Jesus knew how useless it was to say words, even His own wise and strong words, to "ears that hear not." In His parable of the sower He described the obstacles in the human heart for the Word of God, which do their damage at the time of hearing or thereafter (Luke 8:11 ff.). The preacher is indeed unable to add to the power of the Word of God, and it remains the one means of changing the heart in God's directions. But he is in the business of removing obstacles to its hearing. His constant concern must be to find the approach to the hearer and the ways by which he opens his ears and listens. The Word of God does things in the human heart that no other word can do. But it reaches it through the same channels of hearing and attention that any other word must use.

Hard Work

Especially in our age of easy communication the lanes of traffic to the heart are crowded. Like all public speakers the preacher is tempted to look for some simple means by which he can promptly gain the attention of his hearers and clear the track for the persuasive message. He hears them converse in haphazard and meager language and assumes that if he uses choice and fragrant words, they will prick up their ears — or perhaps they will if he outdoes them in slang. He lives with them in a world of routine and monotonous sense impressions; so he assumes that if he can shock them for only a moment with ideas that are unexpected, or if he can tweak their curiosity, or if he can jar them with unusual voice and manner, they will shrug off their apathy and pay attention.

Such assumptions are not wholly justified. The preacher has wonderful things to say, and therefore his language and manner must bear the impress of their wonder. But it has to be language which the people can understand and which they want to understand. When St. Paul observed that worshipers in his own day sometimes spoke ecstatically and others could not understand them, he said that he himself would rather speak five words consciously aimed at the understanding of his fellow worshipers than ten thousand in ecstasy. (1 Cor. 14:19, Goodspeed)

Likewise the method via shock or curiosity is, at bottom, poor approach. If the hearer listens to be shocked, he will stop when the shock is over. If he listens to have his curiosity satisfied or a puzzle solved, he no longer wants to listen when the answer is in. Good approach has to be made of sterner stuff. It has to aim for the long pull.

To the Group

The preacher's task is doubly difficult because he addresses more than one person at a time. The New Testament uses the word "preaching" also of address to individuals; but in this book we are discussing the preaching to groups. No two people in any group are alike. When preaching the Gospel to one person at a time, the preacher can sense his readiness or direct his counsel to the individual need. The pastor-preacher senses that he can reach a hearer often more effectively with his Gospel in the give-and-take of individual conversation than in a group.

Nevertheless, just that is the preacher's business — to reach men in groups. Sometimes the group situation has more exhilaration in it for the preacher than does the individual conversation. Let the preacher not be intoxicated by the magic of numbers, but let him look to the tools of his craft. He still has to make his approach to individuals; otherwise he simply loses people's attention by groups! He has to find and utilize the approaches that are common to them all; otherwise he leaves some untouched. The poor sower sows a spotty field.

A Total Job

At first glimpse it seems to be a dismaying task to render a whole group of people receptive to the message of the invisible God about a Savior who long ago died and rose again to remedy inner needs which they do not care to confront. Particularly for the pastor-preacher, however, the task is easier because he approaches people over a total front.

When people look at a preacher, they interpret his language and pay attention to him because of everything that they know about him. This should make the pastor's preaching especially helpful. He meets people in many areas of life. He comforts the sick and dying, counsels families, helps the needy and doubting, enjoys himself with people at play, buys in the shops of his community, votes at its polls. We shall review this more closely in the closing section below. When people know a preacher, they are looking at his message through a lens ground to their fit by their entire acquaintance with him.

Aristotle's first proof of persuasion was that the hearer find the speaker trustworthy. Our Lord said it even more bluntly: "Ye are witnesses of these things" (Luke 24:48). That means that a preacher is not discussing things that are true in general, or interesting, or entertaining; but he is speaking the repentance and remission of sins laid up in the Scriptures and achieved for men by the suffering and dying and rising again of Jesus, which he himself has found to be coming true in his own life. The preacher is God's loud-speaker, and he speaks the Word of God. But he says it the way a harp makes music: its own being throbs and vibrates with the sound plucked on its own strings by another hand. Witness is a matter of the total life and the entire person of the preacher. Hence approach to the hearer goes on long before the sermon in the pulpit begins, and it continues long after the service is over.

Promise of Freedom

St. Mark tells us that the common people heard Jesus gladly (12:37). Evidently Jesus had achieved a good approach. St. Matthew gives the reason: "He taught them as one having authority and not as the scribes" (7:29). At first sight that looks like a description of a man speaking with a great show of firmness and strong demand for assent. But the scribes did that, too, and quoted the Scriptures and claimed to speak the will of God. The word "authority" here means literally "the power to set men free" — to release from an alien bondage and to bring under a new and higher control.

There is the secret of effective approach. If the preacher can help people realize that his message is a tool for releasing them from the bonds that shackle them to death, then he is speaking with authority. If he can reinforce his message with the spectacle of a man who is himself in the process of throwing off that bondage of sin and fear and entering into "the glorious liberty of the sons of God" (Rom. 8:21), then he is doing his part to make them listen.

Many little things in the preacher's art help to open and keep open the approach to the hearer. They show in his language and appearance and manner and workmanship. But the preacher who wants to reach people for the sake of his calling and to convey the life of God to them in Christ must talk like a man who is called and who is alive and who appears to be frankly anxious to set men free through the victory which Jesus Christ Himself has won for him and them.

Words that preachers use about men's bondage under sin and their liberation through Christ are apt to sound mysterious, even when the hearers are ready to admit that such a bondage and freedom exist. First and last, therefore, the hearer must know that the preacher is talking about him. He has to show him the signs of his bondage which he can tell are really there, his own fears, apathy toward God, lovelessness toward people, irresponsibility toward duty, surrender to flesh and world.

In conversing with the individual the preacher can stop, and silence will underscore the self-searching in the listener. In preaching to the group the preacher must keep talking long enough to bring the sluggish up and must stop in time to keep the agile from wool gathering. The bridge between these two extremes is the preacher's manifest earnestness, his note of pity and concern, that makes it inescapably clear to the hearer: "The preacher cares; it's important. God cares; it's important. It's important to me!" Only so will meaning dawn in the heart of the sluggish and stay alive in the restless.

Even the most experienced preacher will often wish that he could leave the biggest things to the imagination of his hearer. "Can't I presuppose that they know and are thinking about the great standard facts of their sin and God's grace? Won't I simply dull their hearing by saying them over again?" Let the preacher read his own mind with care. He may be saying: "I'm not up to bringing these standard truths home to the people. I'm tired, and so I'll presuppose that they are tired." Let him say them. But let him say them so that they will listen! Let him ceaselessly explore the human resources for hearing and pondering the Word of God. How grateful people and preacher can be that the mighty God is fatherly enough to speak in their language and to employ their mechanisms of learning.

But why shouldn't He? He made them. Let the preacher as a workman for God have enough respect for them to learn to use them.

"A sermon that isn't interesting might just as well not be preached."
How would you respond to these objections, leveled against this
quotation from a great teacher of preaching:

1. He belittles the power of the Word of God.

2. An interesting sermon that does not speak the Word of God is
useless too.

3. The preacher's business is to speak the Word; the hearer's
business is to pay attention.

The doctrine that man co-operates with God in the process of his
own conversion to faith is termed synergism. Isn't it synergistic to
assert that the hearer's attention is an essential part in the process
of receiving the Word of God?

For further reading see pp. 298, 299.

The preacher speaks so that the Word of God will achieve its full meaning for the hearer.

Chapter Eight

MEANING

The preacher uses words. Preaching accomplishes its purpose in people through words. Yet people can be satisfied with less than the full purpose of those words. They may be present because of the pressure of custom or for the sake of enjoying a vague religious mood. The preacher must be sure, therefore, that he is actually using words as tools in the intention of God. He must help his hearers not simply to listen to the sound of his voice but to get the sense of his words and the meaning of his message.

Preaching Must Make Sense

When the preacher speaks his words, they have to make sense. The hearer has to understand the words for the purpose that the preacher speaks them. His words will do that only if the hearer expects them to do so. When people expect preaching to be over their heads, impersonal, doctrinaire, impractical, they won't quite listen. Part of the preaching process, therefore, involves getting the hearer to look for sense and to expect to understand. The preceding chapter surveyed it.

This is so important because the people do not automatically understand the preacher's words in the same way that he does. His message is the end of a long period of preparation, the result of his own battery of skills and mechanisms of handling language, the product of his own insights into theology and human beings. Any group of hearers, even of professionally trained preachers, is composed of individuals with varying insights into Bible or people, manifold mechanisms of thought and speech. We often observe, while conversing with individuals, how words which we thought expressed our idea precisely meant to them not at all what we intended or perhaps nothing. That situation triples in difficulty when we talk to three people.

The Spoken Style

A further complication is the fact that the preacher is more than a writer. He is talking out loud. This has its advantages, of course; for his face and body and hands can reinforce his speech, and he can interpret his words with the inflections of his voice. But the hearer can't stop, turn back, reread a previous portion, look up a word in the dictionary, mull over a hard or weighty saying, quietly relish the mood and impact of a passage; nor can he skim more rapidly if the going is easy. He has to stay with the speaker. Or to put it more exactly: the speaker has to keep the hearer with him, and keep hearers with him who have different capacities for understanding and pressure of interest.

The first great requisite of the spoken style, therefore, is that the preacher takes nothing for granted, that he patiently defines his terms, illustrates his concepts, sets up simple and tangible analogies from daily life to clarify them. Next he must carefully whittle away at his body of fact so that he doesn't offer the hearer too much at a time and yet enough that he doesn't sound plodding or repetitious. Third, he must summarize periodically, help the hearer see where he is, keep the over-all and central purpose of the discourse before him. All of this makes for a style which, in print, actually may look simple and sometimes naive by comparison with the literary.

Preaching Must Make Meaning

But preaching must do more than make sense. Again we say: the goal of preaching is always more than to inform, to relay fact. That preaching convey clear ideas and sound fact is important, but only as means to a further end. That end is meaning. Note the difference between sense and meaning. Sense is the shape of a fact. Meaning is the shaping of the hearer. Sense asks: "Do you understand this fact?" Meaning asks: "Is this fact doing to you what it is supposed to do?" Sense informs the hearer. Meaning strikes him.

The facts of Christian preaching are gleaned from the Bible, a panorama of God's sounding His own will and grace into human hearts so that they changed and change. But preaching is more than reaffirming words from the Bible. Schoolboys declaim the speeches of Patrick Henry or Daniel Webster and meet the demand of their teacher if they understand the words and speak them with intelligence and spirit. But once upon a time those orations swayed human events and shaped the destiny of a nation. The preacher does not enact the role of the schoolboy but of Henry or Webster. God wants to use the preacher as a rifle through which the projectile of the Spirit sinks deep into the heart of the hearer to kill death and explode into life.

As the preacher preaches, the hearer sees Biblical scenes and people of centuries ago. He understands the preacher's remarks about his community and nation, the countries of the globe, the history of the world. But the preacher makes meaning as the hearer thinks about himself. And the preacher is speaking for God! That means that the hearer will grapple with the presence of God in his own heart. Like Jacob at Peniel, he may come away from the encounter sore and lamed — but also with a new name.

Hearers are apt to start listening to the word of the preacher with a bit of inner resistance, for they know that it will not be just entertainment. Even the preacher may shrink from the task of confronting the meaning of God's Word and then, through it, thrusting sluggish souls into conviction and action. He is like an engineer, building a road through a rocky defile, standing at the plunger of a charge of dynamite, half afraid of the upheaval about to come, half expecting that the charge won't detonate at all. Let the preacher brace himself for his task with cheer. "I am not ashamed of the Gospel of Jesus Christ, for it is the *dynamis Theou.*" (Rom. 1:16)

The Preacher Must Make Meaning

Now remember what all goes into making meaning. "Words, words, words," you say? Right, but words surrounded by a man. A dip of inflection, the lift of an eyebrow, the spatter of a consonant, all make for meaning — because they mark a man to whom his own message "means something."

The preacher's alternative is not to make meaning or be neutral. He is always making meaning in the mind of his hearer when he preaches. But what meaning? Watch the making of meaning as a preacher speaks his words. He can say them frozen in posture and face, with no apparent concern beyond wanting to have it over with. No meaning? Yes, a great deal; the hearer is saying: "This is poor, weak stuff; it means nothing to him; I shall sit this out and go home." Or the preacher can flail with his arms and rant with his voice. Much meaning? Yes, but it is this: "Why does he put on that act? He must not mean it; or he must think that his ideas are too weak to stand on their own." The net result, both times, is a roadblock for the meaning of the message itself; and the Decalog would call it taking the name of the Lord God in vain.

Genuine meaning gets packed into preaching when, word for word and idea for idea, the preacher himself has been the target of the Word that he preaches and speaks it because of its discovered meaning. He can't be noisy with his indictment of the Law of God and his preaching of the judgment; for he himself has stood under it, and he speaks it only that he might bring the rescue which he has found.

> Knowing therefore the terror of the Lord, we persuade men; but we are made manifest unto God, and I trust also are made manifest in your consciences. (2 Cor. 5:11)

He can't play the role of a puppet, listless because of inner anxiety or artificially dripping with unction or quavering with appeal, for his Gospel has meant life to him:

> Whether we be beside ourselves, it is to God, or whether we be sober, it is for your cause. For the love of Christ constraineth us. . . . (2 Cor. 5:13, 14)

That Gospel always quickens him into concern for his people. That concern will show differently in every preacher, in his particular combination of the hundreds of signals that reinforce his word — flashing eye, stabbing finger, pleading tone, cheery cadence, play of expression in voice and face.

The test of all of this is what happens after the sermon. When people go home and say, "What gestures! What wonderful words! What a pleading tone!" then probably very little meaning came through. When they talk about themselves, and what they are going to put to work in themselves because of the sermon, and confront each other with the "for-you-ness" of that message sticking out of them like feathered darts — then some preaching must have been going on.

"Pastor, that was a wonderful sermon," said the parishioner at the door after the service.

"That remains to be seen," said the preacher.

We repeat that the ministry as a whole is a great setting for preaching, since the administration of the parish and the routines of pastoral care and the contacts of group work provide myriads of opportunities for watching, and inquiring after, the meaning.

Preaching is a craft. The preacher is a workman. He grows in the skills of his craft, the craftsmanship of making sense and making meaning. He does so in the name of God. For he is actually a co-worker with God (2 Cor. 6:1), a sharecropper for and with God (2 Tim. 2:6). But if the Father is a husbandman that is glorified only when His people bring forth fruit, then God's sharecropper is ever concerned for fruit too. It is part of the meaning of preaching that this concern shows in the sermon from beginning to end and in all of the pastorate that surrounds it in the career of the pastor-preacher.

> Do your best to present yourself to God as one approved, a workman who has no need to be ashamed, rightly handling the Word of truth. (2 Tim. 2:15, RSV)

The preacher needs competence in understanding human nature and the mechanisms of meaningful speech. Basic, however, still remains his own manifest concern for people, the love which binds him to the members of the church and the will to be their servant.

FOR FURTHER THOUGHT

In the light of this chapter, what is imperfect about this theme and major division of a sermon on 2 Cor. 5:18-21: "Paul, an ambassador for Christ" I. He preached the Gospel of reconciliation; II. He led men to righteousness.

Boyhood speech assignments and early preaching experiences tend to build reflexes of self-consciousness which persist in later years. How can the preacher tell when he is overcoming them and is impressing meaning on his hearers?

Under what circumstances does a gesture add to the sense of the preacher's words? to their meaning for the hearer?

For further reading see pp. 298, 299.

SECTION THREE

Types of Sermons

The preaching of the Cross can reach people in formal or casual situations, when they are alone or in groups. When the message comes to a group, we call it a sermon.

Some sermons are preached in houses of worship to gatherings composed primarily of Christian believers. Others, like radio messages or evangelistic talks, are addressed to those outside the church or to the public in general.

Some preachers make a single section of the Bible basic to the content of their message. Others try to preach the truths of Scripture and the Gospel of the Cross without employing a text. We shall not discuss preaching that has no Biblical content at all.

Chapter Nine

PREACHING IN WORSHIP

Most Christian sermons are part of the services in which Christian congregations worship. For most people a "sermon" is an address which they hear "in church."

When Christians worship together, they should have clear purpose, and so should their preacher. They are there not just to enjoy one another's company or to be instructed and edified by a message. Over all is the purpose to commune with God. They lift their hands to Him in praise and thanks. They bring their petitions to Him for one another and for their world. They listen to God, speaking to them by His Word, and they hope through it to grow in their life with God through His Spirit. They speak that Word of life to one another and thus build up one another as the church of God and body of Christ. Preaching helps to carry out these purposes.

Christians speak God's Word to each other in daily life, in the family, at work. In church the preacher is their spokesman.

55

From the Beginning

The first Christians drew their customs of worship from various sources. Many of them had worshiped in the synagog. There they had joined in prayers and psalms and had heard readings from the historians and the prophets of the Old Testament. When a preacher or teacher was at hand, he exhorted or instructed them on the basis of one of these readings. So our Lord preached at Nazareth on the lesson from Isaiah 61. (Luke 4:16-20)

To this scheme the first Christian churches added readings from the sayings of Jesus in the Gospels and from the letters of the apostles. St. Paul counseled Timothy to continue reading these lessons to his people and to link his exhortations and directions for Christian living to these readings. (1 Tim. 4:13)

Christians early had the practice of breaking out, after one of those readings, into conversation which included comments or explanations, thanksgivings and exhortation (cf. 1 Cor. 14:26). Such a conversation was termed a *homilia.* Soon the leader of the worship began to incorporate what he expected to take place in such a conversation into a message by himself, a one-man *homilia* — and thus was born the science and art of "homiletics." It's useful to remember that preaching represents an act in which all the worshipers join.

Preaching for the Church

Very easily the sermon can deteriorate simply to a message from the preacher to the people, in effect an episode set apart from the portions of the service in which people worship together. But for a Christian congregation the sermon should continue to be a means by which each person holds up to each other person's view the praiseworthy acts of God and thus shares with him the royal priesthood of every Christian present (cf. 1 Peter 2:9). The preacher should be viewed as the agent by which all are conveying God's own forgiveness to one another (2 Cor. 2:10); by which all are affirming their common faith in the redeeming work of Christ and by that word of the redemption are stirring one another to love and all good works (Heb. 10:19-25; note *homologia* in v. 23, a mutual speaking), by which all are teaching and admonishing one another. (Eph. 4:11-16; cp. 5:17-21; Col. 3:12-17)

Many Christians are habituated to speak of only two sacraments. Actually the sermon also conveys the forgiveness of sins to Christians by means of the signs and sounds of the spoken Word and is ordained by our Lord for the purpose (Matt. 18:15-20; John 17:14-23). Just as in the Holy Communion every Christian proclaims the redeeming work of Christ (1 Cor. 11:26), so in the word of his preacher-pastor he himself shares the Word with every other worshiper.

The preacher preaches most of his sermons *to* the church, the assembly of worshiping Christians who are being edified through that word to be more fully the body of Christ. But he is also preaching *for* the Christians who in that very act are communicating the power of God to one another. Whether he speaks to the unbelieving world outside the worshiping group or whether he speaks to worshiping Christians, he is their spokesman and agent as well as the ambassador for Christ, who is the Lord and Head of the church. (Eph. 4:11, 12; Gal. 1:1, 2; 2 Cor. 2:10; 4:5)

The Service of Worship

If the sermon is to be a genuine part of a total act of worship, it must relate in meaning and emphasis with the other elements. If the sermon becomes a public address which interrupts worship, or if it does not share the purpose and theme of the hymns, prayers, readings, and responses that make up the rest of the service, it will deteriorate as an act of worship.

Historically Christians have employed two types of worship. One has been called liturgical because it employs forms handed down from previous generations. These forms include responses, hymns, prayers, and stated lessons from Scripture. To each Sunday or festival are assigned certain units which are appropriate and peculiar to it alone during the year. The entire complex of liturgical worship is called the church year, or the Christian year. Our Lord was accustomed to such standard practices in the synagogs in which He preached.

The other type of worship may be called free, because it grants more latitude to the person who is directing the service for the day. We need not here enter the age-old debate whether traditional or free forms serve the worshiper better. The whole contrast between liturgical and nonliturgical is more apparent than real. The moment that two or more Christians try to worship simultaneously they have to agree as to the form their worship will take; otherwise some will soon suffer from bewilderment or inattention (cf. Eph. 5:21). Both the traditional forms and the nonliturgical routines seek to develop variety within over-all customary patterns. Least of all should we attempt to detect less individual participation by the worshiper in the traditional form than in the free. Whichever form of worship the leaders or the congregation employ, all have to work with a will to make the order of worship a means by which the people themselves are worshiping and not merely the specialists who direct them.

Here it is our business to confront the place that preaching has in a service of worship. Even in congregations employing orders of worship laid down in a service book some minor services of a free pattern will be conducted at least occasionally. Under both the free and the traditional systems preaching has at times become an act aside from worship proper, and many churchgoers tended to find either the sermon or the service more helpful or enjoyable. Sometimes the sermon became merely instruction in doctrine or preparation for worship or the Eucharist. Sometimes the worship became a more or less pleasant prelude or postlude giving opportunity to get the people comfortable or to receive the offering of the day; the real business of the day was when the great man entered the pulpit. Either the forms of worship or the sermon, or both, suffered from this cleavage.

The Sermon in the Service

The preacher will do well to plan a conscious correlation between the sermon and the service of worship which is its setting. Nor should this seem to place an irksome burden upon him in addition to the toil of preparing the message. He should learn to appreciate the relation of the sermon to the rest of the service and to grow in the skill of achieving a harmony among all the components of the service.

The relation of the sermon to the service grows out of the fact that it speaks not only *to* the church but *for* the church. It brings the Word of God to the people, the Word of God's judgment and God's forgiveness in Christ. But it also speaks the response of praise and adoration, of the new life and the works of love, of the worshiping group. In itself the sermon already is that response; it describes the response; it stimulates to the response.

If sermon and service are to be unified, the worshipers must see how all the worship, from beginning to end, sounds this Word of God and this response to the Word of God. Every service of worship speaks the Word and brings the sacrifice of prayer and praise. Beyond that general goal, a given service of worship may have a special goal, either in the domain of enlarging faith and dependence on God and adoration for His mercy or in the domain of growing life, consecration, and love. It is important that the special goal for the service be as simple and unified as possible so that the worshiper can focus on it clearly. This unity of purpose of the given service should embrace the sermon too. If the chief thrust of the sermon falls out of line with the rest of the service, then both the sermon and the service suffer. If they are correlated and unified, each element of worship contributes to the meaning of each other one.

This is not to suggest that every item of worship on a given day and in a given service must say exactly what every other item says. Just as a sermon is compounded of goal for the hearer, diagnosis of his need, and preaching of the Cross to the end that he reach his goal, so the individual elements of worship of the congregation emphasize one or the other of these three concerns, and all work together toward the great objective of the hour of worship. Nor do we imply that the forms of worship for a given day of the Christian year must always signal the same special goal; they may vary through the years. What is of importance is that the people are helped to find meaning in service and sermon with a minimum of fumbling. (See Appendix II)

Whether employing traditional forms or whether constructing a free order of worship, the preacher should have the same concern for unity between service and sermon. He is the servant of the church, helping every person before him to amplify and magnify his own message on to every other one. (Cf. Acts 5:12-14)

FOR FURTHER THOUGHT

How valid do you find these statements:

1. The sermon is the chief moment of the service; everything else can fall away and, in the mind of the average worshiper, does.

2. The sermon is the only place in the service in which the Gospel is really preached.

3. The Christian congregation chooses a pastor who is to be the one preacher of the Gospel in any given service.

4. Since people are readily bored by sermons, other devices must be sought by which they will remain attentive to the Gospel; the Sacrament is such a device.

For further reading see p. 299.
Appendix II is on pp. 328—329.

*The preacher is glad to preach
Christ also outside of services of
worship, yet for the church.*

Chapter Ten

PREACHING OUTSIDE OF WORSHIP

Most parish preaching aims at the members of the congregation. The visitor who is not a Christian hears a sermon which is an act of Christian worship. Protestant groups vary in the attempt of their preachers to direct part of their message to non-Christians present. Many pastors have the opportunity, however, to preach the Christian Gospel specifically to those outside the church by means of radio or through evangelistic enterprises. (See Chapter 28 below)

The New Testament gives ample illustration of preaching apart from the service of the church. In the Book of Acts we see the apostles addressing the Gospel to audiences of unbelievers. St. Paul began his work in a given place, if possible, by speaking in the synagog; but he and his helpers often addressed gatherings which had not come together for worship. (Acts 13:15 ff.; 14:15 ff.; 17:16 ff.)

Preaching to nonmembers of the church has sometimes been termed evangelistic. The designation is inept. It is either cause or result of the assumption that the primary Gospel, or "evangel," should be

61

preached to the goal of converting or reconverting people to Christ, while believing and active Christians need something else. But all preaching should be "the preaching of the Cross."

Watch the Approach!

What is the chief difference between the sermon in the worship of Christians and the one directed to nonmembers?

The goals of preaching are the same — that they should believe on Jesus Christ and love their brother. The malady of sin is the same. True, in the believing Christian it is sin which because of remnants of the flesh continues to attack the life of God in him (cf. Rom. 7:15-25; 1 John 1:8-10). In the man without Christ there are not simply remnants, for he is as yet unchanged by the Spirit. Yet in both the new and the old man sin and flesh are the same. Certainly the Gospel of the redeeming work of Jesus Christ and of God's forgiveness of sin and gift of new life through the Spirit is the same to both. Hence the parish pastor can preach helpfully to a visitor who is not a church member or to the community in a broadcast service while he is addressing his own flock.

Nevertheless when we think of the man outside the church, some special problems become evident. The regular worshiper has acquired a language of religious terms which the man outside the church does not possess, for the former is familiar with the Bible and handbooks of religious instruction and the practices of worship. To the non-Christian much of the Biblical mode of speech, Biblical stories and illustrations, and the terms employed in the church's worship, are unintelligible. This means that they are liable to be not merely blanks as he hears them but irritants. To him standard and central terms of Christian preaching, such as faith, unbelief, life, death, God's wrath, God's grace, love, peace, are likely to mean something quite different from the Biblical intention. The more technical terms, such as righteousness and justification, holiness and sanctification, church, world, flesh, spirit, may be utterly bewildering.

But remember that preaching involves much more than making sense. It must always seek to create the set and will to listen. If the regular churchgoer has not been calloused by formalism or habit, he has a helpful set toward preaching; he is participating in grasping the message for his own good and giving it on to the brother. The man outside the fellowship of the church may have only those impulses for listening which lead him to pay attention to any other message — curiosity about its content or its adherents, the recommendation of trusted individuals who have heard it before, and the promise of help for a felt need.

The pastor who preaches to his congregation has already achieved much rapport with his audience because of the pastoral relation. The preacher who addresses nonmembers must frequently start from the beginning or even combat the suspicion that he is at work simply for personal gain. This situation puts the highest premium on tact, transparent honesty, directness, plainness, sincerity. He cannot for a moment seem to be imitating any other speaker. Whatever reputation for integrity he has developed in the community as a citizen and neighbor will be useful, but he must avoid seeming to exploit it.

Particularly in the area of the hearer's malady and need the preacher has the opportunity to shape his message to non-Christians in a distinctive way. He will be most painstaking in exploring the surface symptoms without becoming maudlin or harrowing. This factor of approach makes evangelistic preaching and particularly radio address difficult, and it makes the common touch and the manifest concern of the preacher essential.

Beware of Pitfalls!

The primary difficulty in preaching the Gospel to those who do not know it — and to those who do, for that matter — is the "offense of the Gospel." As 1 Corinthians 1 makes so very clear, this is not simply its supernatural quality. But it stems from the assumption ingrained in the human heart that the one ground of man's approach to God must be the excellence of his behavior. The human being is incorrigibly self-righteous. Hence the man outside the church may find its basic Gospel of redemption in Christ scandalous. Or he may have heard misconstructions of the Christian religion which reduced it to a mere code of behavior, and he imagines that the preacher of the Gospel is simply repeating them. He may harbor the assurance — he can find plenty of help for it — that the Christian code of morality is better than any other, and he may assume that this respect for "Christianity" is faith. Or he may be holding off from membership in the church because he feels that his behavior is as acceptable to God outside the church as within it.

When the man of such mind hears Christian preaching, he is likely to agree with the preacher wholeheartedly in every prescription for behavior, echo in his heart some version of "all this have I done from my youth," and become completely inattentive when he hears anything other than behavior discussed. Or he may construe every analysis of human frailty and sin as the damage of persons other than himself and may enjoy the preacher's lambasting of others. Or he may regard the familiar recommendations to good behavior as sensible, and the theology of redemption as sectarian and optional. Thus the central message, in all of these reactions, remains unheard and meaningless.

Perhaps the hearer accepts the exhortation to Christian behavior. But since he has been inattentive to the Word of the Gospel, which is its one motivation, he proposes to fulfill the preacher's demand by means of the one motive that he knows, his own self-interest or desire to conform or self-satisfaction in doing right or the counsel of conscience. Thus the entire Christian message becomes vitiated.

Hence all preaching to non-Christians has to be unusually plainspoken and acute in pointing to man's basic malady, namely, the loss of God from his heart, and in leading man to the basic remedy, the redeeming work of Jesus Christ. At Athens St. Paul was resourceful in tapping the interest of a difficult audience; but he was ready to lose it rather than to obscure the message of God's judgment and rescue, which was his one business (Acts 17:16-32). Preaching to non-Christians will employ faith goals to a high proportion and avoid the hazards of seeming to recommend a form of behavior without its power.

The thoughtful preacher will discover that a message to those unfamiliar with the Christian religion must often do without ingredients standard in parish preaching: reading a text from the Authorized Version at the beginning of the address or giving extensive quotations in a language not current; quoting hymns or other sacred literature which may be meaningless; referring to functions or projects of the congregation or its denomination; referring to the history of the church, or its year of worship (except Christmas or Easter). Style, illustration, directness, must concede to the limited experience of the hearer without condescending.

For the Church

Having noted contrasts between preaching to the people of the church and those outside, we may still want to remember a basic unity. Many a parish pastor prepares for special approach to the community beyond the church and then discovers that his own congregation is benefiting hugely from the message so prepared. "We never understood so clearly what Jesus means to us." "We really felt the Bible talking to us tonight." "You were really talking to me tonight." After all, the members of Christian churches are living in the midst of only partially Christian communities. They have to be stirred again and again from preconceptions and apathy about the meaning of the Gospel, which they begin to share with the community. The finest warmth of manner and clarity of technique and explicitness of Gospel that the preacher can muster are not too good for the non-Christians of the community — or for the Christians either.

Furthermore the Christians of the parish are in this outreach to their community, all the way, with their preacher. Their words reinforce his message on the radio or in evangelistic services. Their invitation tips the scale in the will of many a person to come and hear the Gospel. Their joy in prayer and praise puts the heart into the components of worship that are frequently attached to evangelistic services and would be meaningless otherwise. Ultimately, the preaching of their pastor to his community is their preaching. He is their mouthpiece, for he is preaching for the church and sounding the call to become members of the body of Christ.

Hence, while we may distinguish types of preaching by the chief targets, the in-church or out-church groups, it is still one and the same preaching. While we may detect special adaptations of the preacher's approach to either, the warmth of his concern will be the same to both.

Widely held is the theory that in the early church the *kerygma*, or Gospel of Christ, was directed to unbelievers; to the Christian congregation the first preachers directed the *didache* or teaching of Christian behavior. Can you make a concordance study of the New Testament to test this theory?

The congregation plans to broadcast its services on Sunday mornings and is discussing problems of budget and abridgment of the service. What objectives of the program are most important:

1. Refresh the sick and shut-ins.

2. Advertise the church to those who habitually stay at home.

3. Bring unbelievers to faith.

For further reading see pp. 297, 299.

In preaching God's Word for its purpose, the preacher will find a text from the Bible helpful.

Chapter Eleven

PREACHING FROM A TEXT

If a sermon is to be "preaching" in the Christian sense, and to be a part of the great tradition of Christian preaching, it will set forth a message from the Bible. This is a purpose of the Bible, to direct the preaching and teaching of the Holy Christian Church through the ages. (Rom. 15:4; 1 Tim. 4:13; 2 Tim. 3:14-17; 2 Peter 1:19)

The preacher may use various devices for drawing on Scripture and for signaling to his hearers that he is presenting his message on the basis of Scripture. The people should be able to see that he is doing so, but he may use different methods for indicating it. This chapter discusses one method, the use of a preaching text; and the next section will suggest the technique for developing the sermon from the text.

Choosing the Text

A preaching text is a portion of Scripture. It can be a single word or phrase. Normally it is at least a sentence, a subject and predicate which express a complete thought. The most helpful preaching texts are usually paragraphs from Scripture, for the average writer employs a number of related sentences to develop a single thought. Entire units of the Bible, such as psalms or short epistles, may serve as texts. Part of the value of a text is that the congregation hears it and thinks about it during the sermon and thereafter; hence the limitations as to length. An entire Biblical book may become the subject of a sermon, but then the sermon will technically grow not so much out of the book as a whole as out of key thoughts and extracts of the book.

A preaching text serves its purpose if it provides at least one of the three primary components of preaching: the goal for the hearer, the diagnosis of the hearer's malady, a statement of God's redeeming grace, which empowers the hearer toward the goal. Where a text supplies only one of these components, the others can be developed by inference from other statements of Scripture. If a text can supply two or even three of these factors simultaneously, it will be especially useful for suggesting and defining the message.

If the preacher is going to use a text, then it should serve his purpose well. Not any chance extract of Scripture will do. It should speak its message perceptibly, and its applications should not be far-fetched. The preacher himself should become the first target of his text and should pray to "behold wondrous things," which emerge as he ponders the text. But he should not have to resort to strained, fanciful, or bizarre explanations of the text in order to make it practical for his hearers. The Middle Ages developed such artificial "modes of application" — the typical, the allegorical — as led to the preacher's pandering to curiosity or strutting with skills available only to the elite. Such homiletical gamesmanship ill befits the ambassador.

Lutheran churches of Europe and America offer their preachers numerous series of texts related to the lessons from the epistles and gospels prescribed for the day of the church year. These texts, termed pericopes, are useful for the major or "common" service of the Sunday or festival, make unnecessary a protracted search for a text, and help in the effort to keep the service unified (see Chapter 9 above). They meet the preacher with the challenge to explore them before he is tempted to foist a preconceived topic upon them.

Even where the preacher employs pericopic texts for his major service weekly, he will have to choose texts for his minor services and special occasions. Also when he chooses a "free text," it is important — if he is serious about preaching textually — that he does not distort the meaning of the text by the topic which he already has in mind. This demands growing knowledge of the Bible and patience in the search for the best text for its purpose.

Using the Text

Preaching to a text is the simplest way of keeping the Bible the source of the message. But it isn't always simple to stay with the text! The text itself is often a segment of a larger work or section, which needs to be taken into account. The preacher wants to preach Christ; if the text does not speak of the redemption, this is no warrant for the preacher to omit it. Hence the preacher must seek to understand his text and to prepare a message that takes its cue from the text on the basis of his total understanding of Scripture, his "theology." This fact makes the difference between textual and nontextual preaching not as sharp as might at first appear. When a preacher uses a text properly, he is like a teacher of geography standing in a dark room and beaming a pencil of light on a spot on a globe. The student begins to concentrate on the spot, but he knows that the whole globe is there.

The simplest device by which the preacher "stays with the text" is that he first asks: "Why is this in the Bible? What was the original speaker or writer trying to accomplish for his listeners or readers?" Some units of Scripture answer these questions explicitly, and for that reason they are most useful as texts, particularly when the announced purpose of the extract also applies obviously to the people who are going to listen to the sermon. To use a text for the goal for which it was originally written or spoken has been termed the direct method of using a text, and every textual preacher should seek to make this method standard. To utilize an idea in a text toward a goal for which the text was not originally written is then termed the indirect method. The preacher resorts to it usually if he has not been patient enough to find the purpose of the text or the best text for his purpose.

Thus Phil. 2:5-11 is a splendid text. By the direct method it suggests the goal "Be humbly self-sacrificing as Jesus was." If it should suggest "Believe in Jesus, who humbled Himself to redeem us," an important goal is set up, but then this text is used by the indirect method. When Matt. 20:28 cues a sermon on Jesus as Ransom for the sins of the world, the method is indirect. When the text is used by the direct method, it suggests, in its context, the goal "The Christian is great as he serves."

Expository Preaching

Preaching which makes a portion of Scripture the cue and definition of its message can well be termed textual. The literature on preaching sometimes makes synonymous with this term the word "expository," suggesting that the sermon is the exposition of a specific portion of Scripture. "Exposition" is the setting forth in preaching of the truth and meaning of an extract of Scripture which has first of all been understood by means of interpretation, or exegesis.

Many writers on preaching, however, use the term "expository" to designate a more limited type of sermons. A few mean by it simply preaching on lengthy texts; most pericopic texts would pertain to expository preaching, in this sense. More generally, however, the term "expository preaching" is used to classify preaching on texts chosen consecutively from a unit of Scripture. Thus in preaching on the Book of Acts, for example, the expository preacher proceeds verse by verse, employing as many or as few for the given sermon as he finds convenient and continuing the next sermon where he had ended the preceding one. Martin Luther and John Calvin presented expositions of entire books of the Bible in this manner in their sermons for weekdays. This method is often employed for Sunday sermons by preachers who do not employ the church year as a guide for the accents of their sermons.

The advantage of this system is that the hearer becomes familiar with extended portions of Scripture and that the preacher must come to terms with the Bible as it speaks to him rather than foist his own accent on the text. The chief handicap lies in the difficulty of unifying the given message. Frequently expository sermons become homilies, restating the meaning of the text and appending observations and lessons. Where expository preachers have employed persuasive techniques, they have usually made each text very brief, have ranged over a wide area of Bible and literature to build their message, and have preached on books which in themselves have strong persuasive method. Preachers in the liturgical traditions have found the expository method useful chiefly in the "nonfestival half" of the church year or in secondary services.

Textual or Topical

The alternative to textual preaching is usually termed topical. This is sometimes assumed to be preaching which does not draw its material from Scripture at all and, instead, gathers subject matter and the central theme from other sources. In this book we shall not use the term "topical" in that way, but rather in classifying sermons which begin in the preacher's mind with a subject or topic to which he thereupon supplies Biblical materials and perhaps even a Biblical text.

Another false alternative to be ruled out in using the terms "textual" and "topical" is that the textual sermon has no specific goal, but the topical sermon has. For the sake of the hearer every sermon should have a single topic, if by that we mean the goal and purpose of the sermon. In homiletical jargon the effort to draw all the elements of the text and sermon into a unity has been called the synthetic method — in the sense of its being not artificial or ersatz but unified. This focus and unity should be quite possible when preaching on any good text. The alternative "analytical" method should, then, not be construed to suggest or allow a sermon to present a series of unrelated observations or lessons drawn from a single text. An over-all unity must still, for the hearer's sake, dominate the goal of the message. Only so can the preacher throw the full weight of his Gospel toward a goal which the hearer will find memorable and practical.

The science of using a text is idle sophistication, after all, unless the text is helpful in thrusting the impact of the Gospel of Christ into the hearer to the end that his own faith may become stronger and his life more consecrated. The Christian preacher has no choice whether to use the Bible or not in his preaching; he will use it. Let him see to it that when he uses Biblical texts, they do not impede the contribution of the Bible to his task and his people but support it.

FOR FURTHER THOUGHT

What is there about a textual sermon that makes it helpful to the man who is preparing it? to the person who is listening to it?

A preacher in a congregation with a liturgical order of service and service book decides to preach on the Epistle to the Ephesians by the expository method. He finds that he cannot make his themes co-ordinate with the propers of the service and the festivals of the church year. What should he do?

Evaluate these statements:

1. The topical preacher reveals disrespect for the Bible.

2. To "preach the text" means to repeat the text in many different ways.

For further reading see p. 300.

*When. the preacher does not use
a text from the Bible, let him still
preach the Bible and the Gospel.*

Chapter Twelve

PREACHING WITHOUT A TEXT

Every sermon of the Christian preacher should speak for God and hence be Biblical. It should speak to people and hence be unified and easy to comprehend, remember, and put into action. We have seen that these objectives can well be realized by using extracts of Scripture as texts for sermons.

To complete the picture we should survey sermons which do not begin with a text or use it to shape their message. Again we remind ourselves that we are now going to discuss Biblical but topically unified sermons, as contrasted with non-Biblical and rambling ones.

In the opinion of many writers on preaching, sermons with the topical method have through the ages been the more successful. It is hard to form an accurate judgment, since the same preacher frequently used both types and since only a tiny proportion of the sermons of Christian preachers have reached print. St. Paul's passion must shape sermons — "by all means save some."

Substitutes for Texts

The average public speaker may be puzzled by the routine of the clergy in preaching to a text. He has been trained to find a "topic" or a "theme" for his address. He has then proceeded to gather materials concerning his subject, arrange them in logical order, and present them in engaging style. He may regard the attempt baffling to make a sentence or paragraph of the Scriptures basic to an entire address. The preacher who is trained in the textual method may gradually prefer it to any other. But he will see opportunities for using substitutes.

Thus the doctrinal formulations of the manuals, creeds, and confessions of the church may furnish themes and topics. The worship of a congregation will be enhanced if its members annually hear a series of sermons on great hymns. We shall see in Section Seven below that when a minister plans a course of sermons on a special subject, he will do well to dispense sometimes with single texts for some units rather than to risk distorting either the message or a passage of the Bible.

In published sermons we frequently encounter addresses with two, three, or more texts. Almost always they represent a topical approach, and the preacher displays the Biblical materials which seemed most useful or striking for the development of the subject.

Published sermons often suspend from texts from secular literature or from the sayings of figures notable in the church, politics, philosophy, or science. This technique may render the preaching of the Gospel of Jesus Christ difficult, and it loses one of the chief values of the Biblical text, its symbolism of Scripture as a source of the message. At once we must admit that Biblical texts severed from supporting Gospel may similarly handicap the preacher who is too sluggish to discern and exploit the whole revelation of God in Christ.

Texts as Mottoes

Many sermons appear in print with a Biblical phrase or sentence at their head. They serve as a motto and sometimes even as a title for the sermon. Actually the sermons themselves may be topical.

When done as a sop to the churchly tradition of texts, the practice borders on the insincere or the showy. Some strong topical preaching with effective Biblical content does employ this practice. The danger is that it may serve the eye better than the ear. It may have more to do with the Victorian essay suspended from a classical quotation than with public address and preaching.

Pertinent to the spoken style, however, is such a text when it supplies a quip or flash which illumines the purpose of the sermon or creates at least one of its major factors of interest. Such a motto text can become a linking device through refrain or other association for the basic unities of the sermon. It is particularly this technique which can justify the use of a textual motto by a serious Biblical preacher.

Under the current interest in new versions and translations, a preaching theme can take its cue from a single concept highlighted by the contrast of a contemporary version with the Authorized. Here, as in all preaching, it is important that the preacher do not lose rapport with many in his audience by seeming to be merely smart. Fashions in preaching literature are fostered by thousands of jaded preachers rather than their parishioners, and it is not the highest compliment to call a man a "preacher's preacher." For the preacher knows that he should keep his ear close to the heart of his people and that this applies not just to their language but to the type and method of the sermon that he uses to reach them. The straight line of talk is the shortest distance between the preacher and his hearer.

Occasions for Topical Sermons

Initial training and denominational customs as well as later experience and habit help to make preachers quite partisan on the subject of "textual versus topical." Their arguments will often employ inferior samples of the one sort pitted against superior products of the other.

Actually the two methods have much to learn from each other, and the wise preacher will keep his skills fresh in both directions. Effective textual preaching begins with continuous application to Biblical literature itself. It puts a premium on the ability to see applications to current life in the Biblical record, and that is precious in every preacher and every Christian always. Topical preaching takes its cues from all the experience of the preacher with people, from all his reading and looking and listening. The textual preacher should have those skills of sensitiveness to life, just as the topical preacher should have the sensitiveness to Scripture.

The shorter the text, the greater the impulse to employ techniques of topical preaching. This is no disaster, and the preacher who is well acquainted with Scripture will appreciate the resources latent in small texts. The preacher who experiments with both the textual and the topical methods should remember to speak language that is applied and interesting when he uses the textual approach, and to offer material that is theological and Biblical when he preaches topically.

Having said this, we are ready to explore the opportunities for topical preaching. Its most obvious field (cf. the previous chapter) is the preaching outreach on radio or otherwise to people outside the church. For them the symbolism of Bible as source is not so significant as for the people who know the Bible. Exposition, sometimes word by word, of beloved Scripture is dear and memorable to the Christian audience, but may interpose a whole layer of thought between the non-Christian listener and the concept at which the preacher aims. True, some of America's most beloved radio evangelists have been textual in their method, but it should be conceded that their texts were short.

In the mind of many preachers the topical method seems to offer more flexibility than the textual. Others feel that topical preaching offers more opportunity to meet the concern of the parish than does preaching according to a pericopic system or by the expository process. To a degree these judgments depend on the proper understanding of textual and pericopic preaching and on the experience of the individual. Most parish pastors will find it necessary to employ both varieties, and subsequent sections will endeavor to give account of both.

Textual Preaching Approached Topically

Both textual and topical preaching have several things in common which are at the heart of the preacher's task. Both give the opportunity to preach the Gospel of Jesus Christ. Both draw the material by which God really helps them from the Bible. Both concern themselves with the relation of people to God. This means that in their final form they are not going to be too different from each other. In fact, it is perfectly possible that a sermon which the preacher begins to prepare by the topical method develops textually.

This is bound to happen when the topic that goes through the mind of the preacher, during his planning for the year or in answer to some of his pastoral care or reading, is in the midstream of Biblical teaching, and he discovers the text that sets forth his idea well. The longer the preacher labors with the Bible, the more apt these discoveries become. Even if he employs pericopic systems for his major preaching, probably half of his sermons will have to be built on free texts, most of which are chosen from the topical point of view.

As the preacher gathers experience, furthermore, even his textual preaching becomes organized in his mind about great families of topics. His sermons no longer stand in his mind as isolated peaks, but he sees the mountain ranges that connect them. He finds that as he phrases the goals of his sermons, he can express them in the nontechnical language of the average hearer or in the terms of theological and doctrinal commonplaces with equal facility. The latter are significant as a sort of thumb index for the subjects of his preaching. Those subjects all concern his people.

"Be humbly self-sacrificing as Jesus was" is a central thought for Phil. 2:5-11. In the preacher's mind it lodges under the topic "Sacrificial Service." When the time comes to preach a sermon or a series of sermons on the subject of the Christian's self-sacrifice, Phil. 2:5-11 stands there to help, whether as a text or as amplification of special points within the sermon.

This review of types of sermons should summarize the task of preaching, not as a laborious plodding through rules and preoccupation with technical routines but as the joyful proclamation of the good news, to the church and by the church and from the church. The Bible, through which the preacher first received the facts of his faith and the witness of God and His Son and the Spirit, stands by as an inexhaustible resource. The preacher develops his skills to use his methods capably rather than to be driven by them.

Does the term "topical preaching" have a bad odor to you? If so, what do you mean by the term?

According to the report of it in Acts 2, is Peter's sermon in Jerusalem on the First Pentecost topical or textual in method? Is it Biblical? Was it preached in a setting of worship? Was it directed to unbelievers or believers?

If you are a preacher, test your memory:

1. What is the topic of the topical sermon you best remember (yours or another preacher's)?

2. What is the text of the textual sermon you best remember (yours or another preacher's)?

For further reading see p. 300.

SECTION FOUR

Preparing the Textual Sermon

Good sermons don't wait for inspiration. Even the most extemporaneous have a process of training and experience behind them. Like a writer or physician the preacher must soberly and steadily apply skills of his craft to his job. Inspiration grows out of the use of the skills, not skills out of the inspiration.

This section describes the stages of building a sermon. It uses the textual sermon as a sample, since it demands as much of the preacher as the topical and since many preachers prepare textual sermons at least in the chief services of their congregations.

Appendix I illustrates with an actual preparation the process described in the next chapters.

If the sermon is to be truly textual, the text must make sense and meaning for preacher and people.

Chapter Thirteen

FIND THE MEANING OF THE TEXT

The preacher who sets out to prepare a sermon on a text has it before him because it may be prescribed in a pericopic system or suggested to him for a special occasion like an anniversary or a dedication. Or it may be a free text, one which he chose in order to preach toward a purpose which he already had in mind. In either case he is saying: "I am really going to make this text basic to my sermon and not let it be merely a motto for it."

Two sets of skills must blend in the first stage of building the genuinely textual sermon. The one is exegesis, discerning the sense and purpose of the extract of Scripture. The other is exposition, making the sense and purpose of the text apply to a group of hearers who are to put it to work in life.

Many of the steps outlined in this and the following chapters are in practice carried on in the mind and not necessarily written out. Nor do they necessarily follow in the sequence outlined. Where the preacher plans his sermons in advance, notes are useful.

81

FIRST STAGE: *Getting Meaning from the Text*

1. *The Text in Its Setting.* — A text is most frequently an extract
of a larger unit of Scripture — a sentence or paragraph from a letter,
or from sayings of Jesus or stories about Him in the gospels, or from an
episode of a book of history, or from the utterances of a prophet or
psalmist. It is helpful to know, if possible, who the original speaker
or writer was and what he was trying to do for people in his time.
The preacher is always looking for relevance; he wants his people to
be struck! Hence he wants to know how the Biblical writer or speaker
was trying to strike people and for what purpose.

In many texts the immediate context, before and after, is helpful.
Some texts, like entire psalms, have no context. The Book of Proverbs
is a loose compilation of individual sayings and aphorisms. The evangelists had various criteria by which they arranged the sequence
of their materials, sometimes topical, sometimes chronological. But
in the longer epistles of St. Paul and in Hebrews the plot and logical
connection is very significant. The total discourse of which the text
is an extract is helpful for understanding the text and for sensing the
practical circumstances and applications.

2. *The Text in the Vernacular.* — Important for the understanding
of the text is the force of the original Greek, Hebrew, or Aramaic.
Yet the preacher will find it useful to begin his pondering of the text
in the language of the people to whom he is going to preach. He is
first and last a preacher; exegesis is a tool in his hand to a more
primary end, and this is that the people hear the Word of God in
their tongue.

What does a preacher do when he ponders a text? He must
discover what it means. But he is not reflecting and meditating well
if he says: "I remember having read this text before. I understand
its meaning. I agree with it. I guess I've finished." This is the
thinking that he is trying to remedy in the hearer who listens to him
read the text. He must move on from sense to meaning (remember
Chapter 8 above). How can he slow down the scrutiny of the text
so that meaning emerges?

Part of the process comes in searching more thoroughly. In complex grammatical sections, what are the antecedents of the pronouns?

What words are modified by adjectives and adverbs? What is the precise meaning of common words like "faith," "grace," "knowledge," "bless," "see"?

The best meditation on a text, the best grappling hook for holding the preacher's mind to the text until it speaks to him, functions as he ceaselessly says to himself: "What does this text have to say to me and to my hearer? How is he like the people in this text? How do his problems and handicaps compare with theirs? What does God have to say to him that he was trying to say to them?" These questions aim at the preaching values of the text. Those values are more than its exegetical difficulties, much more than its curiosities and novelties; they are the cues for the Word of God to the hearer.

3. *The Text in the Original.* — To meditate helpfully on the vernacular, the preacher may wish to use a number of the translations of the Bible. As he does so, he is already taking account of the original language. The Authorized Version is especially helpful for the preacher in that its grammar closely adheres to that of the original. Its Elizabethan English frequently requires retranslation into current terms, not only in apparent cases (e. g., "prevent" for "precede," Ps. 119:148) but in subtler ones (e. g., "discerning," 1 Cor. 11:29, not "seeing" but "recognizing as superior"; "advocate," 1 John 2:1, not "lawyer" but "one who stands by").

Many of the preacher's questions concerning the primary sense of his text will receive helpful answer through study of the original. This does not imply expert exegetical ability, for many helps are at hand. If the preacher can read the original Greek or Hebrew sufficiently to identify root words, standard lexicons will supply great help, and they often suggest the usage for the particular text under study. The original will correct any distortion which a translation may have suggested. To deepen the understanding of even a few of the core concepts of the text will repay the labor with the original.

At this point a thorough commentary may be helpful. A caution is in place if the text is to be the prime mover of the sermon, namely, not to by-pass the meaning and cues of the text to adopt judgments of expositors. So many "homiletical helps" are at hand clamoring to take that short cut. Let the preacher keep the alternative clearly

before him. Shall he use exegetical helps toward sound interpretation
of his text? Certainly. Shall he use expository helps toward preaching
values before he has himself come to a clear understanding of the
text and sought its meaning directly? No. Shall he involve himself
in the reconstructions and comments of exegetes who sponsor the
presuppositions of antisupernaturalism or comparative religion? No.

4. *Amplifying Basic Concepts.* — As the preacher ponders the text
in terms of its setting and of its potential message for his own hearer,
he will begin to harbor a series of basic concepts concerning God
and man and their relation to each other. These concepts will have
to be supplemented in terms of the persuasive purpose of a sermon
(of that more in the next chapter). But already at this stage some
amplifications of the meaning of the text will occur.

Cross references in the concordance, the lexicon, the English Bible,
and the Testament in the original will direct to selections in Scripture
which discuss the specific concept, display its mention or expression
by the same writer or speaker elsewhere, or illuminate its meaning
by incidents. Many of these parallel passages will appear to be arbi-
trary, some in English Bibles even capricious; but some will enhance
meaning notably.

Systematic theology pulls the data of Scripture on given doctrinal
facts together. The outstanding Biblical texts used in the courses
for training church members, or the Biblical data employed in the
confessional writings of the church, or the extracts of Scripture which
are the primary "seats of doctrine" for central concepts, will present
themselves to the preacher by association or on search. He should
think of his text as intersecting, perhaps at a number of points, with
the system of doctrine of the Christian Church and feel himself
employing it to help people grow in faith or in life through that
doctrine.

5. *The Central Thought.* — Careful textual study should bring the
preacher to the point that a wealth of preachable, applicable material
clamors for expression. Even at the desk he should be muttering
paragraphs of preaching at the invisible audience, and the spell and
promise of the text should rest on him as he moves from task to task
in his pastorate. Ideally his chief problem at this point should be:

"How can I preach only *one* sermon on all this? How can I find the devices and angles by which I can rifle this mighty Word of God into my people and pack it into one charge?"

Hence one great step remains at this stage, and that is to determine the central thought of the text, the area of chief accent, so that secondary materials recede and the persuasive thrust of the text appears. Some writers term this the theme of the text and sermon; but since others mean thereby a rhetorically concise and striking title, and still others the topic in the preacher's mind before he ever finds a text, we prefer to speak of the "central thought" of the text.

The central thought, if at all possible, should be couched in a simple sentence. It should be sufficiently positive and practical in content to suggest the goal that the preacher will have for the hearer. If it implies a number of major concepts that will help to shape an outline of the material, good; but at this stage the preacher should concentrate on simplicity and accuracy of the statement rather than form. It should be sufficiently "central" that the great ideas of the text are reflected in it and contribute to it; that, if possible, the uniqueness of this text as contrasted with others of its subject is cued.

One text will sometimes yield more than one central thought. When the preacher has chosen the text to illuminate a topic which he had already had in mind, he will probably not notice alternatives. In preaching on pericopic texts, however, he will frequently discover several options. When correlating the sermon with the propers of the common service for the day, and when planning contrasts from Sunday to Sunday or with previous uses of the text, the preacher will be grateful for these alternatives and will make his choice accordingly. Sometimes the option is between the original purpose of the text (direct method) or another purpose elsewhere validated in the Bible (indirect method). In that case the direct method will always receive the preference.

The supreme purpose in all of the study of the text and the crystallizing of the central thought must be: "I do what I can to get this text to speak to my people, speak the Word of God to them, to the goals of their life." Where that purpose has dominated, the work of the First Stage is productive and potent for each successive one.

If you are a preacher, mentally review the preparation of your most recent sermon to test which of the steps of this chapter were consciously employed.

Do you feel that you are trying to discover what a text says before you plan your sermon, or are you leaning on others to tell you what it says?

When you use helps for constructing a sermon, are they guidance in determining the meaning of the text, suggestions for lessons and applications to the people, or useful quotations and hints for style?

Do you ever use a sermon help to find something "new"?

For further reading see pp. 300, 301.

Note Appendix I, pp. 311–314.

The materials from the text must be used not simply to inform people but to persuade them.

Chapter Fourteen

PLAN TO PERSUADE

Unless the preacher has the right intentions as he prepares his sermon, it may miss the mark. He expects too little of it if he plans simply to get enough material together in order to speak for the customary length of time. Even this problem is formidable for the beginner; too soon he discovers, however, that stopping is as difficult as going on. But the preacher expects too little if he is satisfied after he has found sense and meaning in his text. He now runs the danger of converting his materials into a Biblical lecture. His calling is to persuade people, to change them in the direction which God has in view for them. He himself must plan that persuasion.

SECOND STAGE: *Planning the Persuasion*

If the sermon is to persuade and move the hearer, it must have a clear *goal*. The preacher must be very clear in his own mind what it is and should be able to express it in unambiguous terms.

He should not frame it in answer to the question, "What is my purpose for my sermon?" Too easily he can answer: "I want the hearer to discover the meaning of my text. I want him to apply the Gospel to himself. I want him to pay attention to my message." Those answers concern means rather than goal. Rather should the preacher ask: "To what improvement in faith or life should the sermon on this text lead my hearer?"

Some texts express this goal of improvement explicitly, and the central thought that adequately reflects the text will also reflect the goal. Texts in which the prophets or Jesus or the apostles invite their hearers to believe in God and overcome their unbelief obviously suggest faith goals. Exhortations in the Old or the New Testament to live according to the plan of God plainly suggest life goals.

More difficult is the preacher's problem if the text seems to be simply information about a teaching, or if it is a story, or if it comprises chiefly a diagnosis of shortcomings and sins. In such cases the preacher should be doubly sure to ask: "Will this text and sermon help my hearer to a stronger hold on the grace and mercy of God? Or will it help him to improve his behavior?" Where the preacher has chosen his text himself, he may have had this goal more or less clearly in mind. Where he is working on a text which has been suggested to him in a pericopic system, he may still have to make the discovery.

Simultaneous with the envisioning of the goal of the sermon must be the recognition of the apposite *malady*. Persuasion depends on the hearer's awareness of what he is being freed from and on his desire for that freeing. Hence the preacher should explore the resources of the text for portraying this malady and provide means for diagnosing it.

Often the text is explicit about malady but will imply the goal only by inference. Information goals may thus be unmasked, or cues for more adequate goals may be noted. John 3:16 suggests the goal occasionally: "That my hearer may more thoroughly understand how to be saved." The apposite malady would be: "He does not understand how to be saved." But the text describes the process that keeps men from perishing; hence the goal is that they may live eternally.

The preacher should endeavor to phrase his diagnosis of malady more definitely than a deficiency of the goal. Diagnosis reviews surface symptoms which help to uncover the underlying malady. Note how St. Paul in Eph. 4:29—5:5 describes the goal of helpful speech. His diagnosis of malady is much more specific than "unhelpful speech." It confronts evils on the surface, such as gossip, angry talk, and filthy jokes. But it then explores the underlying and radical difficulty, the loss of the kingdom and rule of God in the heart.

The preacher wants to help people confront their need for his Gospel as quickly and easily as they can; that is persuasion. But he also wants them to desire help, not just from weaknesses or discomforts in general but from their deficiency in the life of God and their judgment under the wrath of God. Most useful are the texts which guide the preacher to make the diagnosis of the underlying malady by means of surface symptoms which the hearer actually can see. Where a text does not provide cues for both processes, the preacher will appropriately supplement from cognate areas of Scripture.

Now the preacher is ready to search for the materials in the text that will actually do the persuading and moving, the *means* toward persuasion, the suggestions for what will really be the preaching in the sermon, the good news.

Many texts set forth Gospel explicitly. The preacher plans to use them. But his purpose is not simply to mouth the phrases or to help the hearer identify sentences of the sermon as Gospel. This would be like suggesting to a motorist that he is equipped for travel because he had read labels on a gasoline pump. The preacher's objective must be to make a firm coupling between the way of life in Christ which the text presents and the hearer's faith and life; to make a living connection in the hearer's mind between the goal which he holds before him and the Word of Christ's redeeming work as the one power for attaining that goal.

Many preaching texts set forth the Gospel with little detail or explicitness. Texts are usually chosen for the sake of the goal which they suggest, and sometimes for a particularly pungent expression of malady. For example, in the epistles, texts setting forth the Gospel are located in sections prior to the application to goals of faith or life. Many chapters intervene in the historical books of the Old Testament, at times, between affirmations of the grace and promise of God. As the preacher plans his sermon, he must make clear to himself how he intends to amplify the teaching of the bare text so that he can fully preach the Word.

Supplementing the Text

As the preacher ponders his text and first notations, he may say: "That's good and hints at much, but it's spare. I'll have to swing in a lot of application and stories and human-interest stuff." He probably will. But first let him fill out the basic persuasive theology of the text. That must come from the Bible itself. The text is useful because it highlights a particular and hence memorable area of Christian purpose or need, a particular thrust of God's own power toward a goal for His people. But the text is only a section of a larger picture, and the preacher cannot afford to have it fence in the essential vitality of his message. True, the sermon should not become untextual, but it should not cease to be Biblical or persuasive or the good news.

The simplest illustration of supplementing a text occurs when it is negative, that is, when it is ample in its statement of malady and deficient in its suggestion of goal. The preacher must make the obverse of malady his goal. Martin Luther acted like a preacher when he began the explanations of the Decalog in the Small Catechism with the words "We should fear and love God that. . . ." But let the preacher find clear Scripture for his purpose.

What if the text suggests no thought of malady? What if it gives cues only for the radical disorder and no surface symptoms, or vice versa? In that situation the obverse of the goal is suggestive, set forth not in negative terms — "Let us not be, etc." — but in practical and concrete concepts. The context of the text, or the theology of the respective Biblical writer as a whole, or the structure of doctrine supporting the given goal, or data of experience concerning surface symptoms for the suggested underlying malady, or close reflection concerning the inner life submerged under the suggested surface symptoms, will provide cues. Then let the preacher find Biblical documentation before he goes on. For example: Is. 26:3 is a lovely text on God's gift of peace to the trusting heart; trust is the goal, underscored in v. 4. Malady is cued in v. 5 with the ironic terms "high" and "lofty," but basic rejection of God underlying such pride emerges subsequently in verses 14 and 18.

The finest art, in which theology and homiletics truly mate, lies in filling out the pattern of Gospel preaching. When the text is meager in affirming basic concepts of God's grace and redemption in Christ, the context in the given book of the Bible or other writings by the same writer may give a cue. Here every preacher should build a theology of the atonement which stands by him as he seeks to give words for the power of God in Christ toward the hearer's attaining of his goal.

Perhaps the preacher is concerned for more ample expression of the Gospel than the text supplies. He may feel the threat of repetitiousness or abstractness. The Scriptures themselves are the source of bewildering varieties of Gospel statement. Sometimes cues are right in the text or context. Thus "truth" seldom means factuality in the abstract, but describes God's faithful plan for redeeming His people (Ps. 85:10, 11; John 14:6; 17:17). "Righteousness" seldom if ever means "sound behavior," but it describes the situation of the man on whom the merciful God has favor (Ps. 85:10; Luke 18:9-14), namely, in Christ. "Peace" seldom means accord or placidity in general, but God's relation with man achieved at high cost (Is. 53:5). Gospel cues for Is. 26:3, considered above, sound through the word "peace" as well as the prophet's direction to remember the entire name and revelation of God's mercy in v. 8. Thus many swift signals of the redemptive plan alert preacher and people to the way in Christ.

The preacher who fills out the persuasive pattern of his text should see to it that goal, malady, and means correlate. If he fails here, he may render portions of his message difficult or meaningless. Every preacher will keep on improving his own working list of complexes of the atonement and their correlation with goal and malady. (E. g., Appendix III)

In the weekly routine of preparing his sermons the pastor will leave most of the process indicated in this chapter unwritten, and he will thrust his analysis and the supplementation of his text directly into the subsequent stages of the sermon. But if he plans to persuade at all, he will patiently and consciously aim to work with adequate materials for the three basic components of Christian preaching.

FOR FURTHER THOUGHT

First Corinthians 13 suggests the goal of loving the fellow man. Where will you find basic Gospel applied to this goal? in First Corinthians? elsewhere in St. Paul? in Scripture? First Corinthians 12 suggests that the love for the fellow man is a gift of the Spirit; hence the Gospel must be directed toward the enhancing of the Spirit's presence. Cues for this in First Corinthians? in Scripture?

Criticize this summary of a sermon on Christian love:

Goal: Love the brother.

Malady: We are all sinners.

Gospel: Pray God to forgive the sin of lovelessness because of Jesus Christ.

For further reading see p. 301.

Note Appendix I, p. 314.

*The preacher shapes his material
so that the hearer can absorb it
easily and retain its essentials.*

Chapter Fifteen

ORGANIZE THE MATERIAL

After the preacher has ample Biblical material before him, can focus upon a central thought, and sees how he can direct the Gospel of Christ to a specific improvement in faith or life of the people, he is ready to arrange a sequence. This process can be tedious and sometimes frustrating. It seldom provides the excitement of personal discovery, and the preacher may wish that he could omit it.

The Hearer Is King

Let no preacher think that he outlines his materials only for his own sake or to satisfy ancient homiletical conventions which may make the sermon dull. As he outlines his material, he will uncover thin spots that need filling out, and he can build a sermon that is uncluttered and easy for him to remember. When that happens, the preacher feels that the outline was useful. Yet above all else he should remember that the first purpose of the outline is the hearer!

The hearer is not reading but listening. Each idea has to come to him in such a way that it stays with him and contributes to the others. The hearer cannot halt the sermon and page back to refresh his mind on a point which escaped him, or reread certain sentences to savor their meaning. For the preacher is talking, and if he is doing what he has planned to do, he is holding the hearer's attention so that he cannot browse.

This means that the preacher has to find a plot and sequence of ideas not simply to fit the materials before him but to fit the hearer's way of thinking. The hearer is like a small boy lying on his stomach watching a freight train come around the bend. First comes the locomotive with its promise of the train behind. Then comes a boxcar, a gondola, a tank car, another boxcar; but whatever it is, each is coupled securely to the one ahead and the one behind, until the caboose says this is the end. Thus all the ideas of the sermon must be coupled together and follow each other in a helpful sequence.

The preacher can remember such a sequence, and most of his labor of memorizing is obviated when the sermon is well organized. But more important, the people will remember it. If they cannot keep the plot and point of the sermon in mind, the hours of labor which the preacher invested were for nothing. If the preacher has to struggle overmuch to remember the sequence of ideas, perhaps to the point of simply reading the sermon to the people, how will they remember?

A good outline is useless, of course, unless the preacher is faithful to it. If he borrows material from extraneous paragraphs and flits back and forth over his plan, the people witness a wreck rather than a train. Outlines are not homiletical whimsy but scaffolding for persuasion.

THIRD STAGE: *Outlining the Material*

Sometimes a text is so rich in closely knit material and the central thought has been phrased so adequately that the segments fall into place like a tangerine's. Those are happy experiences, and each one reminds the preacher that he should never get into the way of a plan that is latent in his text and material. He will probably discover that it is easier to outline texts about which he had no presuppositions than those which he chose to fit an already simmering idea. He will find closely reasoned books like Romans or Hebrews easier to outline than the gospels or books that like Proverbs or James or 1 John employ the leisurely and cyclical thought patterns of the Hebrew people.

The preacher will find it helpful always to use the same scheme of numeration; here and in Appendix I we employ the following:

I. (Roman numerals to indicate the major divisions.)

   A. (Capital letters to indicate major subdivisions.)

      1. (Arabic numerals to indicate minor subdivisions.)

He will remember that each rank must have at least two units, i. e., I has to have a II, if not also a III or IV; A a B, etc.

1. *Plot the Major Division.* — Suppose the outline doesn't "just happen," and the preacher must plan it consciously. Let him start with the major division. In order to stay with the text and the central thought simultaneously, he will use the rule of thumb "Phrase the major division in the language of the central thought." This works in one of two ways. Perhaps one word or phrase of the central thought becomes the "splitting point" of the major division. In technical jargon this is called a synthetic division because the whole central thought is treated in each major division but from a different aspect. Take a rich text like 2 Cor. 5:19, for example, and give it the central thought, "Speak the Word of God's Plan of Peace." The old Aristotelian category of material and form suggests a synthetic division: I. The content of the Word of peace; II. The speaking of the Word of peace. Or focusing on "plan of peace," we can divide: I. God makes the plan; II. We speak the plan.

The other mode of constructing a major division from the central thought distributes the words of the central thought, supplemented for the sake of grammar, over two or more statements in an "analytical" division. The results are often quite similar to the synthetic. Thus the above central thought may yield: I. God has planned our peace; II. We speak the Word of peace.

The difficulty in this business lies in using a text and a central thought simultaneously; it gets easier when the central thought actually puts into words the chief focus of the text. When it does, then this check will help the preacher to use the text throughout the sermon and keep it unified: (a) Does each major division take its cue from the text? (b) Does each major division take its cue from the central thought? (c) Is each major division distinct from each other one?

The preacher need not be superstitious about having always two or always three major divisions. He need not foist bizarre divisions on his material just to escape some stereotype. The freshness of his sermon will not depend on the novelty of his outline, just as architects will not try to make skyscrapers interesting by using strangely shaped girders. Isn't it true that the accent on persuasion, developed in the preceding chapter, will suggest the major division for every text: I. Goal, II. Malady, III. Means? No; check (a) in the preceding paragraph makes that division possible only where the text discusses all three. Even then it may not be preferable, for that division tends to slot all of the affirmation of the Gospel into one section. When the preacher can confront his hearers with Law and Gospel repeatedly in the same sermon without muddling his plan, then he is on the track of a good outline!

Sometimes the first attempt at an outline comes up with a major division that does not concern the hearer: I. The text; II. The application. At the bottom of this may have been a faulty central thought; e. g., 2 Cor. 5:19: "Paul Spoke the Word of God's Plan of Peace." I. Paul did; II. We should. Actually this is not an outline at all; the sermon begins in Division II, and Division I was simply a review of the textual study which the preacher undertook at the start of his preparation. First make the central thought talk about or to the hearer; and then make each major division take up the concern of the hearer. To make this point clearer, to the alternative outlines suggested above on this text we might add: I. God's plan has reached us with His peace; II. God's plan commits to us the Word of peace. To the check list two paragraphs back add a (d): Does each major division concern the hearer?

2. *Fill Out the Divisions.* — The preacher prepares an outline in order to ascertain the sequence of paragraphs of the sermon. In the spoken style a paragraph should seldom be longer than two minutes, 250 words (allowing for extempore expansions). This implies that the preacher is looking for seven to twelve paragraphs for the body of his sermon (introduction and conclusion excluded). Hence the

preacher must expand his major division through subdivisions. If he leaves any one major division unplanned, he is heading for cluttered, difficult, unparagraphed material.

Keep the final plan simple! If you can build sufficient paragraph topics simply by major subdivisions (A's, B's, etc.), you are making the outline easier for the hearer to follow. Minor subdivisions (1's, 2's, etc.) are helpful only if they adhere very obviously to the A and B from which they suspend; and further subdividing into 1's, 2's or even a's and b's is mischievous for preacher and people, unless they merely represent a plot for the development of a paragraph headed A.

Where do the subdivisions come from? The answer lies in the division which they develop and in the text. True, not every paragraph of the sermon will discuss material from the text; Chapter 14 intimated that supplements might be necessary, and some of the outstanding material concerning malady or goal may have to be fitted into the outline without explicit textual cues. The major divisions should be so phrased that subdivisions will be possible. Some will devote themselves exclusively to review of doctrine or narrative of the text, some wholly to application to the hearer. At least one solid paragraph of application to the hearer obviously belongs into each major division. A final check on each subdivision or prospective paragraph topic asks: (a) Does it avoid repeating material used elsewhere? (b) Does it belong under its head? (c) Has it actually discussed the material suggested under its head? As to (c), remember that only the statements of the outline farthest to the right, i. e., those not further subdivided, are the prospective paragraph topics or "particulars" of the sermon; the other outline statements are not going to be paragraph topics.

When the body of the sermon is outlined, run a final check on the whole: (a) Are there enough particulars for a sermon? (b) Are there too many? (c) Do they sufficiently develop the material in the major divisions? (d) Do they adequately cue goal, malady, and means? (e) Do they clearly reflect *this* text, or have the supplements crowded out the unique message of the text?

The preacher's work sheet for his outline often looks badly scrambled. He needn't be ashamed of it. For it reflects the drama of his grapple with human minds as he bends them to hear the Word of God.

FOR FURTHER THOUGHT

Look at 1 John 4:7-11. It describes the process by which God enables us to love one another. A fair central thought is, "Our Love for Others Is God's Gift of Life to Us." In terms of this chapter, which is the most suitable major division:

1) I. St. John's teaching on love. II. Our love for one another.

2) I. God sent His Son to cover our sin. II. Therefore we ought to love one another.

3) I. By nature we do not love. II. God helps us to love.

4) I. Our love for others is a sign of God's life in us. II. God works His life in us through sending the Son to cover our sin. III. Hence we have the power to love.

Apply the check lists of this chapter to one of your recent outlines.

For further reading see p. 301.
Note Appendix I, pp. 314, 315.

Writing the sermon helps the preacher remember his hearer and speak the Word with freshness.

Chapter Sixteen

WRITE

Some preachers will look at the title of this chapter and say: "Write? Why, of course. There's no sermon until it's written out, is there? I would have a bad conscience in the pulpit if I didn't have a firm shape of words in my mind, and that takes writing. Besides — I like to write."

Others will say: "Write? Doesn't a preacher speak? Haven't you said that the spoken style differs substantially from the literary? Isn't it true that when a preacher takes a manuscript into the pulpit with him, either in his brain or actually on paper, it gets between him and the audience? Besides — I hate to write."

Good Writing Helps to Remember the Hearer

This book will not take sides in the dialog above. No preacher worth his salt and with even a little experience in preaching the Gospel should be unable on five minutes' notice to stand up and speak it

99

helpfully and with conviction. Preaching is not writing. Preaching is speaking. Few busy pastors, furthermore, have the time to write out two to six sermons a week alongside their load of pastoral care and administration. Just the same, we shall recommend writing.

We have to be clear what writing we mean. We don't mean writing that stems from the inner demand: "Get that sermon together! Find your padding, ideas, anecdotes, quotations that will puff out the skeleton of the outline so that you can keep going for twenty minutes with reasonable comfort to yourself and your hearers." We don't mean the writing that grows out of the principle: "The manuscript is the sermon."

But we mean the writing that keeps on asking what the preacher began to ask with the first glimpse at his text: What's here for my hearer? In the second stage of preparation he said it more acutely: How can I move my hearer God's way? Even under the drudgery of outlining he was saying: How can I get my hearer to assimilate this message most easily? And now the preacher is still saying: How can I say this so that he will understand me, pay attention to me, hang on to me paragraph by paragraph, and take it along to try out in the days ahead? Writing impelled by that question contributes to good preaching.

Writing is a trial-and-error process. We sit poised over the paper and confront a thought which we want our hearer to get. Now the alternatives come at us: Shall we say it this way or that? How will this paragraph bring up its load and then leave the hearer primed for the next? How can we replace this dull and abstract and technical way of expressing this idea with words that stand up and walk and light up in technicolor?

Much of this must happen, of course, also when we are not writing. Even after the manuscript is finished, it still isn't the sermon, for it stays in process until right in the pulpit it is finally hammered out with special energy and concentration. Not every sermon has to be written out, for the preacher can think of the hearer and what words reach him even without writing them. But the value of writing is that some of the false starts and inferior alternatives are discarded before it is too late. Writing tends to shorten the length of the sermon, because its chaff gets winnowed out over the typewriter rather than by wind that blows from the pulpit. Writing, furthermore — and its electronic counterpart of advance recording — gives time to discard threadbare or inexact expressions, to test the perspective and pace of the message, to "try it out for sound."

FOURTH STAGE: *The Working Brief*

Preaching is speaking. Therefore anything done in preparation for preaching should be speech preparation. Somewhere in the writing process, therefore, the preacher should have the feel of the charged and concentrated communication that is speech. This implies that one draft of the sermon should be in one sitting — and fast. Every preacher must find his own routine for this. One swings a pencil over foolscap, another types eighty words a minute (don't mind the overstrikes!), a third may speed up the process still more by extemporizing into a dictating machine or tape recorder. Much in that first draft must be improved, and we speak of that in the next chapter. At this stage — write.

Such a one-stop performance is possible only where one stage of advance preparation has intervened. This is the working brief. Set it up concisely and orderly. It should not be overlong; if it can't be mounted on one page single-space, then keep a major division to the page. Some of the components:

1. *Clear particulars.* — The final paragraph topics suggested on the trial outline should be clarified and improved. If they are complete sentences, they will be more helpful. If they are phrased in questions — and this applies to the central thought too — the answer to the question is part of the particular.

2. *Definitions.* — If any concept needs definition, now is the time to set it down. This involves noting the most important and striking exegetical values of the text, core doctrines, and any correction of misconceptions that the sermon must provide.

3. *Application.* — All of the sermon is to do things to hearers. Wherever the preacher expects to bring goal, malady, or means to the hearer — and the great majority of paragraphs will do this — he should note it explicitly on the working brief if the paragraph topic does not make it sufficiently apparent. Central thought and major divisions

should be phrased in terms of the hearer, and most paragraphs will follow suit; the only exceptions are those which develop Biblical background or analogies for the sake of arriving at subsequent application. All through this process the preliminary outline may need reworking to provide for adequate outreach to the hearer.

4. *Illustration.* — The preacher wants to make the sermon visual. The hearer's mind should be a screen on which scenes play in which he himself has a part. The best illustration is application, anything by which the hearer feels struck. Many other illustrative devices will help, however, to make unfamiliar or intangible concepts come alive. Some may occur to the preacher already at this point and can be cued into the working brief.

5. *Biblical amplification.* — The preacher can read his text and outline in two minutes. He plans the sermon to take twenty or more in order to give the hearer opportunity to reflect on the concepts of the sermon and to understand them amply. That means that the compact structure and the technical definitions of the material have to be "opened," the way a tightly printed paragraph must be reset with more lead between the lines and white space. One of the most important means for "opening" the paragraph is to insert Biblical material parallel to the text or supplementing the text. Not everything will do. Stories and doctrinal passages must not be too familiar or too unfamiliar. They must be apt and not derail from the main track. The working brief will indicate some such material so that the preacher will not stop his writing to page around for faintly remembered materials.

6. *Non-Biblical amplification.* — By this time the mind of the preacher begins to teem with recollections of hymnody, pulpit utterances, current and past reading, that may serve to amplify or underscore or add interest, and his files will yield further grist. Very brief notations will serve as memoranda.

7. *Introduction.* — If the preacher is thinking about his people, he has for days already been searching for a primary approach to the sermon, an introduction. If some ideas have come, he may note them.

8. *Conclusion.* — In many ways the last five minutes of the sermon will be the most important. For days the preacher has been muttering

climaxes and conclusions. He will indicate possibilities on the working brief. Sometimes challenging applications or illustrations are of a sufficiently summarizing nature to belong in the conclusion.

FIFTH STAGE: *The First Draft*

A good working brief has caused the preacher, while he has been preparing it, to mumble sentences to himself, tense with its climaxes, and to enjoy its plot. He can stand up and preach the moment that it is done, except that the resulting sermon will be long and a bit tumbling. When there is no time for writing, the working brief goes directly into the "memorizing" stage. (See Seventh Stage in Chapter Twenty below)

Many writers on preaching advise young preachers to write out their sermons during the first ten years of their ministry. We have observed, however, that busy or self-confident pastors will by-pass writing in their younger years and then begin to write as they discern need for self-discipline, for freshening language and overcoming stereotypes, for safeguarding the proportion and testing the coherence of the sermon in advance.

This adds up to the counsel: Write the sermon, write at least one each week; but — write the first draft in one quick sitting. Otherwise the proportion is lost, the enthusiasm for grappling with the hearer's attention cools off again and again. True, the first paragraphs will be clumsy and wooden, and the last hurried and tiring; they will take special reworking anyway. Don't waste time finding the most felicitous phrase, don't pick up something else and stall, but write. Much of the central three quarters of the first draft will be surprisingly apt. Don't come to a halt over special problems of content or because of the boresomeness of some passages. Simply try, honestly and straightforwardly, to put the message together for the hearer. Keep asking, "What do I want to say?" and then say it as if one of your people already were sitting on the other side of the desk.

The first draft may be too long or too short. It will have many deficiencies. Some paragraphs may actually remain unfinished. Leave room after each paragraph for the first critique; write triple-space, put in good margins, write legibly enough to reread, for you are going to manhandle much of this draft later. But whatever its shortcomings, it served a tremendous purpose. It crystallized preparation up to this point; it was the first test run of the sermon; it was speech on paper or on tape. This means that it was preparation for speaking.

FOR FURTHER THOUGHT

In response to reactions to this chapter:

"I don't find it possible to write to an outline at all. I can write the sermon first, and then discover what my outline was."

Good; can you then improve the outline that you discover you used and rewrite according to the improvements?

"I can't get started."

Is your trouble something aside from preaching altogether? work habits? preoccupations of parish? bad focus in the workroom?

"I'm too slow."

Until we become skilled, we are slow at any process. Are you giving yourself enough practice?

For further reading see p. 301.
Note Appendix I, pp. 315–321.

The sermon matures and improves in the preacher's mind to the very moment that he preaches it.

Chapter Seventeen

REWORK

The foregoing chapter promised to discuss writing the sermon. But it said very little about it beyond suggesting that when the preacher has explored and organized his text and prepared a working brief, he should sit down and write or talk it through. Is this all that there is to writing?

Certainly not. In one sense there can be no writing without revision. This applies to writing of any sort and for any purpose. Few serious authors write perfect copy, and those who do hammer it out slowly, and then they are writing for the eye. The preacher's first draft was for the ear. It was one quick attempt, and as he wrote it he knew that some spots sagged, some jargon was abstract, some paragraphs were poorly coupled to their neighbors. But the preacher is trying to reach hearers who are still ahead of him. The student rejoices in his first "sermon manuscript" and cherishes it as a minor miracle. But the maturing preacher knows that the sermon isn't done until it's preached.

SIXTH STAGE: *Rework*

If the preacher can hold to a good routine, he will try to leave twenty-four hours between finishing a first draft and returning to it for reworking. His judgments will be less fatigued. Both the excellencies and the deficiencies of the trial run will embarrass him less. Even then he will approach the review in several stages.

1. *Quick check.* — Right on the first draft — hence the triple space — make preliminary notations. Look at the language. Cross out excess words like adjectives and impersonal constructions; shift passives to the active; break up some of the complex sentences into simple ones; replace, or at least mark for further concern, the abstract or technical or tired verbs and nouns.

Now run through the whole thing a second time, and see whether the manuscript as a whole reflects the working brief. Perhaps the latter was poor at some spots; note whether the basic plan needs improvement. Did the preacher get carried away by his own enthusiasm as he was writing, and did he neglect good planning in the working brief? Are the people in his mind? Does he carry his heart for them on his sleeve? Is the heavenly Father having His way about showing forth the message of His Son for the sake of His Spirit's working? How are the proportions? Is the main-line track clear? Are there bad derailments?

2. *Paragraph check.* — The chief advance of the first draft over the working brief was, obviously, the individual paragraph. Ten or fifteen lines of type now stand where three were before. Does everything in the paragraph talk about its topic? How about the sequence of sentences? A good paragraph works with a plane rather than an ax; each sentence lays down a shaving beyond the preceding one rather than jump far ahead and splinter the idea over again. Does the paragraph frankly and helpfully tell what it should, signal its topic near the start, and if possible tie up its story in a summarizing sentence or other device?

Even more important are the questions about the content of the paragraph. It's for people! Does it help them? Can they understand it? Do they want to? The preacher worked for many hours with Bible and grammar and lexicon and perhaps commentary and doctrinal handbook. He had time for memories of the church and its worship and its literature to come to mind. But the hearer will just begin to follow him; will he be able and willing?

The chief answers to these questions lie in application and illustration. Analogies, whether the one-word kind or the kind extended through the portrayal of whole human situations, have to thrust the abstractions and the intangibles into focus. Are there enough of them? too many? People are fatigued by obscurity, but irritated by the delay to get to the point. Often the preacher uses an illustration because he has thought so long about his subject that he is bored, and he hopes to whet curiosity by obscuring the purpose for which he is telling his illustration. But most of the time he is merely puzzling or dangling the hearer. So: is the purpose of every illustration clear — preferably before it is used? Where an idea needs more firming up, where can we get something to do it — Bible? the experience of the majority of hearers present in their own family or community or parish life?

Does the paragraph actually apply its teaching to the hearer? Or has the preacher been carrying the application in his mind and merely presupposing that the hearer thinks about it? Or is the application pedestrian, excessively hortatory, condescending?

Where the purpose of a paragraph is teaching and doctrine, does it talk in the high terms of God, or is the thrust for faith and life left unclear? Is the holy thing used like a blackboard pointer? Some of the techniques which the preacher has learned at considerable cost in working with children or newcomers to the church he can wisely invest in preaching to the church as a whole.

3. *Transitions.* — While writing the first draft, the preacher may have felt that some of the paragraphs hung together poorly. Perhaps he left the problem unsolved in order to get to the next point, or perhaps he extemporized new and unplanned paragraphs into the draft to make it hold. Now is the time to ascertain what was wrong. If the particulars are in proper sequence, little transitional language should be necessary, except at major divisions. Perhaps a paragraph failed to end on its own topic and thus made the shift to the new idea difficult. Perhaps the outline is cumbersome; it's harder to move from IA3 to IB1 than from IA to IB.

4. *Introduction.* — As the entire sermon takes shape and its applications clarify, the approach to be used in the introduction emerges. False or double or wordy introductions can be discarded. If the hearer is really king, then the standard opening for a sermon should be: begin with the hearer. Tell him why it is a good idea that he should concern himself with the sermon and its subject. If early paragraphs in the outline deal with the hearer's need and problem, tell him the purpose of the sermon and get into the analysis of need quickly. If you have discovered a startling quotation or story that fits the thrust of the entire sermon and seems sure-fire stuff for the introduction, stifle the impulse, and save it for the conclusion. You got yourself under way pondering the general setting and immediate context of the text or the day of the church year for which you are preparing. But only the most disciplined portion of any audience will respond to such materials with genuine attention at the very beginning, and so you will save them for the body of the sermon.

The big purpose of the introduction is to make the central thought and goal of the sermon clear and to promise helpfully that it will be discussed. Now is the time for the preacher to wrestle for a statement of the central thought that is brief enough to be memorable and meaningful enough to be distinctive. The introduction need not forecast what the major divisions will be if they are obvious components of the central thought. If the central thought has a concept that needs definition and explanation, the introduction may be the place to provide it in ways that will not make hearers uncomfortable for their ignorance but grateful for the help. The entire introduction should be friendly. It should display the preacher's good will toward his hearers and his own appreciation for the opportunity to present a helpful message. It should not shock, or bore, or entertain, or make promises which will not be fulfilled; it should introduce.

5. *Conclusion.* — The last five minutes of the sermon are the most important. What the people remember of the sermon and how it moves them to goals is what it did for them. Hence the last minutes of the sermon must convey its most memorable Gospel, its clearest imperatives for faith and life. The plan and structure of the sermon prior to the conclusion here carries the greatest load.

The concluding paragraph must get out of the way of the doctrinal and persuasive climax of the sermon which preceded it. The end has to come early enough in the sermon and the service that people still have the energy to hear and think, of course. But more: the conclusion has to swing the attention once more on the goal for the hearer and on the power of God in Christ to reach it. The hearer knows that the sermon is over — and wants its living to begin.

The conclusion will therefore pull the strands of the sermon together once more — in one braid. This is not to imply a stereotyped summary or bald exhortation. Often the preacher can link conclusion and introduction through a common phrase or picture which helps him to "put a ribbon around the sermon." Save the most memorable illustration, provided that it pertains to the goal and means of the sermon, for the conclusion. Use poetry only if it deeply moved you, if its one-time and out-loud telling will move the hearer, and if you can look him in the eye as you say it.

6. *Style and language.* — If the preacher has time to rewrite the entire sermon after so much reworking of individual sections, well. Then he will be able to concentrate on a few over-all factors. He will want to listen to his language, test the sound of his lines, rearrange the order of words, shape cadence sometimes to be rough and compelling, sometimes easy and transparent, but never artificial or pulpiteering. The preacher is speaking not merely to people but from people; he has to sound like the man they all would like to be as they talk to their brother. He is not writing a play to declaim. He is rather filled with the concern to use words in such a way that people will not be conscious of words but of the Word of God. Even the finest job of rewriting has not "finished" the sermon. The preaching is still to come!

Much of the preparation of a textual sermon looks tedious and diffuse in print. But it telescopes in practice, it picks up speed with skill. That speed does not come with omitting or by-passing the essential ingredients, but it comes with sure handling of the tools of theology and language. The preacher's goal is not to be good, or fast, or comfortable, but to speak the Word of life. The finest skill is not too good for that goal.

Look at one of your recent manuscripts, or listen to a recent tape. Think about the language. Do people hear that kind of language anywhere else? Does it sound like you? Is it the most direct and simple way of saying what you have in mind? Can you catch yourself making words to bridge over spots where you are fumbling or stalling?

People think in pictures. Make a census of words in the above sermon. How many of the nouns evoke pictures in the hearer's mind? How many of the verbs imply motion and action?

Analyze several illustrations in the above sermon. Is their purpose clear? Does the hearer know why you are going to tell each?

For further reading see pp. 301, 302.
Note Appendix I, p. 321.

SECTION FIVE

Delivering the Sermon

The preacher knows that preparing a sermon is not preaching it. He still has to speak it to people. The old word for that speaking is "delivery." It implies that the prepared address now arrives at the destination.

Good preaching shares the qualities of all effective and persuasive speech. In addition it has its own unique plus: it speaks the Word of God, it is driven by love for people.

In his anxiety to deliver the sermon to the people, the preacher must see to it that he lose neither the qualities of good public address nor the plus of Word from God and love for people. Either failure means that the cargo is not delivered but lost in transit.

The preparation of the sermon climaxes, and the whole person of the preacher shares, in the preaching.

Chapter Eighteen

PREACHING THE SERMON

Look again at the Biblical words for "preaching," noted in Chapter 1 above. They mean "telling," "proclaiming." We have been discussing what the preacher does before he tells. But now comes the telling! This is the high moment. This is one of the most rewarding tasks in the pastorate. Now the Word of God which has been churning and seething in the mind of the preacher is ready to thrust out into the heart of the hearer.

The Preacher's Tools

The sower in our Lord's parable had a bag around his neck, hands for scattering the seed on the soil, and feet to carry him from spot to spot. His counterpart, the preacher, has similar equipment for putting the Word into people. He walks about all week, but during the service of the church he stays on a platform or in a chancel or behind a pulpit or lectern. Sometimes he wishes he could move into the audience and sit down next to some person who looks sleepy or

troubled or doubtful; but in the decorum of the service he has to con-
note his desire by means short of that.

His whole person is the means! He is not just a loud-speaker fas-
tened to a pulpit, but he is a man. He speaks a message which has
stirred him first and which shows its effect over his entire body. His
concern to reach the hearer likewise shows all over him. His voice
and speech are primary, for he has to communicate by means of the
spoken word. But the rest of him must work in harmony with his
speech. His face and arms and hands flex and relax in keeping with
his message. To keep necks from craning and heads from bobbing
he stands in one place, yet he feels the concern of his task over his
whole body. When the entire organism of the preacher works together, the hearer is not conscious of all its parts, nor is the preacher
who is skilled at his craft and wrapped up in his purpose. The effectiveness of the message depends on the hearer's thinking about the
message and not about the processes of language and speech by which
it reaches his brain. Hence the preacher's whole self must work together smoothly and unobstrusively.

Preaching Signals Ideas

Preaching must make sense, we said in Chapter 8. The sermon is
useful, not via magic or some spiritual osmosis but only as it hits the
hearer's brain. The preacher's speech must tune each hearer's mind
so that he sees each scene and thinks each fact exactly the way the
preacher intends.

The carrier wave of the message is the voice. Hence it must be
ample so that the hearer doesn't strain, pleasant or not overloud so
that he doesn't cringe. Inflections of the voice are pointers which
signal important ideas; hence the voice must be flexible and able to
employ a wide range of notes on the musical scale. The preacher must
be able to control the force and pressure of his voice and to vary its
quality so that his moods will not distort or hamper his tone; tensions
must not strain the larynx or the opening from the mouth to the nasal
cavity, mellow and relaxed moods must not cause the voice to weaken
or become breathy.

The voice conveys ideas by words. Tongue and lips produce
a variety of shapes to the cavity of the mouth and thus produce

vowels; tongue, teeth and gums, lips, and pharynx cause blocks of the voice or friction of air to produce consonants. The speaker must produce vowels and consonants efficiently and pleasantly and in keeping with the best usage of his hearers. Otherwise they will begin to think about how he talks rather than what he is saying.

At this point ideas only begin. Now words must be grouped into phrases, phrases into sentences, sentences into larger structures of thought. The preacher must signal the relation between individual words, or between ideas expressed by groups of words, by means of speeding up or slowing down the rate at which words and ideas strike the ear; by altering the pitch or key of the voice or the quality of its tone; by facial expressions and, if other methods are insufficient, by movements of the hand and body. The sermon is delivered not by handing the hearer a roll of tape inside a package but by unrolling the tape and playing it through the receiver of the hearer's mind so that the ideas stand in proper perspective and hang together in a chain of persuasive thought. That playback is the preacher's speech.

Preaching Signals Meaning

Preaching does more than convey ideas and facts. It persuades people. They are not mere spectators of a program which they are seeing on an inner screen, but they are a part of the program; they are to find themselves being changed in the very process of their listening. How does a preacher through simple spoken words produce meaning and change in the hearts of his hearers?

Preaching makes meaning through processes grooved by God in human nature and in the theology of His Word of redemption. The preacher must himself first be swayed and changed by the message which he speaks. If he is truly preaching, this has involved more than his mind, and he is doing more than remember ideas and launch them at eardrums. The change took place in his own heart before he ever opened his mouth to speak. When he preaches, he now reflects this change across the whole mechanism of his person. He has been the target of the projectile of God's love and grace. He has seized upon God Himself with a new grasp. He is battling his own flesh with new determination. He is charged with a fresh concern of love for people, and the hour of preaching is its opportunity. This grasp on God and purpose in life shows through his whole body.

Thus the preacher's voice stirs to the experience not just of preaching but of God at work on people. His muscles tense or relax in keeping with the urgency or the comfort of his message. Hence as he stands before his people, his whole presence is a reinforcement and demonstration of the message. As they look at him — and this is why preaching is different from distributing literature — they are drawn into the same total inner and surface response that he displays. In psychological terms this is called empathy, that the speaker shares in the same total response that he proposes to produce in his hearers and that his own response tends to reinforce the equivalent in them.

Let us remind ourselves at once that this is more than psychology. This is witness. Here lies the urgency of the pleading and beseeching which St. Paul describes himself as practicing toward his hearers (2 Cor. 5:18-21). In God's scheme the preacher is one who himself experienced what he preaches and preaches as one who has experienced it. (Luke 24:44-48)

Controlled Application

The preacher makes meaning in the hearer, however, not simply by giving him the demonstration of a changed person. He is there to help the hearer change too. That has been the goal which has dominated his preparation of the sermon. It must dominate its delivery likewise.

What more can delivery do than the sermon does? If the sermon is planned to persuade, if it speaks Law and Gospel, if it sets up a salutary goal before the hearer and diagnoses his deficiency in reaching it and gives him the power of God in Christ to achieve it — what can the preacher do more than to say it?

To begin with, he can see to it that his delivery takes nothing away from the sermon. Obviously, muffled speech or gobbled articulation will remove much of the simple substance and fact of the sermon. But the goal and purpose of the sermon can fade in the hearer's mind, a helpfully planned message can be left sounding aimless or mawkish, if the preacher's speech and manner has no apparent goal for the hearer.

At this point the age-old debate enters the scene whether the preacher should be emotional in his manner. Actually he has no choice. The human organism operates in a bath of mood and emotion in every waking moment. Every speaker is always emotional. The only question is whether the speaker is going to reflect those emotions which are appropriate to his purpose. Emotion is the physical response to inner tension or relaxation. A sermon should have the high purpose of changing hearers from the clutch of weakness or darkness to life and light. The true preacher responds to his hearer's plight in terms of his own personality. He has God's own gift of life and light for the hearer and reflects his intense concern that the hearer should share it. Some men are more overt in their response than others, but none can be devoid of inner feeling or surface reflection if they mean what they say.

True, if the preacher does not have the appropriate response for reasons to be discussed in the next chapter, he will not solve his problem by artificial unctuousness — people call it "hamming" — or bluster or gyrating gesture. For people will, even without thinking, discern that his emotion is the anxiety that he will be caught being unresponsive to the Law and Gospel of his own message. Why he should fear that may have a number of reasons, but all of them will distort his preaching.

Wouldn't it be wonderful if all preaching sounded as though a dam had given way and the good news were now flooding out upon the hearer in an irresistible tide? Perhaps; but certainly not always. For people have to be led and not simply overwhelmed. They are there, as Paul reminds us in 1 Corinthians 14, not to be spectators of the preacher's ecstasy but thinkers with him of the Gospel of God. The preacher's speech does more than launch a tide. It guides a stream of living water. If at times he worries about his preaching and thinks of himself as a cracked conduit, he should remember that God brings the water not through aqueducts and tile but through water carriers, of whom he is one. Let him stop to drink and then walk on again with his precious burden.

The preacher standing in the pulpit about to address his people may find a number of different moods battling in him for dominance. Can you single out any of these? any others? Which are strongest?

1. I wonder if I am going to be able to remember what I wrote.

2. I'm tired, and I wish this were over.

3. I like it when people have to sit still and listen to me; this will be enjoyable.

4. I believe this will really help the people today.

5. Some of this will be fine; but I worry about some thin sections.

6. I used to be afraid of this as a student, and I still am.

7. I prefer making a sick call.

Listen to your tape. Does your speech have a "one speed forward" quality?

For further reading see p. 302.

The preacher should be constantly aware of improvements he can make in his speech and delivery.

Chapter Nineteen

IMPROVING DELIVERY

Preaching is a skill. We are skillful when we can repeat a process again and again, each time with increasing effectiveness and ease. The skillful preacher is not merely good; he is improving. What happens when he fails to improve? The answer is that he must be practicing mistakes.

If the preacher should improve at his preaching, he must therefore be able to examine himself, forestall mistakes, and correct them as they occur. Later we shall have much to say about self-criticism (Section X below). At this point we want to look particularly at the business of improving speech and the delivery of the sermon.

A man's speech is very personal. He wants to say, "I am what I am." He wants to believe that he cannot change, for the worse or for the better. But he can. New mistakes and deficiencies can pop up at any moment. But the old ones can be pinched off too. He need not stay the way he is.

Self-Consciousness

Most speech difficulties arise from self-consciousness. The public speaker is particularly the target of it. He needs the good will of the individuals to whom he speaks. The preacher should have the constant concern: "Is my hearer understanding me? Am I helping him to change mind and heart for the better? Is he feeling the impact of my Gospel and the Word of God?" Instead he may begin to ask: "Does the hearer like me? Am I going to make a good impression on him? Am I going to be able to remember what to say? Am I going to make a fool of myself? Am I going to be as good as I was last time?"

These are inner reactions which the preacher hardly admits even to himself. Many of them may be submerged reflexes from adolescent speech courses. Yet they affect speech in a very direct way. The entire manner of the self-conscious speaker tends to become brash and pompous. He may inwardly feel shy and inept and uneasy. But he paces about with vigor, speaks brusquely or showily, flails with his arms and thrusts himself into the forefront of his performance, so that his hearers notice him rather than what he says.

Other mechanisms of speech suffer. The self-conscious speaker tries to be too careful about his vowels and consonants. Perhaps his tongue will become so tense that the consonants produced by the quick flick of the tongue against the gum ridge will sound limp. The "a" in "rasp" or "man" will be so tense that it will become blatty. His speech will become pedantic in quality because he will mechanically give the same quantity to accented and unaccented vowels instead of diminishing the quality and length of the latter; thus the mispronunciation "Save-yore" for Savior is almost a trademark of the pulpit. He will worry about the sound of his own voice, and if he is a tenor, he will depress its average key to a husky level because it sounds higher in his inner ear than it does to the hearer.

"What do I say next?" is the constant anxiety of the self-conscious preacher. Thus his mind drifts from the words which are on his lips to ideas which are still ahead. The result will be that the pitch changes and inflections of his voice will be absent-minded. In the standard English sentence a major peak of inflection comes close to its end. But the preacher anxious about his supply of ideas will normally miss that inflection because he is already probing his memory for the next sentence. The result will be that half of the major ideas of his address lack the point and underscore of inflection that they deserve. The unskilled oral reader commits the same fault; he drops his voice toward the end of the sentence instead of inflecting the major idea (radio people used to call this pattern read-y or the dropsy). Often every sentence will end on precisely the same tone on the musical scale, and hearers will pick up the rhythm. Many preachers try to mask their absent-mindedness concerning the final half of their sentences by employing a particularly melodious downward slide; a few, by giving many sentence ends an upward inflection. Since the average sermon has more than two hundred sentences, the net result is an overpowering monotony which has been called, sad to say, pulpit tone.

Abnormalities

All the above difficulties can emerge with the organs of speech themselves functioning normally. From self-consciousness or other difficulties a further battery of disorders may arise which involve improper functioning or deterioration of voice and breathing.

The preacher must be heard. In order to direct his voice over his entire audience or to give special emphasis, he may use what he thinks is a stronger voice but what is simply the pressure of his breath against his larynges as valves. The result is a rasping and wheezing sound, since the larynx functions as a vibrator when it is relaxed and the breath is controlled by lungs and diaphragm. This wheeze is unpleasant, but worse, it may become the source of irritations and disorders which have been dubbed "clergyman's throat." The climax is the formation of laryngeal nodules which must be removed surgically. A preacher should seldom feel more strain in his throat when speaking to a large audience than a small one; he should adjust by breathing more amply and possibly by raising the average key of his voice slightly.

Speaking involves the use of many muscles of throat, diaphragm, and chest. As the speaker becomes fatigued through speech or his other activities, his muscles may lose tone. This will hamper speech because of poorly controlled breathing, distorted quality of the voice, poor posture, and impaired co-ordination.

Improvement

In theory the recipe for eliminating self-consciousness is simple: Remember the hearer! Applying the recipe is complex. Good delivery depends on close thinking and devoted concern for the hearer long before the actual speaking begins. If the preacher practices concern for his hearer throughout his preparation, reminds himself that everything he is doing he does as God's servant of people, constructs a message which from its opening words on is utterly for the sake of reaching and persuading people, then the actual delivery of the sermon will not be something startling and different from the work at the desk, but it will be simply the climax of a process that has fought self-consciousness all the way.

Some special handicaps deserve a special alert. One is the sense of insecurity about remembering, the problem of memorizing a manuscript, and this is the subject of the next chapter. Another is the introduction, normally a peak of anxiety and therefore a special hurdle. Writers on speech have given various suggestions how to bring a set of relaxation into the pulpit and defeat the reflex of anxiety about getting started. Some preachers memorize their opening paragraphs with special care so that they feel less uncertain. These suggestions probably begin at the wrong end, and they may cause the preacher to concentrate on being elaborately, self-consciously easy and relaxed — not much of an improvement! Most of the remedy comes in the final stages of preparing the sermon. Let the preacher make his introduction brief, let it be a simple recommendation to the hearer why the sermon will be worth his while and what it proposes to do for him. Let him plan the introduction so that it gives him the opportunity to stand before the hearer as a friendly witness to Christ rather than a practitioner worrying about his own prestige.

Errors in articulation and pronunciation must be brought under conscious control, if necessary by actually practicing the fault in order to replace it with improvement. Dictionaries are important, and the introductory chapters on articulation have special value. Many other helps for speech are available. The preacher's voice and mood will usually be at their best if he has spent the moments prior to the sermon joining the congregation in a hymn, thoughtfully and prayerfully, rather than in a final huddle with himself pawing some paper or hacking and gargling.

The preacher uses brain and muscle. This means that he should train for his task with the same devotion that the boxer or baseball player applies to his. This means sleep. Too many parishes listen to preachers spent and fatigued with last-minute preparation and a short night's rest. The steward of God's mysteries is also a steward of the body which is his tool. He will husband and refresh his energies so that his message will have the maximum of controlled impact. In phase with sleep must be proper habits of food, elimination, recreation, and bodily exercise. The entire preaching process will benefit, for memory will function more smoothly, words will come more accurately, the muscles in face and upper body will co-ordinate better. The preacher should undergo regular medical examinations and take the physician's advice. If he has the slightest thought that smoking may harm his voice or concentration, he will refrain. Sport or relaxation — good for breath and sleep — aid preaching.

Even these few lines on this subject sound unrealistic to many a practicing pastor. He may feel that his task is too complicated for clearing the priorities and giving preaching the place that this book suggests. Certainly, the priorities in the pastorate are never just for liturgical preaching, but for the Gospel proclaimed by every means possible across the whole front of the pastor's calling. Below (Sections IX, XI, and XII) we shall have more to say about how the entire program of the pastor correlates with the preaching, both in demands upon it and in power for it. At this point we want to face the fact squarely: badly prepared, limply or absent-mindedly delivered sermons are probably worse than nothing. For they train listeners to inattention or to hostility toward the Gospel. They set up an association in the minds of the unwary between theology and triteness, religion and a noisy unctuousness. The preacher has no call to irk men on account of himself but to plead with men in Christ's stead. He may indeed have to feel weak and tremble at the thought of his inability; but he has no business shamming, for he speaks the Word of God in the name of God, and the people die unless he carries out his mandate from God.

Do you normally employ the best pitch for your own voice? You can measure it approximately by finding your lowest possible note, counting the number of notes on your scale up to the topmost (including falsetto); then locating your optimum key about a fourth of the number of steps from the bottom. Now begin reading in a forceful tone, on that key only; gradually insert inflections equally above and below that note. This should suggest where your easiest speaking voice should lie.

Listen to your own preaching on tape. How about the last note of each sentence? the cadence on the last four or five syllables? Is it the same, or is it varied?

Make a list of speech discomforts that you face in preaching, and check them against a good current book on voice or speech.

For further reading see p. 302.

Good delivery depends on re-
membering not just the address
but always the people who are
addressed.

Chapter Twenty

PREPARING DELIVERY

If the preacher wants to deliver his sermon to the people, he has to be thinking about them. If he forgets them as he is speaking, the sermon will strike their ears with the invitation to think and worry about the preacher or to admire him and try to keep listening to him rather than to the message.

The preacher will be concerned for people during the delivery of his sermon only in the degree to which every previous stage of preparation has found him consciously concerned for them, trying to find a message for their purpose and need, struggling to phrase a message that will plumb their hearts and bring them help. Wherever the preacher flags in that purpose, the message will lose power.

Turning the People Off

It is so easy for the preacher to flag. He is tired and busy and must meet many deadlines in his job. When he is listless and preoccupied, he fails to stay alert and resourceful for the inner purpose of his preaching. He worries more about himself: "I need only ten more minutes' worth." . . . "This doesn't look very interesting, but I'll say it briskly and cover up." . . . "I can't compress this, but they have no right to be in such a hurry." Such attitudes produce a shabby manuscript, and the final preaching loses its hold. For the hearer is sitting and watching the preacher cover up or wishing that it were over, instead of reaching out to grasp words to make him alive.

Even though preachers want to do a good job at every other point in their preparation, there is one spot where many of them on purpose turn their minds away from the hearer. That is the stage before entering the pulpit and after the form of the message has come into shape. Chapter 17 above suggested a sixth stage of preparation, the reworking of the final draft. What comes next? For many a preacher the answer is not "Keep on remembering the hearer" but "Start remembering the sermon."

Many a preacher makes the Seventh Stage of his preparation the memorizing of the manuscript by rote. He may have this habit from high school days. He may have the actor's facility of "learning a quick book." Others find at least some of their sermons adapted for verbatim memorizing. The practice seems reasonable, for it safeguards fruits of thought and expression produced at long labor. It seems to prevent awkward pauses. The preacher with an average memory, however, will invest an inordinate amount of time in a stage of preparation which adds nothing to the message. And it forgets the hearer! Think of a pleasant story that you would like to pass on to others. Relish it in your mind, chuckle over it. Then write it out, and commit the words to memory. Now tell it in the words which you had written. What happens to the chuckle? Either it fades, or it becomes artificial. For you aren't thinking of the story and its fun, but of the words you had determined to use.

Other preachers totally omit the Seventh Stage. They take the revised manuscript into the pulpit and read it aloud. Some insert a step of retyping the manuscript so that its grammar shows and its moods and inflections can be signaled to the reader; this is a useful device on radio where the preacher is obligated to reproduce his manuscript exactly. Some preachers do well at reading. Some audiences resent a preacher who reads from the manuscript, others are trained to prefer it. Thus the debate, whether to read the sermon in the pulpit or to "preach without notes" will probably go on.

Preachers who are untrained to read aloud or inexperienced at it often make their hearers inattentive because of the read-y or absent-minded inflection described in the preceding chapter. Material memorized by rote will usually sound the same way. Sporadic efforts to use a brisk high pitch at the start of every new sentence will usually only intensify the monotony of the same low key at the end. Only the most skilled reader succeeds in maintaining adequate eye contact with his audience.

The preacher who habitually reads his message to his hearers meets his chief handicap, however, in the Fourth and Sixth Stages. He expects the labor of recall to be no threat, and so he does not fight for the most simple and direct expression or for the most closely knit sequence of particulars. The result is an address which he could never repeat except by reading — and one which the audience could never remember except by rereading. Great preachers who have read their manuscripts in the pulpit, and there have been many, took the style of language and the mentality of their hearers into account and wrote sermons rather than essays.

SEVENTH STAGE: *Practicing to Remember People*

Suppose the preacher takes seriously the principle that he must remember the people. Suppose he has put himself in their place through all the stages of preparation previously outlined. How can he keep on thinking of the people and not succumb to a new anxiety: "How shall I remember what to say?"

Remember how foolish it is to stop now. "You're getting hot!" the children shout when the searcher is getting close to the hidden object. As the day and hour of preaching move closer, the preacher's nostrils begin to dilate, and his pulse quickens, and pleasurable shivers run up his spine. Why? Because everything to this point has been locked in his imagination. But now he is going to confront people, one or one hundred or one thousand, in the moment to which the Lord God called him and for the purpose of sounding forth that saving call! Now it's really the time to think of the people!

The process is much the same as the Sixth Stage, discussed in Chapter 17. There the preacher went over and over his materials with pen in hand and tried out new versions of whole paragraphs on his typewriter. Now he pushes back from the desk, and his eyes no longer focus on paper. No preacher uses the same method as another or even the same method in all his sermons. One will want to mull over the entire manuscript again and again in his mind, envisioning the hearer. Another wants to enter the pulpit to try out many of its paragraphs "for sound," to people the pews with imaginary hearers both appreciative and critical. Others like to put the manuscript away and start thinking the sermon through, paragraph by paragraph, with nothing in their hand. If they become derailed or blocked, if their attention wanders, they note it carefully; for here a link is open and the train uncoupled, the shining thread of the discourse is tarnished, too many alternatives for transition present themselves. Then they pull out the manuscript again, or perhaps only the working brief, and note improvements. If some paragraph is too slender or abstract, that is a good reminder to fill it out with living tissue — for the sake of the people.

We call "functional memorizing" the process of going through the planned sermon repeatedly, with the people in mind, until its structure is solid and its expressions are meaningful. How often? That depends on how much time is at hand for preparation, how easy and inevitable the outline of the sermon has been from the Fourth Stage on, how vivid the relation of the material to the people. In textual preaching an added aid to memory is the text itself. The particulars of the sermon seldom follow in the order of the words in the text, but the ideas are there, clamoring for treatment from the page of the open Bible.

With a sermon of average difficulty — where there has been time to do some reworking of the manuscript — the first review of the sermon in its final preparation for delivery may take an hour or more. For the mind will sort out by-paths, test previously developed sequences, fumble for better illustrations, and possibly derail completely a time or two. The few Biblical quotations or verses from poetry that are to be stated verbatim will need close memorizing. The second run will be much briefer, and if the time is up, the preacher can concentrate simply on sequence and a few troublesome paragraphs that tend to overlap. A third run, if there is time, will usually approximate the length and many of the words of the final sermon. The last run or two can be very brief, since the mind will signal entire paragraphs as clear and ready and since the speed of thought is three or four times that of speech.

Do you take the manuscript into the pulpit with you? Do you prepare some notes, like the first sentences of each paragraph, or the propositions of the major divisions, or the trial outline, and take them along?

The most pragmatic answer is obviously: "Do anything that will put you at ease toward the people." But in justice to the covering principle of this section we should reaffirm: The sense of safety comes not from something outside of you but from the simple structure of the entire message, simple for the sake of the people. If somewhere in the preparation that structure was too complicated to remember, it's never too late to whittle it into shape. The practice of carrying an outline into the pulpit may weaken the preacher's communication with his hearers, but worse, it may weaken the patient intention to make those propositions inevitable and easy to remember before the sermon is ever preached. And that they must be if the people are to get the plot and vitality of the message from one-time hearing.

Look, the preacher is in the pulpit! Is anyone in doubt about what he is thinking? His mind is crowded with words, details of a message. Does he step softly so that he will not dislodge them before he begins? No, for he has been waiting to talk to his people. He feels the pressure of a message which he is anxious to give them. He knows most of them from daily acquaintance in the neighborhood, in pastoral care, and in church work. He rejoices to have them together in one act of worship. He rejoices, for he loves them, and he knows that the Word of God in Christ is just exactly what they need. He is their servant and speaks that Word not just as their teacher but as their spokesman. He is the servant of God, and God will help him to preach the Word with boldness.

Does this chapter recommend functional memorizing because

1. It saves time as compared with rote memorizing?

2. It gives the preacher the right to garble his words with a good conscience?

3. It makes speech smoother and therefore easier to listen to?

4. It implies close effort at every stage of the preparation toward making the sermon easy for the hearer to remember?

5. It stresses thought for the hearer, which rote memorizing does not?

6. Reading a sermon aloud is homiletically unsound?

At what stage of preparation do you find your thought for the people most vague?

For further thought see p. 302.
Note Appendix I, pp. 321–327.

SECTION SIX

The Topical Sermon

Section Four reviewed the preparation of preaching which grows out of a text from Scripture.

Many sermons, however, take their first cue from an idea in the preacher's mind — a "topic." He moves on to develop a Biblical sermon around it, with or without benefit of a single text from the Bible to define or shape it.

Most stages of preparation are the same for both the topical and the textual sermon. Special problems and difficulties should be faced and safeguards erected.

Most preachers will find it helpful for themselves and their hearers to cultivate skill in both textual and topical preaching, provided that "topical" still implies "Biblical."

131

*The preacher will appreciate ad-
vantages of topical preaching but
will beware of its pitfalls.*

Chapter Twenty-One

ADVANTAGES AND PITFALLS

The textual sermon finds its theme and goal in a text. The topical sermon begins with a theme and goal in the mind of the preacher. The difference is not absolute. Every textual sermon must build around a single goal to be persuasive. Every topical sermon must work with teachings of Scripture to be persuasive in the Christian sense — "preach repentance and remission of sins." In this book we do not discuss preaching that dispenses with Biblical ingredients altogether.

The chief differences between the two methods of building a sermon lie in the gathering of primary material and in organizing it. The Second, Fifth, and Sixth Stages discussed above in Section IV are much the same in both types of sermons.

"I Have an Idea"

"I have an idea for a sermon," says the preacher. This is likely to be the beginning of a very good sermon indeed. For it is close to his own experience. The idea is probably the crystallization and summary of a number of random thoughts which have now merged in his mind in the shape of a topic. Those thoughts rose to the surface and began to nag for treatment perhaps while he was reading the Bible, or while he was reflecting on the state of his people and parish, or as he was scanning the news of the day or reading helpful editorials or a great novel, or as he was pondering poetry or art.

The preacher who is skilled in the textual method and employs the pericopic approach to most of his Sunday morning sermons will also "get ideas." Some are left over as he has to discard secondary goals while preparing a textual sermon. As he plans his preaching by the year (note Section IX below), he observes areas of Biblical doctrine, or life in the parish, or national or community concerns that need special treatment, and he begins to plan entire courses of topical sermons. (Note Section VII below)

What is a "good idea" for a sermon? It's hard to say, for ideas seldom stand still. It may be a flash of insight into a teaching of the Bible. It may be a turn of phrase in a headline in the newspaper. It may be the fragment of a conversation during pastoral care. It may be an unexpected word in a new translation of the Bible.

Advantages

If the preacher is a man of God, the preacher-based idea may indeed suggest a sermon. For the preacher is interested in it. Sometimes the interest is due to novel phrasing or a quality of surprise, and he may have to brace himself for the disappointment that after all he hadn't enough substance in hand for a whole sermon. But often the interest is a spark from the anvil of his ministry. The surprise may be due to the discovery of an important word of God that is just beginning to disturb and exhilarate the preacher, and he wants to share the impact. If he can keep that spark alive and in an entire discourse help it kindle imagination and will of the people, high witness and great preaching should result.

Another advantage of the topical method is that the idea is likely to be unified. Memorable ideas for preaching seldom attack via the route of abstraction or theological generalization. This means that they may be concrete in their segment of human life or vivid in their focus on a particular religious value. One of the greatest difficulties in textual preaching comes at the very beginning — to find a unified goal. Unless that hurdle is cleared, the entire sermon will be diffuse and impractical. In the topical method the unity seems to come already installed!

Where Topical and Textual Meet

If we could imagine a preacher who employed exclusively textual routines in preparing his sermons, we would find that he still had some acquaintance with the topical method. For whole classes of preaching texts suggest the topical process.

By this we do not refer to one-sentence texts excised from a close context. Usually the preacher draws in so much help from the context that he is actually preaching on the larger section as his text.

But we do think especially of Biblical narratives. They are in Scripture to give the preacher a swift review and summary, a case history, of man's life under God. Only seldom does a Biblical story suggest more than one preaching idea. In the case of the parables of Jesus, with the possible exception of the parables of the sower (Matt. 13:3 ff.) and the vineyard (Matt. 21:33 ff.), ludicrous results accrue if goals are multiplied or applications are drawn from many details. Preaching on a narrative text, accordingly, has a strong affinity with the topical method. The text suggests a core of application to the hearer but gives few cues for filling out the discourse.

Pitfalls

Topical preaching is not foolproof. A topic is not unified simply because it is brief. A compact phrase may mask a metaphor that applies to many situations. The preacher is stirred by the theme "The Blessedness of Faith." His sermon then lists a series of fruits of faith of which some concern the approach to God, some the trust in God, and some the "fruits of faith," or the life of love. Both diagnosis and goal become diluted in the hearer's mind because of the broad range of ideas. Or the preacher is fascinated, as have been many before him, by the music of the sentence — actually it is a text — "The Spirit of Man Is the Candle of the Lord." He exploits the figure to describe the radiance which God sheds through people, and the way that people are consumed in the service of love. Again focus and goal are weakened.

The preacher should be sharply critical of an engaging caption — the trade calls it a "preaching angle" — which may set off so slight a train of association that it will not give the thrust for a genuinely persuasive sermon. He should be sure that he is handling more than an illustration of one idea within a sermon, more than a factor of interest attaching to a single paragraph. He need not throw the item away. It may become a memorable conclusion for a sermon on a more adequate theme. Properly explored and attached to more substantial Biblical materials, it may grow into a refrain or an echo that will underscore the plot of a thoroughly helpful sermon.

The Christian preacher should be especially edgy about topics that have the ring of popular currency but are poor legal tender for Biblical concepts or refuse to correlate with the way of life in Christ. Such phrases jump into popular interest from the news, or advertising, or popular psychology and psychiatry, and the pulpit often exploits them until their interest has worn out or until it gets on alien ground. The Christian religion itself has suffered from the stress on "peace of mind" implying physical comfort quite irrelevant to the peace which Jesus gives and on His own terms. "Freedom" is a good word in theology and also in politics, but not in the same sense; and the preacher finds himself hoodwinked into stressing human autonomy at the expense of dependence on God. "Faith" degenerates too frequently into a hypnotic self-confidence — "first we must have faith in ourselves. . . ." Often the pat phrase becomes oblivious of the primary needs of people and the common clay of reality. The "adventures" and the "challenges" of faith neglect the prosaic and plodding battle between flesh and spirit; the "beauty" and the "glory" of the recommended goal lie beyond the sense impressions that they suggest. The result is that the man in the pulpit doesn't seem to be the kindly and compassionate pastor whom the people know from bedside or deskside.

Topical preaching takes its cue and fills out its material frequently from the pastor's reading or rhetoric rather than from Scripture. Such a sermon may mirror the preacher's interests, and his adeptness with words, and tacitly invite the audience to be spectators of it. Unfortunately many published sermons, aiming to provide grist for the mills of the little parsons, reveal a distance between preacher and people. Sometimes the distance is cultural: the preacher's quotations from literature and his analogies borrowed from his reading are beyond the level of his average hearer. Sometimes the distance is one of thought forms. People think in practical and concrete terms. But the preacher multiplies his words by the device of abstraction or technical classification. The concept "love" gives him the chance to review *agape, philia,* and *eros.* The justice of God gives him the cue for paragraphs on contrasts of Jewish, Greek, Roman, and contemporary law. Gradually the people view preaching as the business of watching the pastor browse among his quotations — a sort of reverse on the relation of shepherd and the flock.

The primary pitfall of topical preaching is ultimately that it may not have enough to say. It may have to speak helpfully about minor problems; it may have to fill out its bulk through literary devices. If the preacher can fortify the topical method by finding the helpful text to support it, well, then the First Stage previously discussed stands by with fountains of material. The Second Stage should be critical and painstaking, so that the planned material will genuinely preach the Gospel of Christ to human need. Otherwise the preacher will find himself multiplying words and particulars in an outline which either will run roughshod through the hearer's capacity for attention or will be broad as the heavens and never quite down to earth.

Almost every preacher, nevertheless, must employ the topical method frequently. Let him be patient at remembering his task while he is doing it. Let him remember his call to preach Law and Gospel to his people. Let him remember the people, the limitations of the preaching situation as well as its advantages, the abilities and the handicaps of the human mind. Let him make things easy for himself and his people. He has plenty of hurdles to overcome in the basic offense of the Gospel and the skittishness of human attention, without adding to the difficulties of the preaching hour with a mass of random language concerning things within and beyond the experience of his people — things that do not pertain to the work of God's own Spirit in their hearts.

FOR FURTHER THOUGHT

Chapter 26 below describes some average situations suggesting the use of topical sermons; also note Chapter 34.

What would you suggest to remedy the ambiguity of the goal in the topics listed under "Pitfalls"?

What is the simplest way of keeping a topical sermon from becoming non-Biblical?

Suppose the topic "The Peace That Jesus Gives" works in your mind. How would you go about finding a good text to fit it? How about "Our Freedom Under God"?

How recently have you read or heard a topical sermon? Was it Biblical?

For further reading see p. 303.

*Material from many sources helps
the preacher construct the topical
and the textual sermon alike.*

Chapter Twenty-Two

GATHERING MATERIAL

This book does not use the term "topical" to represent non-Biblical preaching or even all preaching without the use of texts. By "topical" it means the preaching on a subject which the preacher has begun to develop before he turns to a text to define it.

As the preacher goes about filling out the material of his topic to arrive at a reasonably complete and helpful message, he draws on a number of sources. One is the Bible, which he may exploit by choosing a text or by other means. Many other sources supply material at the same time, and to survey them has purpose also for the building of the textual sermon.

Topical Sermons with Texts

The simplest method of tapping Biblical resources for a topical sermon is to choose a text that unfolds or highlights the topic. This brings us back to the subject of choosing texts. (Note chapters 11 and 12 above)

Perhaps the topic going through the preacher's mind is really an echo of Scripture, a reflection of a Biblical narrative, a pregnant theological phrase. Choosing the text is, then, simply a matter of finding the passage that cued the topic. Sometimes this search will be disappointing. We remember savoring a topic on the atonement, "Jesus Wrecked the Wall," i. e., between man and God. Search led to Eph. 2:14, but it speaks of His destroying partitions between men and men. The man who is accustomed to textual preaching does his best if he finds the thoroughly appropriate text for his topic. Then the First Stage outlined in Section Four yields a useful harvest.

Professional and devotional experience with the Scriptures, through the years will lead the preacher to whole areas of Bible which yield texts for previously considered topics. Thus Ephesians portrays the mutual edification of the church, Psalms the church at worship or under adversity, Colossians or Romans or Hebrews the various pictures for the atonement, 1 Peter the church in its witness to the world, John the atonement as God's bringing His plan of life for the world to come true, Ephesians and 1 Peter the calling of the Christian. With each new sermon and each new experience as a teacher of religion the preacher gains more facility in using the Bible as a source of topics and a source of supply for each topic.

Another kind of text for topical sermons serves as a cue or underscore for only a phase of it. Ultimately the motto text discussed in Chapter 12 fits here. Preaching literature affords interesting examples of this process, but the lay listener seems to profit less from it than the professional reader.

Biblical Topics

Common in the literature of preaching is the topic taken directly from the Bible: "The Frustration of Moses," "The Cruse That Never Fails," "Weighed in the Balance and Found Wanting," "David, Saint and Sinner," "Jesus the Carpenter," "Almost Thou Persuadest Me," "The Slave Who Became a Brother."

Frequently such topics capsule a Biblical character or incident rich in preaching values. As the preacher develops his sources from Scripture, he will do well to restate in less fragrant and more literal terms exactly what he proposes to mean for his hearer by the topic.

A sermon on a biographical topic is not a sermon if it proposes in more or less interesting fashion simply to review a chapter from a life story. It becomes a sermon as it sets out to help hearers. Topics that refer only to a person in history, or that are chiefly negative or diagnostic in their suggestion, are therefore not the central thought of a sermon.

The topics above will therefore look something like this at the start of preparation: "Though we properly incur God's chastisements for thwarting His plans, His mercies never fail at the end"; "God's care for His people never fails at the point where they need it most"; "God's righteous judgments upon the nations remind us to seek Him in repentance"; "The battle between flesh and spirit drives us to humble dependence on God's mercy"; "Our Lord's share in our humanity strengthens us for our calling"; "The seriousness of God's call in the Gospel must penetrate our resistance and apathy"; "In the church of Christ all are brothers." — Note that these statements are for the preacher, not the public. As he labors to phrase his message for the people, the conciseness and charm of the "topic," if any, may return to the scene; its phrasing may enter into the major divisions or, properly amplified, into the advertising of the message for the day.

Even the busiest preacher will discover that he will never be at a loss to discover Biblical topics as the Bible becomes to him more and more populated with flesh-and-blood people like those of his parish and as the Biblical record unfolds its insights into human nature or the divine plan and he discerns the pungency of its expression. When to employ topical sermons and thus to put this material to work is a question to think through in annual planning. (See Chapter 34 below)

Materials from Non-Biblical Sources

The topical sermon needs more than its topic; it has to have meat on its bones. The Bible is a primary source. The preacher will develop the skill of using many other sources, some of them indirectly Biblical, both for arriving at topics and for filling out the discourse.

Such a primary source are the materials of the church's worship, its hymns, canticles, responses, and prayers. The more familiar they are, the less aptly do they capture interest, and hence they play a less important role in introductions and conclusions than elsewhere in the sermon directed to average listeners. Quotations from the utterances and incidents from the lives of non-Biblical figures in the history of the church — fathers and saints, poets and pioneers, missionaries and philanthropists — can be apt and striking. The preacher should remember that his average hearer is not interested so much as he himself in Augustine or Luther, Thomas a Kempis or Ziegenbalg, Evelyn Underhill or John Mott. Hence the quotations will have to be short, and the preacher will use them at points to which the interest of the hearer is already geared.

Christian art is a useful source of material for preaching, provided that the words about it sound like more than filler, that the preacher can actually communicate his own appreciation to his listener, and that somewhere his hearers have the opportunity to see and hear what he is talking about. To address a placid Midwestern audience on a segment of the ceiling of the Sistine Chapel, or on the theme of victory suddenly inserted into the meditation on the crucifixion in Bach's *Passion According to St. John,* may be little more than showmanship and cultural strutting. Different it is if the pictures appeared in a recent issue of *Life* magazine, or if a parish group recently had an open meeting with the recordings of the *Passion,* or if the people heard it on the radio. We have attempted whole courses of sermons on familiar religious paintings, and the people present took a print home for further thought; but we found that the goal suggested in the story of the picture needed patient textual unfolding if the Gospel was to be preached at all. How boring, to say nothing of harmful, references to Holman-Hunt's "The Light of the World" and its "latch on the inside" have been through the years, only long-suffering listeners can tell.

Quotations from literature can fill out the structure of a sermon helpfully. But they will have to be brief, and usually the people will absorb the idea better if only the point is quoted directly and the remainder paraphrased. The quoted writer has to be close to the people and must demonstrate the ability to express himself helpfully to the ear. The doggerel that passes for poetry in the newspapers or the pedestrian assertions about morals and God by scientists and politicians are usually substandard, and the people often find them trite before the preachers do. The preacher gleans his helps from literature as he himself reads. What excites him and causes him to say, "That's good for my people," is worth jotting down quickly, and the best of it will be remembered without copying it. Anthologies of quotations are seldom useful for more than stimulating us to be alert in our own reading. While we are on the subject: Let the preacher take pains honestly to credit the source of his quotations. If he has to do it too frequently to sound well, then he has too many of them.

Pastoral care and conversation suggest topics and supporting ideas. Quotations from conversations are often more usable and pungent than the literary ones and have the advantage of the preacher's own discovery. Obviously he will have to refrain from using any that might cause hearers to be embarrassed, or to try to identify who is quoted, or to resent that somebody else got the distinction of "making the sermon today." Also when aiming at diagnosis of people's shortcomings and the sins of community and parish, the preacher needs to be unfailingly kind. He needs the saving sense of humor, which doesn't mean that he tries for a laugh, or that he belittles wrong or jokes about it, but that he has a kindly awareness of human frailty, beginning with his own. The kindness lies in the will to help.

At the heart of all the material that the preacher introduces into a sermon, whether from the Bible or outside of it, must be his intention to help people with the Gospel of God. He has been called by Him to speak the message of His love and the mercy that never fails. Whether he has to labor hard to find enough to say and goes far afield for his materials, or whether he strikes a lode in Bible or elsewhere that makes him wish he could speak all day, he must view his materials never simply for the sake of finishing a sermon or interesting the people, but always for helping them find God and put His power to work in their lives, through Jesus Christ and His Spirit.

FOR FURTHER THOUGHT

What *is* the trouble with Holman-Hunt's "Light of the World"? A cue is Rev. 3:20. How do you preach "means" in this figure?

Review your practice in using manuals of illustrations or quotations. Are they starters? Do you quote them verbatim? How do you acknowledge sources? How do you signal to the ear what quotation marks do for the eye?

Have you ever tried a literary quotation or a popular saying for a sermon theme?

What helps do you find useful for finding texts to fit topics which you already have in mind? Do you build notebooks of texts or file them topically?

List advantages and disadvantages in asking people of the congregation to submit topics for preaching.

For further reading see p. 303.

Whatever method the preacher uses to build his sermon, let him make sure that he will preach Christ.

Chapter Twenty-Three

SPECIAL PROBLEMS

Whether the preacher approaches his sermon by the textual or the topical method, let him be sure that he is planning to preach! Otherwise the textual sermon becomes a lecture in exegesis, the topical a review of literature. To test whether a sermon really preaches, we have to apply two criteria to the finished product simultaneously: How much of it helped the hearer ponder Jesus Christ as Savior and Lord by virtue of His death and resurrection? How much of it caused the hearer to think about himself and his own relation to God in Christ?

The preacher can't apply the criteria and then plod back into the pulpit after the sermon is over and pour spiritual vitality into it from a little red can, with the shamefaced explanation that he had run dry. He had his chance. The curious quickening of interest in Holy Communion in recent years, by pastors and people alike, may be due in part to its uniform affirmation of God's mercy in Christ, in saving contrast to many sermons which precede it.

Freshness

The beginning preacher has one paramount question: "What shall I say?" The practicing pastor begins to ask: "How can I keep it fresh?" That question is as vital to the topical as the textual method. Under the latter the preacher feels himself going stale because his outlines are too similar and his exposition becomes pedantic. But the topical preacher, enjoying the sensation of letting the chips fall where they will, may discover to his dismay that he is using the same chips over and over.

In part the same remedies apply to both ills. The closing sections of this book survey the self-disciplines of criticism, growth, and concern for people. These self-disciplines must steadily refresh any preaching. At this point let us say to the topical preacher: Don't let the reservoir from which you dip your themes become too small. He has his ways of being alert to his parish; he has his skills of finding "angles" in his reading. Staleness sets in not just when he finds himself without topics but long before — in the period when he is still preaching in many different ways but on the same basic ideas. Planning the topical sermons in advance will help to forestall this tendency, for then the preacher will see just what he is trying to do in a year's space and how hard he is making it for himself to speak brightly and interestingly when his crisp themes actually are masks for the same eight or ten problems of his people.

Let the preacher fight to understand his own themes! The fact that the statement is novel or brief is no guarantee for its precision and concreteness. What does it really mean? What does it mean in terms of Bible, of God's way with man in Christ Jesus? What does it mean for the hearer? Where is it going to take him? What is it going to do for him? What Biblical counterpart is behind the conventional American abstractions of "freedom" or "faith" or "soul" or "peace of mind" or "righteousness"? A clear answer to these questions will sometimes lead to scrapping the whole idea, and sometimes to the discovery that new light from God's Word may dawn on preacher and people.

In general the preacher will safeguard freshness, paradoxically, by discovering his topics not through signals of language and "angles" and novelty but through the search for helpful truth. The file folder labeled "Topics for Sermons" may become choked with novel take-offs on newspaper headlines, human interest stories, incidents from biographies old or new — and they may concern very few human problems. Rather think of people, reach under the surface of people's lives, let the Bible tell about God's thinking concerning people, and many topics will come to the surface. Then try to clothe the topic in striking language. If thinking about people is dull and the prospect of helping them lacks freshness, then the preacher has arrived at the point where astonishing titles for sermons will hardly rescue him. The safeguard for fresh preaching comes from thinking about people and expanding the mind and heart to their panorama of difficulty, whether you look at them directly or through the vision of the Bible.

Outlining

At first glance the topical sermon seems easier to outline than the textual one. Each major division in the latter is a three-ply affair: 1. It has to say something about the central thought; 2. It has to say something about the text; 3. It has to say something about the hearer. In the topical method each major division simply says something about the central thought, doesn't it?

Not quite. Each major division of the textual sermon is three-ply, so that the text and its preaching pervades the whole discourse and so that every part of it will persuade people in the desired direction. Those purposes do not stem from tradition or abstract principle but from the mandate to preach the saving Word of God for repentance and to redeem the time. That same mandate and stewardship applies also to topical preaching. Hence the topical sermon will have divisions which are at least two-ply: Each has to employ material of the topic; each has to take people in the direction implied in the topic.

But that means that the topic must indeed state or imply a goal. The purpose of the sermon is never merely to while away the hearer's time, to inform, or to please. Yes, his time should be well spent, he should receive valuable information, he should want to listen. But the purpose of the sermon is to change him into the direction of stronger faith in God or of fuller life under God. Also the topical sermon must therefore have a topic or a central thought in which a goal is latent or expressed, a goal for the hearer.

More, it should be one goal. Often the lack of unity in topics is due to the ambiguity or vagueness of religious words at their heart — faith, grace, peace, joy. This vagueness is compounded when the topic should at one and the same time convey a fact and underscore a mood. "The Blessedness of Faith" is an ambiguous topic because both "blessedness" and "faith" have various meanings. When the words in topics are Biblical, goals can be unified frequently by employing Biblical meanings consistently.

Suppose that the preacher has had a Biblical phrase gnawing in him for some time, and he is ready to preach on it: "The Beauty of Holiness." His first discovery will be that he had been thinking of the excellence of proper behavior, but the Scriptural terms are talking about the place of worship. So he comes up with an outline of this sort: I. The beauty in nature; II. The beauty of personality; III. The beauty of worship. The trouble is that I and II have little goal for the hearer; perhaps the whole sermon is in III. Applying the Second Stage (Chapter 14 above) forces him to choose the goal either of appreciating communion with God as the highest experience in life, or better, to share God's goodness and mercy in worship. Now for a major division try the conventional negative-positive: I. Our substitutes for beauty; II. Our realization of God's grandeur through worship; or better: I. God offers it to us; II. We rejoice in it at worship; III. We can take measures to safeguard it. Some such treatment multiplies opportunities for affirming the Gospel in one and the same sermon and moves the hearer in a practical direction. But everything depends on a clearly envisioned and unified goal for the hearer and on adequate Biblical insight. Sometimes a good text will help to lead in the right direction from the start. Ps. 96:8-10 pulls a wealth of material into the orbit of the above theme.

The apparent freedom of the topical method sometimes leads the preacher to overelaborate his outline. The rule of thumb "Not more than fifteen particulars" is just as important for the topical as for the textual method; so is its brother "Try not to indent beyond the major subdivision" (get along with A's and B's and dispense with 1's and 2's).

Behind these maxims lies the principle "Keep it easy for the hearer." The topical sermon should be just as easy to remember — both by preacher and by people — as the textual one. But this means that it has to be built to remember. The goal is the thing. Amplifying a subsidiary idea too extensively by accumulating a number of paragraphs around it will spoil the perspective. The Biblical preacher has abundant materials to draw from and a good conscience as he uses them. Hence when he darts from item to item under a topical construction, he may be oblivious of the fact that the people are limping many particulars behind him. The best bond for holding together the several purposes of each major division of the sermon is simplicity. Also homiletics has its law of parsimony. Simplicity must reside in ideas, not in similarly sounding phrases, in alliterations and catchwords.

In actual practice the skills of textual and of topical preaching merge. Whether the text or the idea comes first, the Christian preacher will find it possible in most cases to implement his subject with a Biblical text that guides the direction of the message and that will give it a depth which his own unaided reflection would not have reached. "Give attendance to reading," St. Paul told Timothy (1 Tim. 4:13), and he probably did not mean literature in general but the Sacred Scriptures in particular. He went on to couple with this practice the pastor's ministry of strengthening and exhortation. We need not speculate whether St. Paul preferred preaching on the basis of single texts to operating with the total resource of Scripture; for he reminded him elsewhere that the total was at his disposal (2 Tim. 3:14-17). Whether the preacher begins with the choice of topic or with the choice of text, that total resource will always be there and used.

The review of both textual and topical preaching methods emphasizes the complex craftsmanship of the preaching ministry. It sets out to do a simple thing: Get people to listen to the Gospel of Jesus Christ. All the arts of speech and persuasion, Biblical interpretation and world literature, insight into human nature and history, contribute. How sad if the preacher misses his aim in the multitude of his helps.! How wonderful if he can save men "by all means"! (1 Cor. 9:22)

FOR FURTHER THOUGHT

Think of the topic "The Freedom of the Christian Man." Can you find a good text for it?

What do you think of Luther's outline: I. He is free from human bondage; II. He is free to be man's servant. How does this fit under the text you chose?

What do you think of this major division: I. In the church; II. In the state. (In the home, too, maybe?)

Look at one of your recent sermon outlines that gave you trouble. Did you have too few or too many particulars? What bothered you about it — its triteness or its difficulty for memory?

Try to outline the sermon of a famous contemporary topical preacher. Any hints for your own practice?

For further reading see p. 303.

SECTION SEVEN

Sermons in Courses

If one sermon can lead hearers toward a helpful goal, several on the same subject should do it better. Hence preachers present at least some of their sermons in courses or series.

The Christian year provides a framework of worship in which all sermons share the common support of contemplating the life of Jesus. Preaching to pericopic themes, however, is not exactly serial.

The secondary services of the church provide abundant opportunity for series of sermons. Properly planned and executed, such preaching can enlist churchgoers to attend several services weekly, deepen their spiritual life, and enhance their understanding of the Bible and the heritage of their church.

Courses of sermons have much use in the church, but offer special difficulties for the preacher.

Chapter Twenty-Four

THE COURSE OF SERMONS

Preachers dream of sermons that work with dramatic swiftness. Unbelievers turn to Christ. Church members rouse from slumber and jump for the exits crying, "God wills it!" Mass methods of the revivalists seem to suggest that the dream might come true.

Actually the pastor-preacher settles down for the long pull. He brings the Gospel to his people and his community across a long front of the people's own witness, his individual pastoral care, his group work, and finally his preaching. He looks for ways by which any sermon can supplement and be supported by others. "Come again," he says at the door after the service; he means it desperately!

To put sermons into courses or series is one device for reinforcing the single sermon and for telling the listener that there is more to the subject than one sermon, more that he should hear. A course of sermons helps the hearer to put together more material on a single subject, and the preacher to help him do it quickly.

In the Common Service

At this point enters one of the contrasts between preaching to a church year or constructing an independent plan. Liturgical churches employ a program of worship for each Sunday morning with ingredients, in part, assigned for the particular service. About half of the year disciplines the people to reflect upon the birth, life, death, and resurrection of Jesus and the sending of the Spirit. The other half focuses on the great themes of Christian discipleship in faith and life. Where the preacher correlates his sermon with the sermon for the day, he will find few opportunities for extending the discussion of the same theme over more than a few consecutive Sundays. A few possibilities occur, and in exploiting them the preacher does not imply that the sermons in a topical series are for that reason more exciting than the others.

At the start of the church year the four Sundays in Advent have over-all themes of longing for the return of Christ, steadfast hope and faith in God under difficulties, awareness of the human need to which the mercy of God in Christ responds. The note of "preparation for Christmas" either anticipates moods of Christmastide or distorts the Biblical concept of "repent ye" into means instead of goal, and should be used sparingly.

Epiphany and the variable number of Sundays in its cycle provide one of the best settings for serial preaching in the church year. Two keynotes interrelate: Christ displays the Father at work among men through His ministry; Christians display Christ at work among men through theirs.

The Sunday mornings in Lent prior to Judica and Palm Sunday are not "Lenten" in the sense of contemplating the suffering of Jesus. Especially if a course of Lenten sermons is in progress on Sunday or weekday evenings during Lent, it is important to keep the distinctiveness of these Sundays. The weeks following Easter and leading to the Ascension have a unified quality, although the preacher should see to it that he does not lose the message of the Cross in stressing the Ascension.

Experts in the liturgy suggest cycles for the Sundays after Trinity, not all of them realistic. Many pastors plan courses for this season since they feel that its Sundays are less distinctive than those of the "festival half." But summer Sundays are not the best time to find average Americans in their pews through four consecutive weeks.

We repeat: these observations do not apply to preachers whose congregations do not use a service book with traditional propers or to any services other than Sunday mornings.

In Minor Services

The preacher thinks of no service as "minor." He probably gives special care to the sermon for a smaller audience, to compensate for the reduced support of mass participation. That is why the preacher is glad to use the device of the course to reinforce any individual sermon preached in the secondary services of his church.

Both liturgical and nonliturgical communions provide special services during Lent, on Sunday or weekday evenings. They are aimed particularly at members to help them meditate on the redemptive work of Christ and to strengthen their life in Him. Often the church brings a special invitation to the community to attend these services, and numerous nonmembers respond. In either case the Lenten sermons need to be rich in contemplating the redeeming work of Christ, and they must help to discipline the attention and concern of all who are present.

Some churches conduct special evening services during Advent. The preacher should shape his course into sufficient contrast with the mornings.

A frequent opportunity for special courses of sermons is given by the evangelistic program of the church, either on its own premises, in neutral quarters, or on the radio.

Where the congregation is alert to its opportunities for worship and spiritual growth, many other evening services on Sundays or weekdays will be arranged. These provide a splendid opportunity for serial preaching.

Advantages of the Course

The sermon course gives the opportunity to dwell on one subject and reinforce one goal more amply than a single sermon can do.

Thus a course of sermons can widen the insight of the congregation into the Bible as a means of God's grace. Courses of the type described in the next chapter will help the people to focus on a special area of Scripture, to gain at least a preliminary insight into practical applications for their own life, and to be led to more careful reading of Scripture at home or to participation in class study.

Other courses of sermons can be shaped to train and co-ordinate the thinking and life of the church in the direction of basic beliefs and duties. Often these courses can be synchronized with projects or programs of the congregation and can be supplemented by special institutes or training classes. Types of such courses are exemplified in Chapter 26 below.

The Christian Church is a company of worshiping people and has been so through many centuries. Hence it has a culture of art and hymnody, a treasury of saints and sanctified experience to remember. In any group of Christians much must be done to bring all up to a minimum standard. A course of sermons in one of these areas is useful, especially when the sermon is supplemented with actual sharing in the experiences described. Chapter 27 below discusses some opportunities and gives a few samples.

Sometimes special groups of the congregation are recruited for particular projects of service. Their training sessions will be attached to brief services of worship, and the preaching of these services can be important and memorable.

Problems and Handicaps

All of the advantages of serial preaching depend on the same condition and proviso: that all of its units are really preaching. People have to receive the grace of God in Christ, and they have to pay attention. Courses of sermons achieve these objectives only at the expense of conscious effort.

Where courses are built around a central topic or theme, as many of them are, the temptation is there to utilize a standard program for the units: I. What our topic is all about; II. How people tend to misunderstand this topic, or, the disasters of misunderstanding; III. Some Biblical experiences with reference to this topic; IV. The Cross is our only help etc. Thus a series of sermons on one of the great doctrines is liable to resolve into individual addresses, some of which deal with weakness or sin or misunderstanding; others with virtue, knowledge, and achievement; still others with forgiveness or grace. The result is that some units of the series will be sermons without preaching, and the Gospel will not be sufficiently linked to needs and goals.

Another difficulty is that the preacher luxuriates in the opportunity finally to get to the bottom of a topic. He works carefully at it, he enjoys it tremendously. The sermons come out with much pressure and detail; they approximate fervent lectures. But the people can't keep up. Most courses of sermons are scheduled for evening services. People have less capacity for sustained attention at the end of the day than mornings; this means that the sermons in evening services should be shorter. This is a double burden for the preacher who is excited over the discoveries of his course.

Another problem is that the units seem to repeat themselves. Many a Lenten preacher has found that the fifth or sixth unit out of seven begins to sound thin. In general we have found a topical series hard to manage beyond four or five units. Biblical series can be different, but they have to be planned with exceeding care lest they unduly repeat themselves. The purpose of a sermon course is to give reinforcement to one fact that all units have in common. When one unit no longer gives reinforcement, it is actually not serving its purpose. It is cooling or dissipating rather than amplifying the warmth of the whole. Each unit of the course must confirm a central fact, but each must do it in a different way.

A final problem concerns choosing texts. Frequently the preacher begins his planning with the over-all idea and with a number of subtopics and now looks for texts useful for developing each unit. He finds them promptly for one or two items of the series; others continue to elude him. Rather than post his series with texts that are only partially appropriate, he would do better to preach the entire series without announced texts. For, first and last, the preacher's aim, also in his courses of sermons, must be to give men the life of God by faith in Christ Jesus. His sermons are not to become sociological or theological or cultural lectures. Nor should people witness a mere token use of texts. Let the preacher preach.

A preacher wants to give a course of sermons on "The Blessings of Discipleship" and comes up with two plans. Which is preferable? I. What discipleship is. II. Following Jesus. III. Bearing the Cross. IV. Power for discipleship; or: I. Learning of Jesus. II. Denying self. III. Witnessing to Jesus. IV. Bearing the Cross.

Often a single text seems to be the basis for an entire course of sermons. Is that good or bad? Advantages? Disadvantages?

What is goal, and what is means, in the Savior's or the Baptist's word "Repent, for the kingdom of heaven is at hand"?

Where was Jesus going in John 16:5 (cf. Heb. 4:14; 9:12, 24; 10:20)?

For further reading see p. 303.

*The textual approach is useful for
numerous courses which help to
mature knowledge and life.*

Chapter Twenty-Five

COURSES WITH THE TEXTUAL METHOD

At first glance courses of sermons seem to grow most simply out of central themes. They are obviously developed by the topical method. Many courses, however, can be planned by means of a basically textual approach. Such courses, properly planned, can enlarge and deepen the meaning of the Bible for preacher and people alike.

If preaching should be true to its basic purpose, the preacher will constantly remind himself, as he plans such courses, to aim at basic problems of his hearers. He will consciously avoid merely outlining or restating sections of Scripture and rather seek to preach Law and Gospel to definite and unified goals of his hearers.

Books of the Bible

The textual approach can be applied to courses on books of the Bible in several ways. One is the expository method in the classic sense, preaching through an entire book with texts following consec-

utively. Where the book is a compilation of sayings or incidents not
wholly related to a common core, as the synoptic gospels, Proverbs,
or the Psalms, taken in sequence, the series of sermons becomes
a "course" only through the literary accident of being drawn from
the same book. Texts from the historical books of the Old Testament
may sometimes be devoid of preaching values unless they are very
long or unless they are subjected to much fanciful interpretation.
For most books of Scripture an expository treatment may draw out
to a tedious length.

Closely knit books with pervasive Gospel content, on the other
hand, lend themselves well to the expository treatment, e. g., the
Gospel of St. John and the epistles. A pastor of our acquaintance
successfully synchronized Ephesians with the church year. A few of
the epistles and the short historical books, and many individual
psalms, lend themselves to brief courses in secondary services.

A useful variant of the expository, verse-by-verse method is to
develop a series of disconnected texts from the same book for a course
of sermons. The connecting link of such a series may be simply the
title of the book: "Great Texts from . . ." "Highlights from . . ."
A notable volume arranges texts from Isaiah for the major services
of an entire church year. Not just a visual or literary but a factual
and inner unity, that of the book itself, will bind the units of the
series together logically. The preacher will plan his units to contrast
with one another as well as with other sermons being preached in
the same week or period. This method is especially welcome to the
preacher who finds certain stimulating texts passed by consistently
in the regular lessons or the pericopic systems being employed in
the morning services. Modifiers attached to the title of the course,
e. g., "Beautiful Texts from . . ." or "Amazing Assertions by . . ."
may divert attention of the hearers from the persuasive values of
the sermons.

Especially helpful is the course of sermons which treats four to
eight texts from a book of the Bible through which a major lesson or
purpose of the book is driven home. This method can put a whole
book of the Bible into the forefront of a congregation's thinking. If
the series of sermons can have as its setting the entire book, read

aloud in the service of worship or studied in a parallel Bible class, marked deepening of spiritual life will accrue. Thus Jonah can be read in four consecutive services (Chapter 2 by two readers responsively), and a series of sermons can be preached on the general theme "God Employs Frail Witnesses." I. He directs them when unwilling (1:1-4); II. He sustains them when undeserving (2:7-9); III. He blesses their imperfect message (3:4, 5); IV. He seeks to purify their grudging witness (4:2-4). Such a series would co-ordinate well with a month's institute on evangelism.

First John can serve similarly, although the chapters are longer. It may have to be broken up for reading in portions of the individual services, and it may need the help of contemporary versions. A covering topic can be "Love Is Practical." I. God's own bond between us in the church (1:3); II. Our contrast from the world (2:10, 11); III. Composed of painful giving and forgiving (3:16, 17); IV. God's gift in the heart (4:7); V. God's power for victory (5:4).

Philippians can be especially warm in this treatment: "What It Means to Be Joyful in Christ." I. To pray for the fellow Christians' spiritual health (1:9-11); II. To serve them in the mind of Christ (2:14-16); III. To sustain them in faith in God's mercy (3:14, 15); IV. To share true contentment with them (4:18, 19).

Even larger books can be brought into the scope of a short course of sermons, by working out cuttings for reading that will give a connected and interpreted picture and by choosing texts that correlate with each episode. Job, Hosea, Hebrews suggest such a treatment.

Themes from the Bible

The textual method goes to the Bible for themes rather than for material on previously chosen themes. A familiar illustration is the process by which many a preacher plans his special Lenten sermons. He will read the history of the Passion of our Lord, in one of the gospels or in one of the composite versions assembled from the four gospels. As he does so, certain situations with a common core emerge. He needs six or seven units, depending on the custom of his congregation concerning the observance of Ash Wednesday. The most obvious and widely used set of seven texts presented directly in the record is the seven words from the cross. Many preachers find it hard to discern kerygmatic implications in "I thirst" or "Behold thy mother," but they are there. In this series, as in others compiled for Lenten preaching, short texts set into a narrative drive many preachers far afield for material and application. The published literature displays a curious aversion for full and applied preaching of the atonement. The seven words should be a reasonably explicit antidote.

Other sayings of Jesus in the Passion history form valuable Lenten courses. Some are cues for topical rather than textual preaching. The metaphors customary in hymnody are sometimes drawn on to achieve application — we betrayed, denied, mocked, scourged, crucified, forsook. The resulting accents cluster about malady rather than the atonement. The history of preaching provides many exhibits of distorting the intended purpose of the Gospel narrative and associating the cross with indictment for sin rather than God's forgiveness of sin, or at least of preaching its indictment so vividly that the message of the atonement sounds pale by contrast.

Once we began to prepare a Lenten series by asking the question: How did Jesus Himself foretell His Passion and its purpose? Obviously a topic was already at hand for the course: "Jesus' Purpose in Dying on the Cross." The textual process stepped in, however, in that there was no conscious prediction what the answers would be. The texts and their goals came out of a reading of the four gospels themselves: I. To save us, John 3:14, 15; II. To gather us, John 10:15, 16; III. To free us, Matt. 20:26-28; IV. To forgive us, Matt. 26:26-28; V. To secure us, John 14:2, 3; VI. To sanctify us, John 17:19. By hindsight we discovered that this process gave sharp and independent definition to some concepts which before had seemed simply synonymous with others and that this was a course of sermons on the metaphors of the atonement. Had it been worked out topically with texts traditional for the purpose, this preacher, at least, would not have been as interested as he was.

This incident will illustrate the fact that a sermon course can frequently merge the topical and the textual approach. The preacher begins with a topic for the course, but he proceeds to develop subtopics by finding texts first. Building a course on the theme of a Biblical book, described above, uses this process. Thus the theme of contentment, suggested in Philippians 4, can be expanded into an entire course by scanning the epistle itself on the subject and framing themes after the texts have been found: 1:12 ff., the experiences out of which contentment grows; 1:21 ff., contentment with life or death; 3:7 ff., contentment with God's kind of righteousness; 4:6, contentment in prayer; 4:11 ff., contentment in hunger and abundance; 4:16 ff., contentment for the sake of others. The first and fourth texts correlate closely, and four units emerge: I. It depends on God; II. It shows in prayer; III. It can stand both hunger and abundance; IV. It is concerned for others.

The concordance will offer a large variety of texts on a topically chosen theme, which can then be sorted according to their inner contrasts or comparison and ultimately be developed textually. Thus good texts emerge under the caption "free": John 8:33 ff., from sin, through Christ; Rom. 6:18, 22, from sin; 6:20, from righteousness; 8:2, from death; 1 Cor. 9:19, from men for men; Gal. 5:1, from the indictment of the Law and the self-rightousness through the Law; 1 Peter 2:16, for the proper service. Resulting units can be "The Christian's Freedom" I. From sin for God; II. From unrighteousness for righteousness; III. From death for life; IV. From the Law for the Spirit; V. From selfishness for people. Note that it would be a disadvantage to have one unit on John 8:33: Free through Christ; for that has to be explicit in each sermon.

Some of the most satisfying experiences of the preacher's ministry come out of his preparation of sermon courses. He himself learns new approaches to the Bible and gains new insights into it, and he feels unhampered by the tight schedule of the Sunday morning plan. His people react with good cheer. One of the chief joys, by contrast with the single sermon where the task is to strip excess material away and keep the impact as simple as possible, is the pressure actually to confront a concept for all that it is worth and to find new things, not simply in expression but in the Word itself. The textual method keeps sending the preacher back into the Scriptures for his material. Let him see to it that his people will be helped by them and not merely fascinated by his technique.

Look at the suggested course on 1 John above. Which unit really belongs into every one of the other four?

What trait of the Book of Job renders much of its material unlikely as a source of texts for preaching? What portions would be useful?

What do you think of this course of Lenten sermons: "Jesus' Death Shows Us How to Live": I. Walking with courage; II. Speaking with kindness; III. Cherishing with love; IV. Praying with fervor; V. Suffering with resignation; VI. Obeying with faithfulness?

Try building a course on "The Church Is Christ's Body" by finding texts in the concordance and developing themes later.

For further reading see pp. 303, 304.

Chapter Twenty-Six

COURSES WITH THE TOPICAL METHOD

The textual process is a constant stimulus to the spiritual and theological growth of the preacher. His mind expands, and his insights deepen, as the Scriptures speak to him, and this they do as he prepares pericopic or expository sermons and their counterpart in courses, those which are built by the textual method. The people grow under such preaching as the preacher grows. Yet situations arise in the pastorate where the minister senses that he and his people need instruction in special fields, edification and maturation in specific areas. As he reflects upon the status of his church and as he plans his total preaching program, he isolates these areas and sees subjects for preaching to implement these concerns. Such preaching uses the topical method.

Doctrinal Series

The deficiency of the parish which can be analyzed most easily is its doctrinal understanding and competence. The pastor senses that his people are not making use of some doctrines which are difficult, like predestination or the problem of evil, or others which wear out and become meaningless, like Baptism, justification, and the love of God. He feels that some practical questions of daily interest should have an answer in basically theological and doctrinal terms — the Christian vocation, church and state, for example. He finds that the subject exceeds the bounds of a single sermon. So he plans a course. He promotes the interest and attendance of his people by stressing the importance of Christian doctrine both for the sake of personal faith and for the purpose of conversing helpfully with others.

At this point it is necessary to stress even more with reference to the course of sermons what has been our constant refrain concerning the individual one: sermons are not simply to inform. The old classifications of pastoral, inspirational, devotional, and doctrinal (subdivided into theological and catechetical) sermons are misleading if they suggest that any sermon may omit doctrine, may be devoid of pastoral concern, may leave the will to worship untouched, may fail to teach. If people plan to hear a course of sermons on a great doctrine and their purpose is simply "to know more about it," they are likely to come short of the great goals of faith and life. With Bible classes or discussion groups the pastor will do well to correlate courses of sermons on great doctrines in which content and understanding receive chief stress, while the sermons function in periods of worship in which the people help one another eat and drink Christ for the sake of the life which is His gift.

We have described the textual approach to a doctrinal series thus: Pursue the doctrinal concept or Biblical term through the concordance, and sort out the resulting texts in order to arrive at a series of distinct phases of the subject. Frequently, as a preacher plans a course of sermons on a great doctrine, a number of subtopics suggest themselves to him before he ever turns to the concordance. After he has the subtopics and titles for the individual units, he then begins to look for texts and the Biblical development of each topic. This is actually the topical method. This writer has found that for him the process frequently resulted in developing a series of themes with texts from the epistles of St. Paul. Behind this lies the historical accident that the categories of Protestant theology were originally framed with

Pauline emphases: sin and grace, justification and sanctification. Useful as these categories are, they leave out of account many of the sayings of Jesus with their accents on the Kingdom in the heart, the clash with the rule of material things, or Christian discipleship.

An unfortunate theological folkway is the assumption that "doctrine" applies to the domain of faith and salvation, for which Biblical materials speak with much detail — God, man, Christ, the Spirit, Word and Sacrament; while the domain of living draws for Biblical statement on "practical" sections of Scripture which have a lesser doctrinal prestige: the calling, the life of love, the relation of the spiritual to the secular. The preacher will do well to prepare sound and rich theology for his serial preaching on the most practical of subjects.

The preacher whose mind is charged with Scripture and not merely with the abstractions of dogma will be able to construct courses that serve not simply to portray doctrine but to bring the power of the Gospel to bear on people. He will find it helpful to alternate, for example, between textual and topical series for Lent. Without turning in advance to Scripture at all, he will be able to enumerate subtopics for a course on "The Meaning of the Redemption": God plans it; Christ pays its price; men are freed from bondage; men are freed for service; the church looks forward to its consummation; the Word makes us partakers of it; the church proclaims it to others; the Sacrament shares it. With care and further reflection there emerge mutually exclusive yet consistently evangelical topics for which texts are readily available.

Doctrines which people find difficult or which they love to argue about are normally not suitable for courses, since the hearers have a set for debate or for mental clarity rather than for being changed. We have tried whole courses like "Five Disputed Doctrines" — predestination, Baptism, creation, Communion, justification — and wondered why the rest of the hour's worship seemed to accomplish more than the preaching. Such subjects need discussion in a study group. On the other hand, "Justification" can cue a course with Biblical refreshment and goals of faith properly coupled: The just God wants us to be just; we have no capacity for being just, God must account us so in spite of ourselves; faith in Christ's redeeming work justifies before God; God's reminders of our own incapacity help to lead to His way to be just; having been once accounted just, we need God's help to continue so; when we are just before God, His fruits begin to come. The texts for such a course are available from the entire New Testament or from a single book like Romans.

A course of sermons on one of the chief fields of Christian teaching will clarify the thinking of new members of the church and refresh the veterans. The Decalog is a practical series, although the preacher needs to be resourceful to apply adequate Gospel motivation to each unit, and he will probably group the Commandments to compress the series. The articles of the Apostles' or the Nicene Creed provide convenient cues for serial preaching. The petitions of the Lord's Prayer are unusually apt for preaching that merges textual and topical methods.

Practical Concerns

In all his preaching the pastor is concerned for people. No matter how Biblical or textual his approach to the given sermon has been, he will arrive at explicit application to his people, just as the original documents of Scripture aimed at people. Hence the year-round Sunday morning program of preaching will have a practical emphasis. Nevertheless the alert pastor will see areas of need which require special attention. Worship services with sermons do only part of the job. He will plan study groups, short institutes, or Bible classes on special topics, or programs for acquainting the parish with projects in the area and throughout the denomination, to co-ordinate with the worship and the courses of sermons. Since those courses direct themselves to areas envisioned in advance, their method will be topical.

In most urban centers the tempo of church work accelerates after summer heat or vacations. Courses of sermons for autumn therefore concern worship, or the functioning of the church in the place, or Christian education. In the area of worship the general theme "Worshiping God Together" will suggest: The definition of worship; the purpose of worship by the Christian group; the concentration of mind and faith in God required for true worship; the Word of God in worship. "God's Business in God's Church" suggests: the work of the church; where Christians carry out the work of mutual edification in the church (family, congregation); modes of mutual edification in the church; its witness to the world. Texts for worship present themselves in the Psalms; for the church, in Ephesians.

Other courses of sermons helping to renew activity in the parish and taking their cue from the beginning of the school year build around the congregation's program of Christian education: Its core, the Bible; its purpose, the building of life in people; its method, sharing God's gifts through His Spirit; its agents, all the members of the church with the help of leaders and professional church workers.

In a church year, when sermons for the morning services are based on Gospel texts, a special course of sermons on personal witness or evangelism is helpful between New Year and Lent. Its material can be drawn from the Book of Acts or First Peter. The weeks following Easter are valuable for swinging the dynamic of Lent and Easter into the life stream of the congregation by means of special courses of sermons in secondary services, coupled with appropriate study groups and reading shelves and films, on the Christian family, or the Christian vocation, or Christian citizenship. The seasonal interests of thanksgiving, charity, and stewardship make special services and institutes on these subjects possible in October and November.

In plotting courses by the topical method the preacher may often find texts for several units but not for others. He will find it better to preach Biblical materials but without a special text altogether than to assign and announce a text which does not really pertain. This will serve him better than the device of quoting dual or triple texts; for thus the attention of his hearer will not be drawn to a focal point as well as by the simple announcement of the topic of the sermon. But always let the preacher patiently search for the Biblical grounds for his theology and preach them amply.

The preacher will feel a sense of fitness and proportion if each sermon of a course has approximately the same length and depth of treatment. But more, his people will not be fearful of future tedium if previous units have been crisp. "Make things easy for them" and "Give them something to think about" are not incompatible axioms.

FOR FURTHER THOUGHT

If you schedule a portion of the Passion history into each of your special Lenten services, how will you correlate a course of sermons with each reading — by the textual method? by the topical method?

We tried courses of eight or nine sermons in secondary services annually on one of the Chief Parts of Christian Doctrine from the Catechism — Baptism, Third Article, etc. — with study guides, Bibles in the pews, page turning to references. What was the risk for preaching? How could the plan be improved?

What is your criticism of an autumn series of sermons on the theme "The Officers of the Church": I. Elders; II. Treasurer; III. Trustees; IV. Voters; V. Members.

For further reading see pp. 303, 304.

Many topics of special interest cue courses of sermons that convey the Gospel effectively.

Chapter Twenty-Seven

MISCELLANEOUS COURSES

In addition to the standard topical courses of sermons discussed in the preceding chapter, the resourceful preacher will develop many which are not directly suggested by problems in the understanding or life of the parish. Often he will devise them with the frank intention to create interest through sermons not too obviously doctrinal or practical. This intention is praiseworthy, provided that he aims for interest not just in sermons but in the Word of God and the preaching of the Cross. Such courses should alternate with types that make more substantial demands on the self-discipline of the hearers.

Biographical Courses

Courses on characters from the Bible give opportunity to exploit the Scriptures, train people to alertness when they read them, and use the textual method. Bible characters, both the memorable and the obscure, fit into the portrayal of God's relation to man and man's response to God's Word and will. A standard Lenten series focuses on scenes and incidents in the concluding hours of Jesus' ministry. The miracles of Jesus and other events in His life help to explore His character and meaning as Redeemer. The Book of Acts provides numerous courses of sermons on the Christian witness, the inner functioning and growth of the Christian Church, and the march of the Gospel; all center in the actions and speech of flesh-and-blood people. Close reading of the Gospel narrative will document sermons on individual disciples of Jesus; the supplement of later tradition often becomes fanciful. The characters and experiences of individual prophets may be depicted by patient exploration of their own writings. Outstanding characters of the Old Testament — Moses, David, Elijah — may individually become the topic of an entire course.

The value of a course of sermons depends on the support that each unit gives to a central idea. Hence a course on David, for example, should single out one quality applicable to the hearer, e. g., saint and sinner, man of action and man of adoration. Units for the latter paradox can be: the preparation in youth and maturation; the insight into the Word of God; the tests in the crises of life; persistence till old age and death. Suitable texts emerge from the historical books of the Old Testament and the Psalms. Similarly one focus on Moses is better than a course on Moses in general, provided that each unit will have applications for the hearer. For example: "Moses, Exemplar of God's Guidance." I. Through false riches to the true; II. Through partial obedience to the perfect; III. Through humbling to leadership; IV. Through petulance to faith; V. Through ignorance to insight. Individual units then deal with the entire sweep of the story of Moses, assembling data from numerous incidents in the narrative, or each can be textually developed from a single narrative for each case.

It should be an axiom that biographical courses will preach the Gospel in each unit. Suppose that "Paul, Warrior for God" suggests: I. Once against God; II. Conquered in conversion; III. Battered but not beaten; IV. Steadfast to the end. I and II in this scheme should be merged and the ample material distributed over several more units: striving to win people; fighting against Satan. An additional unit, using the sword of the Spirit, should probably be canceled and its concern with means distributed over all the rest.

The literature of preaching is full of sermons on obscure characters from Scripture — the young man who fled without his garment, Jephtha's daughter, Achan and Elihu and Eldad and Nabal and Paul's nephew and Peter's wife. A series entitled "Obscure Characters of the Bible" is hardly useful. It isn't really a course of sermons at all, for its units propose to support one central fact about their subjects: they are obscure. The course gambles on the most slender of motivations for interest — curiosity, and it may draw the hearer's attention to the ingenuity with which the preacher multiplies enough words for a sermon from a shred of mention in Scripture.

Conversely, not every personage whose story is amply told in the Biblical record is for that reason a candidate for a course of sermons; e. g., Absalom, Ahab, Judas.

Biographical sermons will be useful if they are interesting in terms of the hearer's own life and if without hindrance they bring the Gospel message to the forefront of the hearer's attention. Thus Lenten sermons surveying the characters of the Passion story can become excessively moralizing and denunciatory when they are made to focus on human evil to the exclusion of the meaning of the Cross and the mercy of God.

Can the great figures of the church since the apostolic age be made the subject of courses of sermons? The cultural values of such sermons may be rich; the strain on the preacher's ability to reach the hearer's personal faith and life, severe. Where the preacher operates with Biblical texts, he is liable to reduce the mention of the historical character to little more than an illustration; where he takes his text less seriously, the application to the hearer's life may become oblique and unevangelical. Perhaps the purpose of such biography can be achieved by a straightforward narrative, with brief appreciation, in the course of the service, after which the textual sermon makes only brief reference to the biography. Thus a series of sermons on the Christian mission, in Epiphanytide, could have its accompaniment of brief biographies of great missionaries; a series on Christian welfare could have an accompanying set of accounts of Christian philanthropists like Francke, Müller, Wichern, Passavant, Buenger. This treatment would serve well parallel to sermons related to Christian art.

Courses on Hymns and Art

Great hymns are useful as courses for sermons, since the hymn is one of the chief means by which Christians admonish one another, and yet they are prone to join in them thoughtlessly. Some great hymns are in themselves good material for an entire series of sermons, each based on or utilizing a text which summarizes a given stanza or thought of the hymn; the entire course should focus on the chief aspect of the hymn and not just its name. Thus "A Mighty Fortress" can be treated in four units of which each considers a stanza. Better would be a treatment in which all stanzas are the subject of each sermon, "A Hymn of Victorious Faith": I. God is the fortress into which we flee for refuge (Ps. 46); II. The devil is the adversary whom God will vanquish (Eph. 6:11-13); III. The Lord Jesus Himself fights the decisive battle (Rev. 19:11-16); IV. By full dependence of faith we share God's might and victory (1 John 5:4, 5). These central thoughts might well be replaced by quotations from the hymn.

Other courses of hymns can be built around a central theme so that each unit helps the congregation to concentrate on a different hymn. Thus: "Let Us Sing to the Spirit of God": I. That He may give us the light of God's presence ("Come, Holy Ghost, Creator Blest," Rhabanus Maurus — Edward Caswall; 1 John 2:20); II. That He may bless us together in His church (Luther, "Come, Holy Ghost, God and Lord" or "We Now Implore God the Holy Ghost," 1 Cor. 12:4-7); III. That He may preserve us with God (Schirmer-Winkworth: "O Holy Spirit, Enter in," Matt. 13:23 or James 1:18-21). Such a series may give opportunity to help the congregation appreciate and practice unfamiliar hymns.

In Chapter 22 we discussed individual sermons on great pictures. A whole course on pictures ought to be given only seldom, and its function will be achieved only if the people can look both at the picture and at the preacher. For the occasion has the dual purpose of deepening cultural sense and preaching the Gospel of Christ. Splendid art reproductions are available on slides, the average parish owns equipment for projection, and the preacher may plan to speak while the people look at the screen. Certainly he should help his people see Christian art frequently, and brief comment will be helpful; but he should not convert a sermon into a lecture on art, nor will the people look at the same picture very long. During a sermon related to a picture either a reproduction should be in their hands, or a slide projection should have preceded the sermon itself. The value of the picture for the sermon is only slight, for preaching must achieve its own visualization and concreteness by word of mouth. The course of sermons on pictures will help the hearer, however, to develop valuable associations with art which he will enjoy for years to come.

In this connection courses on the symbolism or art of the church building and its equipment will be useful. Entire Lenten series are capsuled in symbols of the Passion incorporated in many chancels.

Courses on Forms of Worship

Valuable courses of sermons will help the people employ and participate in the forms of worship. Whole series with obvious Biblical support can review the Common Service, or the orders of matins or vespers. Such services will be useful for practicing the participation of the hearers; but the preacher should take care that he does not lecture on the liturgy but that he preaches to repentance and remission of sins. Quickly sung and forgotten elements of worship such as the Gloria in Excelsis or the Te Deum can be segmented into notable series of which each unit underscores a total accent. Thus the Gloria in Excelsis can be termed "Our Adoration of Jesus Christ": I. We join the angels in it (Luke 2:13, 14); II. We praise Him as the Son of the Father (Matt. 3:17); III. We praise Him as Redeemer (John 1:29); IV. We acknowledge Him as Lord (Eph. 4:8-10).

Similarly the Magnificat, Benedictus, and Nunc Dimittis can serve as textual courses. The Benedictus is peculiarly useful for a series in Advent and will serve to allay the assumption that John the Baptist preached only the Law.

Courses of sermons put the resourcefulness of the preacher to the test. This means that he must work hard to keep them from being merely a display of ingenuity. His best technique must first and last help the people to find the grace of God at work in them in their daily lives.

What do you think of a series of sermons on the Magnificat during Advent? What do you think of a series of sermons on Holy Communion based on the Nunc Dimittis?

What do you think of a sermon in a series on the life of St. Paul which concludes: "Thus we have seen how God can bring us to our knees in adversity so that we are driven to despair. Now come next Wednesday evening, and hear how God lifts us up again."

What do you think of a sermon on the Suffering Jesus which contemplates a picture by Rouault and points out the bad art in comparable paintings by Von Carolsfeld, Carlo Dolci, or Hofmann?

Every sermon in a series has the same goal. Why should people listen to more than one unit in it?

For further reading see p. 304.

SECTION EIGHT

Accents in Preaching

As the preacher works with the Bible to shape his preaching, he finds that it offers special accents of concern and of application to the people.

As he seeks to understand and reach the needs of people, he finds their problems drawing together into patterns that outline the goals of his pulpit messages.

The chapters of this section illustrate how theological accents correlate with practical goals: Justification (evangelism), the calling (the daily life of the Christian), the church (worship, giving), the family (family life and marriage), the Christian hope (comfort in trial and death), and prayer. These will serve to demonstrate the process by which many other accents can be envisioned and applied.

177

*Faith for justification is both be-
gun and preserved as the preacher
speaks the Gospel of the Cross.*

Chapter Twenty-Eight

PREACHING TO THE GOAL OF FAITH

Among the primary goals to which the preacher leads his hearers
is faith. He means more by faith than simply believing that God exists
or simply acceding to the truth of certain teachings about God. Saint
James vigorously combats this distortion (2:19). Least of all will he
let his hearers mingle with their concept of faith "having faith in yourself" or expecting the best of other people — current ingredients of
American folk religion. He seeks to build the faith which clings to
God and His promises carried out in Christ and by which man stands
under the favor of God and lives the life of God.

The Target of the Word of Faith

The preaching which intends to bring hearers who have not known
Christ to faith in Him is often called evangelism. The term suggests
that its cardinal ingredient is the Gospel of Christ preached to the
goal of faith. It is a good term; for nothing but the Gospel can bring

people to faith. Moreover, when the man without faith listens to the Christian preacher aim at goals of behavior, he may imagine that he is qualified to attempt those goals without the life that is God's gift, unless the preacher is explicit and ample in his affirmations of man's malady and God's remedy in Christ. Hence evangelistic preaching concerns itself predominantly with the goals of faith.

But the Christian preacher speaks also to Christians. They, too, need rich clear Gospel to lift them from the little to the larger faith, from self-righteousness to trust in God's mercy, from boredom or apathy in worship to sincere adoration and praise. While they live in this world, Christians constantly face the trials of faith, and God Himself is concerned that they nourish their faith and have shepherds to lead and feed them. If "evangelistic" preaching aims at faith, then much of it concerns established Christians as well as unbelievers.

The Importance of Faith

The preacher must help the hearer understand why faith is so important to him. It isn't just a nostrum for peace of mind or a good conscience. It isn't just a condition to be fulfilled for entrance into the church. Faith is important because men have to do with God, who created them to be, among all created things, His representatives and reflectors (Gen. 1:26-28). He proposed to be the power behind the actions that would fulfill this plan (Eph. 2:10). He entered into a covenant relation with His people in the Old Testament age that they might so act (Ex. 20:5; Lev. 19:2) and has that same intention for His people in the new age (Jer. 31:33; and John 15:1). He fixes His people with an unflinching scrutiny and judgment. (Note Chapter 4 above)

Yet man as he is born into the world is incapable of standing under this judgment; he is condemned (John 3:3; Ps. 51:4; 90:7 ff.). Severed from God, he lives of himself in more or less open rebellion against God's plan (Eph. 2:1 ff.; Rom. 1:18 ff.; 3:9, 10), the state of sin. After this life this condemnation issues into another existence of indescribably dreadful but conscious death from God. (Is. 66:24; Mark 9:43 ff.; Luke 16:19-31)

But the judging and condemning God has at the same time the will that man be righteous and live (Rom. 3:26; Ezek. 33:11). What does it mean that man is righteous? Popular language in every age has made it mean ethical behavior that satisfies the judgment of God; at the heart of this definition is the error of the people who sought to put Jesus to death. Another construct is that "righteousness" is a quality of sinlessness which God puts on man's account. The Bible of both Testaments, however, means by "righteous" the situation of the man who stands under the favor of God. He is "upright" indeed, but not because of the ethical quality of his deeds — that is a result and not a cause — but because of something in God, and that is His mercy, God's favor toward the sinner who has not earned it (Ex. 20:6; Num. 14:8; Deut. 4:29-31; Ps. 32; 36:5, 6; 85:10), God's "judgment" of rescue and saving, God's forgiving and not imputing the sin to the sinner.

Mercy, however, is not a thing to be earned, for then it is not mercy. It is simply to be sought and grasped (Rom. 11:6). Man's uprightness before the judgment of God therefore is possible only as he reaches out with the clutch of faith and grasps God's mercy. (Luke 18:9-14; Ps. 123; 130)

Barriers for Faith

Only God can give faith; only His Spirit can cause man to clutch God (1 Cor. 12:3). One way that God does it is through preaching; it is "the Word of faith" (Rom. 10:6-17). But man not merely disbelieves; he casts up barriers against the Word that brings to faith. He finds the Gospel of God's mercy contrary to his own ideas of justice. (1 Cor. 1:18-23)

One barrier to faith is idolatry, the trust in things, the lust of self-indulgence. In the Old Covenant God's people defected to the worship of images and had to be aroused to their peril by the prophets (Ps. 96:5; 115:4; Is. 57:5; Hos. 14:8); in the New, they struggled against the lusts of the flesh and world and still had to be alerted to their menace. (Matt. 6:19-34; Acts 17:23-31; 1 John 2:15-17; 5:21)

Another barrier is self-righteousness, the assumption that human behavior renders upright before God and cancels the need for mercy; its constant companion is pride. The prophets inveighed against it (Is. 1:10 ff.; Jer. 2:35). Jesus Christ went to the cross under the resentment against His warnings (Luke 11:44 ff.; 18:9-14). Hence if the preacher wants his Gospel of mercy to be heard, he must preach the Law that indicts men for their sin (Luke 15:7; 1 John 1:8 ff.). His Word of Christ will create and sustain faith in God's mercy; he must use God's own means of penetrating the barrier for listening to it.

As he does so, he must see to it that he raises no additional barriers. Job's clumsy friends first tried to comfort him and then drove him to self-righteousness by their denunciations. The whole Mosaic covenant was a device for helping God's own people to confront their continuing need for His mercy (Rom. 7:5-12; Gal. 3:24). But the Law is badly preached when it causes people to review their own goodness to bargain for God's favor; or when hearers imagine that the discomforts of its denunciation are a penance which appeases God. It has one great purpose — that men say: "Tell me your Gospel!"

The Word of Faith

Now comes the Word of faith. We have said that the preacher must prepare the hearer for it by helping him see the idolatry and self-delusion of any faith in things or in self. The preacher must help the hearer see that he is not gloating over his predicament but is standing by to help and has but one concern — that the hearer reach out and grasp the mercy of God. Now he preaches the Word that gives and strengthens that faith. He preaches the Gospel, and it has many modes of portrayal. (Cf. Chapter 5 above)

May the preacher use phrases like "Believe," "Believe the Word of the Gospel"? Isn't that what St. Paul said to the Jailer; "Believe on the Lord Jesus Christ, and thou shalt be saved"?

Certainly, provided that he knows what he is doing. Exhorting to believe in Christ is not preaching the Gospel; it is announcing the goal which the Gospel will help to reach. Such exhorting and announcing is good indeed, provided that it signals: This is important; now get your help to do it. St. Paul spent the rest of the night speaking the Gospel to the Jailer "and to all that were in his house" and then baptized them (Acts 16:31-34). The Word of reconciliation not merely pleads with men to be reconciled, but it says:

He has made Him who knew no sin to be sin for us that we might be made the righteousness of God in Him. (2 Cor. 5:21)

So, preacher, don't confuse goal and means; and don't presuppose, but preach!

Another mayhem committed on the Word of faith is that the preacher says: "All you have to do to be saved is to believe. Now believe! If you believe, you will be saved." Such "iffy" preaching draws the attention of the hearer away from the message that is going to work the faith and instead causes him to focus on his own mind. Furthermore, it is liable to make him think of faith as an inner assent to, and agreement with, the doctrine of the Gospel. But faith is a hold on God Himself and on the promise of His life, and the doctrine of the Gospel is the means by which the faith is wrought and preserved. Let the preacher say: "I know that you have trouble to believe that God is your Father and Christ your Savior. But it's a matter of life and death that you do. God Himself wants to help you reach and grasp Him and make Him your own one source of life. He does so as we bend our minds and thoughts to what He once did to make you His own and give you life. Let me tell you what He did." And then let him preach the redeeming work of Christ as the act of God's mercy, the forgiveness of his sin, the source and the nurture of his faith.

Pleading for Faith

Christians use the word "faith" till it wears thin. Preachers easily say it unthinkingly. They may think of their Gospel as a set of words to be remembered and agreed to, of their preaching as the refreshing of people's memories. But faith is the victory that overcomes the world (1 John 5:4). The man that says, "Yes, God, you have redeemed me through Jesus Christ," is the man whom God views with His favor. To stand in that relation with God is a precious platform from which every other gift of life and power for duty is reached. Hence the preacher does more than reaffirm statements to be believed. He wrestles for the attention of his people. He labors to be thought well of so that nothing will interfere with his Gospel and calling. He goes into travail for them over and over that they might be born to God. Hence as the preacher aims for the faith of his people, he goes out to them with the Word of Christ's work in his heart and lips. He takes infinite pains to be the representative of Christ. For he is charged to lift men who withered under the blast of God's judgment upright to see His mercy and be glad, His mercy in Jesus Christ, our Lord.

FOR FURTHER THOUGHT

Has this chapter helped to meet the questions after Chapter Five?

What do you think of these summaries? Do you prefer one to the rest?

1. The Gospel must always be preached in the past tense: Jesus died and rose again.

2. The Gospel must always be preached in the present tense: Jesus wants to live in you today; live for Him.

3. The Gospel must link past and present: Jesus died for all men and rose again that we might live now and forever.

4. The Gospel must be preached timelessly: God's victory over sin hasn't happened until we conquer sin; Christ gave the pattern.

Do you find it harder to see what faith goals of preaching are for believers than to see what they are for unbelievers?

For further reading see p. 304.

The call of the Gospel summons and sustains men for a growing and fruitful life in Christ.

Chapter Twenty-Nine

PREACHING TO THE GOAL OF LIFE

As pastors shepherd flocks of Christians, they will sometimes ask: "Isn't faith without works dead? Isn't doctrine without life meaningless? Is it right ever to preach without also summoning to action?"

Those questions reveal a valuable insight. This writer feels that goals of faith are important in preaching, just as the autoist will check his fuel line or carburetion even when he is not setting out at once on a journey. Preaching to the goal of faith is prophylaxis, repair, and safeguard for maintaining the relation with God which the Christian needs for his whole existence. To single out faith in God as a goal, provided that by "faith" we mean the living hold on God and not bare assent to information, is a device of persuasive speech. Yet it is altogether true that the ultimate purpose of the atonement is action; "faith . . . worketh by love" (Gal. 5:6). Most of the themes of the Christian year, as set up in the traditional lessons, aim at the enabling of the Christian life (thus Christmas, Titus 2:11-14; Easter, 1 Cor. 5:6-8).

185

The Shape of Life Is Love

Good preaching makes the goal clear to the hearer. A clear goal of Christian preaching is that men should live their lives under God and with His powers, that Christians as they have been reclaimed for that life should be fruitful for God (John 15:1; Eph. 2:10; Phil. 2: 12, 13). For God has set them apart for His service and purposes (the true meaning of holiness, Lev. 20:7; 1 Peter 2:9). All of the purposes of God sum up in that men should love as He loves. (Rom. 13:9; 1 John 4:16)

Love is neither a feeling nor an abstraction. The man with Christian agape sacrifices himself for the good of the next person, with a determined will and at the expense of personal pain and life itself, according to the example of Jesus (John 13:15, 34; Phil. 2:2-8; Matt. 20:20-28). Love reaches its peak in the attempt to convey the life and love of God to others, through forgiveness, nurture, and witness. (Matt. 18:18; 28:19, 20; Gal. 6:1 ff.)

Love Functions in the Calling

The life of love is concrete and practical, the visible proof that the invisible God is at work. The New Testament pulls God and His workman -together into one concept when it terms the life of service a calling (discussed with reference to the preacher's work in Chapter 2). Christians are the called ones through the Word and power of Christ's redeeming work (2 Tim. 1:9). But they are also put into a situation where they themselves are the calling ones. The New Testament terms by "calling" both the situation of being related toward people whom we can reach with the call (1 Cor. 7:10-24) and the action of calling with the call by which we have been called (1 Peter 2:21; cf. 3:15; 4:9-11). The New Testament describes the many facets of the calling in extended sections like Ephesians 4—6 and 1 Peter 2—4.

Christians occupy several callings at the same time. Marriage is the opportunity to nurture with the love of Christ (Eph. 5:22—6:4; cf. Chapter 31 below). The conversation of Christians with those inside and outside the church conveys the grace of God (note 1 Peter above; Eph. 4:25—5:4; Col. 4:5, 6). The gainful occupation can be the setting for calling (1 Cor. 7:21-23; Col. 3:21—4:1). Citizenship, even in the civil order, gives the Christian an opportunity to reflect the will and mercy of God (1 Peter 2:11-17; 1 Tim. 2:1-8; Rom. 13). Outstanding as calling is membership in the Christian congregation, to be considered in Chapter 31.

Preaching Alerts to Obstacles

The preacher can paint charming pictures of the calling. He can help his people meditate on the examples of Jesus Christ or of the saints at work about the Father's business. But he must remember that goal and example only introduce the preaching. He has to supply fuel and motive, and he has to give the hearer the mind for the intake. The hearer will turn his attention off promptly when the preacher speaks unrealistically or sentimentally about the calling.

This side of the grave the calling never functions without handicaps. The Scriptures are a potent resource for portraying the maladies that beset the Christian as he tries to do God's will. To speak the Gospel to ears that hear, the preacher must speak the Law that underscores God's will and man's failure. True, he must do this not in a constant chatter of faultfinding or a pessimistic refrain, "But you don't do this, do you?" With patience and sympathy he must help the hearer confront his constant need for replenishing the grace of God and for refreshing the life of God so that he may apply himself faithfully to the calling in which God has placed him.

The first obstacle for the calling is that the flesh persists in the Christian even after he has been reborn. "Flesh" denotes the endowment of human nature when it is disengaged from the rule of the Spirit of God (John 3:6). Also in the Christian the flesh is the source of a host of impulses, desires, and concerns which fight against the life of God at work in the inner self. (Gal. 5:17-21)

The Christian lives among people in whom the flesh is active; many of them have not yet received God's own power for life. Human culture and civilization operate with impulses of self-gratification and pride that are the opposite of the Christian calling (1 John 2:15-17). To keep order through pain of penalty the people of the "world" construct agencies of law, which serve God's own design for protecting human beings (Romans 13). Yet despite their valid purpose they can

obscure the motivations of life and love which are to move Christians
in their callings and thus are liable to support the flesh. (1 Peter
2:13, 14)

Flesh and world are driven by self rather than by God, and they
serve the prince of this world, the devil (John 12:31; 14:30; 16:11;
Eph. 2:2). These forces are hostile to the calling, and as the Christian
succumbs to them, he not simply pursues regrettable ends but tampers
with the plan and will of God. (Eph. 5:6-14; 1 John 2:15-17)

Preaching Gives Help to Living

As the preacher diagnoses the obstacles for the calling, he wants
his hearers to come to the point that they say: "You are so right, you
read my mind, and I should do what God wants me to do — help me!"
He looks as if he wants to help, and he has promised to do so. He
does. He preaches the Gospel.

This does not mean that he simply says: "You are a sinner, but
God will forgive your lapses in the calling; believe in Him, and you
will be saved." That is preaching the Gospel to a goal other than the
one that he has promised to help the hearer reach. Nor does he preach
the Gospel by saying: "Now remember that Christ died for you. You
ought to be grateful that He did, and out of gratitude you should give
yourself to God and Christ in service." That link between Gospel and
goal has hoary precedent. But the Scriptures are quite silent about it.
Just at the moment that the hearer should be reaching out to take
strength for his task from God Himself, he is asked to think about an
inner mood which, like all moods, tends to vanish when you start
looking for it. Different, of course, is the frequently recommended
act of thanksgiving. (Note Chapter 33 below)

The preacher preaches the Gospel to the goal of life when he
causes the hearer to think about Jesus Christ and what He has done
to stir the Christian to life. Paul tells Titus that he should move the
people in Crete to do good works by reminding them of the grace
of God which has already appeared in the redeeming work of Jesus
Christ and has freed them for good works (2:11-14; note Jesus' parallel,
Matt. 20:28). Another complex of Gospel preached to the goals of life
and calling is the one set up in Romans 6. Conveyed through the

Gospel and Baptism, the act of Jesus' dying puts the death and life-lessness of the hearer to death; the act of Jesus' rising confers the same life upon him which God gave to Jesus. Another complex of Gospel preached to life and good works is Jesus' own depiction of His redeeming death as the means by which the Spirit of God is sent into the hearts of God's people. (John 3:15, 16, related to v. 2; John 16:7, related to 15:12-17)

Hence the preacher sounds a note of sober optimism about the Christian calling. He makes it clear that through Christ and the Spirit great things are already at work among Christians, and despite the clash between flesh and spirit in the inner man, they will increase (John 14:12, 13; Gal. 5:17-25; Col. 3:1-17). Hence the goals of Christian life can be preached with the strong imperatives, "Do," "Live," "Love," "Grow." For they are rooted in God's own indicative of the completed act in Christ (Eph. 2:10). Like the imperative to faith, the imperative to action is valid if and when, in the hearer's mind, it is coupled with the cross and resurrection of Jesus. For in Him — our life is literally "in Him" — we shake off the bondage of the flesh from day to day and embark anew on the tasks of love.

This means that the preacher can risk even the most trying area of guidance, that of helping men live the life of God in the "natural" or "secular" orders. He can help them love their neighbor in citizenship for God's sake and not just penalty's (Rom. 13:5; 1 Peter 2: 13, 16); to share in marriage as people set apart for God through Christ (Eph. 5:32; Heb. 13:4); to earn money as the implement for love toward men (Eph. 4:28). This preaching will not seek too sentimentally to erase the distinction between sacred and secular, to praise labor because God made the soil or eating because God made the food; but it will seek to keep creation and redemption together. The full possession of the life of God awaits unveiling in the coming again of Christ at the Last Day. But already here Christian lives can find refuge and refreshment in that Christ, His death and rising, and the preacher's word of Christ can mightily foster that death to death and that perseverance to life (Col. 3:1-10). Thus eating and drinking, family and friendship, toil and citizenship, can become settings for the display of God's saving presence. (1 Cor. 10:31; Col. 3:17)

What do you say to the parishioner who responds to your sermon: "But you can't make me want to pay my taxes!"

What does 1 Tim. 2:1-8 suggest as to God's purpose for government:

1. To keep people comfortable?

2. To make Christians rich?

3. To preserve international order?

4. To facilitate the preaching of the Gospel?

How can you preach the Gospel so that a man will want to fit into the democratic process and be an officeholder if he has the chance? text?

What is the positive goal apposite to "Don't use bad language"?

The Word of Christ keeps men fit for mutual responsibility in the church, which is the body of Christ.

Chapter Thirty

PREACHING TO THE GOAL OF CHURCH

Most of the pastor-preacher's sermons are for members of the church. They employ him to carry out a complex variety of tasks of which preaching is only one. The preaching of the Gospel of God, however, does much to make and keep the people a church. The New Testament is rich in suggestion for such preaching.

The Meaning of the Church

People who are not members of churches associate the name with a building, or an organization with pastor and officials, denominational affiliation, and the fellowship of good sociable people. The members of Christian churches are apt to share the same superficial judgment. In the scheme of Jesus and the apostles, however, the church is a group of people who are bound to Christ by faith and who by love are mutually responsible for maintaining that faith in one another. The vertical and horizontal dimensions of the church give it the structure which is most aptly pictured in the Bible as "the body of Christ" (cf. 1 Corinthians 12). The relation in the church between Jesus and the members, and among the members, is capsuled in the term *koinonia*, which is often translated "fellowship" or "togetherness" but actually denotes a sharing to which all participants contribute. Because of their common hold on Christ and His life the members of the church can serve one another as the channels and agents by which this life reaches and sustains all.

In practice this mutual concern and provision takes place as the members of the church "admonish" one another in times of need. This means that they speak not merely warning and rebuke but the forgiveness of sins from God (Matt. 18:1-20). Hence each Christian exercises a never-ending care toward every other one (Gal. 6:1-10). It involves concern for both the physical and the spiritual need at one and the same time, and the member of the church seeks to omit neither. (Matt. 25:35-40; Acts 2:44, 45; 2 Cor. 8:1-7)

Christians worship together and thus convey the Word and life of God to one another in sounded Gospel, sung thankfulness for all of God's gifts, and signed Sacrament (1 Cor. 11:23-30; Eph. 5:18-21; Col. 3:1-16). Thus they become a company of royal priests in God's design, interceding for one another and bringing one another to God as spiritual sacrifices. (1 Peter 2:4-10)

The Goals of Preaching to the Church

The preacher will find his preaching useful for defining and at the same time implementing each member's place in the body of the church. He will do much of this preaching in the standard chief services of the week. Many special services give additional occasion for preaching to these goals: confirmations and reception of membership classes; reconsecration services and gatherings of the organizations of the church; dedications of buildings of the church and their anniversaries; installations or anniversaries of the church's professional workers; choral services and the recognition of the church's music. Annual courses of sermons will be vital on phases of the church's doctrine and the concerns of its members toward one another.

A major goal of preaching to the church is worship. Constant churchgoing develops thoughtlessness in worship; the "busyness" of much church work lowers the eyes and hands of the people. The Psalms provide glowing words to describe the awe and reverence, the dependence and faith of the worshiper as he looks up to God. As worshipers gather together, they help to enhance one another's adoration of God. Here the sermon for the day will frequently draw attention to the Introit or Gradual or Collect in affirming the high goal of the hour together and of the worship of the people as they are alone and in their families. The message of a great hymn enters the sermon by echo or forecast.

One of the most common impediments for achieving mutual sharing in worship is the tendency of people to individualism; they imagine themselves in lone communion with God, though sitting with others. Here the "one body" of Col. 3:15, the "one another" of v. 16, the "edifying of the church" of 1 Cor. 14:12, the "let us consider one another" of Heb. 10:24, become calls to fellowship. The preacher will know how to train for sharing the Word with one another also in those portions of worship most easily disfigured by individualism, namely, listening to preaching and receiving Holy Communion. (Note 1 Cor. 14:15 coupled with 15:1 ff. and 15:58; 1 Cor. 10:16, 17 and 11:18-33)

Every church should be a company of Christians conducting many programs for the help of all. This help should be not just sociability but edification of spiritual life, not the huddling into special interest groups but the expanding purpose of strengthening the weak and comforting the lonely. Such mutual help is a pervasive motif of Christian preaching (James 1 and 2; Ephesians 4 and 5). The intercessory prayer of Christians needs much stimulation; of this more in Chapter 33. Preaching will frequently summon the hearer to share more consciously in it right in the service of which the sermon is a part.

Special programs or projects of the Christian Church in the place receive the support of preaching. Outstanding among them are Christian charity and welfare. Our age too easily loses itself in the false alternative of surrender to programs of secular security or freedom to acquire wealth for self; Christians need the summons to personal responsibility for their own (1 Tim. 5:8). Our Lord's glowing words

at the last Judgment have been quoted in behalf of a universal human-
itarianism (Matt. 25:40). Gal. 6:10 applies there; but Matthew 25
speaks of love within the body of Christ and to the brethren, as do
Matt. 10:40-42, Mark 9:41, 42, or 1 John 3:16, 17.

The Christian preacher wants to enlist his people for Christian
witness and evangelism. Average hearers promptly grade themselves
as "able to talk" and "unable to talk." The church prepares for witness as it trains its people to support one another's faith and witness.
St. Paul's contemporaries knew that when he spoke of putting on the
"whole armour of God," he thought of no solitary act, but of a troop
of soldiers helping one another into their breastplates and greaves
(Eph. 6:13-18). So the church today has to be enlisted person by
person, not just for telling the story to those on the outside but for
helping one another to the life and word that tells it. Parallel to this
program is the support of missions. Far from being a fund-raising
project on behalf of a national or area denomination, preaching to
the goal of support for missions is a part of the Christian community's
rallying itself for God's business.

The same technique applies to the most routine and burdensome
of all church work, gathering money. Some of its funds pertain to
welfare and missions, but most of them support the church plant and
the payroll of its workers. The preacher must properly interpret the
function of the church's paid workers and its buildings as part of the
process of mutual edification. He enlists his people not just in "giving"
but in the common business of soul care and building the body of
Christ. (Gal. 6:6; Eph. 4:11-16)

Preaching the Gospel to the Goals of the Church

Preaching to the goals of the church is always practical, and so
the preacher may not be tempted here to speak to goals of information
as easily as in some other areas. Here he is in danger of mere blatant
exhortation or of linking the energies of people to their task through
group loyalty or self-interest and of by-passing the motivations that
are in the plan of God.

If men are to worship the heavenly Father, they must confront
Him as merciful and adorable through contemplating the work of

Jesus Christ, His Son. Our Lord gives a remarkable illustration of this principle in John 13—16 (particularly 15:1 ff.) when He places Himself and His redeeming work before His disciples as the enabling of their mutual love and commitment. St. Paul inserts the dynamic of the Gospel into his own counsel to salutary worship (note 1 Cor. 15:1 ff. in its sequence on 1 Cor. 14). Splendid cues appear throughout Hebrews, climaxing in 10:1-25.

Christians are to be concerned for one another's welfare utterly through pondering God's love in Christ. This is the monumental function of 1 John, especially 3:16 ff.; 4:7-16. St. James suspends "religion" or the religious service of care for the needy from the gift of God's Spirit through "the Word of truth" (1:17-27). Ample for entire courses of sermons is the case study of the first church in Jerusalem in the Book of Acts (2:42-47 is a summary). Christian giving receives exquisitely evangelical motivation in 2 Corinthians 8 with its picture of the Macedonians who gave beyond their power. First they gave themselves to the Lord and did so because of the grace of the Lord Jesus Christ and His perfect gift (v. 9). This section portrays a most churchlike mechanism of Christian influencing the brother Christian through the demonstration of his Christ-centered faith in action, an echo of Heb. 10:24.

The witness in life and speech to those who have not known Christ receives its most explicit discussion in 1 Peter. The propulsion for it through the atonement receives painstaking and repeated emphasis. (1:2, 11, 18-21; 2:3, 6, 21-25; 3:18-22; 4:1, 11; 5:10)

Jesus Christ discusses money with practical realism as a thing to be invested shrewdly and with long-range vision, but for the sake of the heavenly relation of men toward God, a relation in which the Christian is joined with his brother (Luke 16:1-13). Thus all giving shares in the dynamic set up in 2 Corinthians 8, and the preacher should stimulate to it with the clear call of the Word of Christ's redeeming work. In that method lies the corrective for the many semi-materialistic motivations for giving that have invaded the church in our time.

The Christian preacher always speaks for the church. He is always a spokesman for its people; he is always seeking to win men for its fellowship and strengthen those who are in it. How important, then, that in that preaching where he most plainly functions in his calling, the address to its people, he never fail to use the power of the Cross!

FOR FURTHER THOUGHT

What do you say to the Christian who asserts: "I'll have to witness just by my behavior, for I just can't talk religion."

Do you like it when people say: "Pastor, I come to church just to hear you; I can't wait for the rest of the service to be over."

How do you react to this thinking: Christians are simultaneously saints and sinners. Some of their motives for giving are spiritual, some fleshly. We are grateful for all of the money that they give, from whatever motive, for we need it all in the work of the church.

Study the metaphors of the atonement which St. Paul uses in First Corinthians as he tries to build up the unity and the functioning of the church there.

For further reading see pp. 304, 305.

*The church begins in the home,
and the preaching of the Gospel
keeps it unified and helps it to
witness.*

Chapter Thirty-One

PREACHING TO THE GOAL OF FAMILY

The parish pastor is deeply concerned for the families of the church and the community. The malfunctioning family pulls down what the church and its worship builds up; the functioning family supports what the church sets out to do. Hence he preaches about family life, and more: he preaches *to* it, to the end that families fulfill the plan for which God made them. The growing edge of the church in the community is its families, for their neighborliness and spirituality are exhibited on the front line of living and thus are the church's primary witness.

Membership in the family is in an exact sense a calling. We have already identified it as such (Chapter 29 above). Preaching to it has rich Biblical cues.

God's Goals for the Family

Good preaching makes clear that its goals for the family are God's own purposes. In courtship and marriage, conception and birth, God's own creative plan and power are under way (Gen. 1:26 ff.; Heb. 13:4). The family is there not just to bring children into the world but to nurture them. In God's plan, however, the physical and the spiritual are not to be isolated from each other. Man's rebellion against God produces a fatal split in this plan; physical begetting and nurture hand on a life without the Spirit (Gen. 3:1 ff.; Ps. 51:5; John 3:5). Nevertheless God purposes to use the families of His people to begin and sustain His kind of life in their children. (Ps. 127 and 128; more explicitly Eph. 5:22—6:4)

Thus the family becomes uniquely a calling in the sense of being an agency which hands on God's call (1 Cor. 7:10-15). The members of the Christian household sustain one another with the Word of the Gospel and thus deserve the appellation "the church in the house" (Rom. 16:5). They witness to their surrounding world in the normal routines of aid and hospitality. This outreach must be sincere, resourceful, and coupled with the words that interpret life as stemming from Jesus Christ. (Phil. 2:14-16 coupled with 4:2, 3; Rom. 16:4; 1 Peter 4:7-11; 3:1-15)

Difficulties for the Christian Family

Preaching not merely alerts to the goals of God for the family and draws blueprints for its living, but it seeks to preach the Gospel in such a way that it will be heard. This means that with sympathy and imagination the preacher helps his people confront their need for ongoing nurture from God Himself and then seeks to meet that need with His Gospel and to outline its continued use right in the family structure. Contemporary culture exaggerates courtship and mating and thus renders the steady responsibility for care and growth relatively obscure. The church and its preaching must serve as a counterpoise.

The family is a "natural order." Not only Christians have families or marry, nor are they the only people to have satisfying marriages and healthy families. Conversely, all of the strains and difficulties that beset families invade theirs also and thus are a trial for faith itself. Christians in families ask: "I believe in God and go to church; why do these things happen to us?" Pastoral care responds with 1 Cor. 10:13; preaching explores the meaning of trials of faith that strike the families. Particularly will it alert to the meaning of trial in the hand of Satan: it tends to divert attention from God and focus on human survival or satisfaction. In an expanding economy housing absorbs effort and attention. Young people mate early in view of the uncertainties of the armed services or prolonged education, and their responsibilities multiply sometimes before they are ready for them. Our age has an easy conscience about infidelity and magnifies the sensual while minimizing the total ingredients of marriage. The more earnest the sense of obligation of parents to their children, the more trying will be the stresses and sometimes the neuroses and anxieties of both parents and children.

A special group of problems set in at mating but continue to threaten solidarity of the family. They come in the shape of "mixed marriage" and the establishing of a home in which man and wife are not equally committed to Christ. The preacher knows that he cannot carry out his responsibility in forestalling these situations by sermons alone; but also in them he will have to show himself sensitive, patient, and realistic toward the strains which threaten his hearers.

The diagnosis of family problems must be much more than mass counseling or psychiatry. It has to be a reasoned and penetrating unfolding of God's own plan for nurture going awry, of blocks and deficiencies that threaten the life of God at work among his people. (Note Eph. 5:1-7 in the context of 5:22 ff.)

In many families a problem of increasing difficulty is the obligation toward the elder generation. Much of this is understandable in the light of economic problems and disparity in personalities. But the preacher must help his people to be alert to the basic plan of God and the violation that is latent in many minds. (1 Tim. 5:1-16)

As with all preaching of the Law, the preacher must warmly and sincerely make clear that he is there not to reproach but to help, that his diagnosis alerts to the need for God's help, and that help will be not just a soothing of conscience but a replenishing of power to meet difficulties in a practical way.

Preaching the Gospel to the Goals of the Family

The family is an arena for the Christian calling. It is the basic cell in the structure of the church. Hence the cues and modes of

Gospel preached to the goals of calling and church apply also to the preaching to the family. (Cf. chapters 29 and 30 above)

Especially pertinent are the affirmations of Gospel which make use of the picture of life and its nurture. One of the most moving of them directly links the atoning love of Jesus with the love of husband and wife in the church, namely Eph. 5:22 ff. In that context the phrase "nurture and admonition of the Lord" is instructive. It does not imply acts of moralizing or authoritarian rebuke but the process by which the life in Christ is made to sustain the individual and to overcome the erosion of world and flesh (cf. also John 15:1-10). That process involves thrusting into the consciousness of people the redeeming work of Jesus Christ, His self-giving to the end that God be Father.

Sermons directed to the goals of the family will both preach and prescribe the Gospel of Christ. The hearer will hear it in church, and he will take it home to use there. The physician may give a diabetic an injection of insulin and then instruct him how to repeat it at home. Just so the preacher will preach the Gospel to his families and then counsel to practice the same mutual feeding, the same consuming of the flesh and blood of Christ (John 6:53-56), at home in family worship. But the preacher must remember especially in this process not to let package terms like "the Word" or "the Bible" or "the Gospel" replace patient and explicit unfolding of the story of the atonement applied to the person who is listening.

Special Opportunities for Preaching to the Family

Currently much attention is being given to sermons for children. They are planned for worship in weekday or Sunday schools, or as separate ingredients in services which also schedule a sermon for adults, or in services frankly replacing the attendance of children in parish worship. Any experience which preachers can share with one another in making the Christian message concrete and perceptible to the child is useful. As is the case in all sermons directed to a special group of Christians, preaching to a group of children has to make clear that they are part of the larger church and that the goals outlined to them are to be realized in their lives with adults and in their families as well as in school or playground.

A helpful bridge between the special requirements of children and the responsibility of maintaining the goals of church and family is the "family service." This is the name given to a Sunday morning service in which children are present with their parents; where a parish conducts several services the same morning, it is possible to shape one of them in this direction. The structure and materials of worship and the themes of preaching vary but slightly from the standard order. The chief differences involve the care to speak in terms of the child's mentality, to leave nothing about the sermon or the service unexplained, and to choose visual data which are within the scope of the child's mind. These qualities of worship and preaching are highly welcome to adults, too! This deliberate encouragement to the family pew makes possible much direct application to needs and problems of the family, the obvious common denominator of such a service.

Full-length sermons have almost vanished from Christian weddings. Even brief wedding addresses can serve a splendid purpose. The congregation needs to develop a culture that makes weddings unostentatious and spiritual in purpose if they are to be suitable settings for preaching. The preacher will have to determine whether he is preaching to the assembly or addressing only the bride and groom. Texts are often suggested by the couple and may have only general relevance. Where the choice is the preacher's, he has not only Eph. 5:22 ff. at his disposal but the whole range of Biblical narrative.

Mother's Day gives the cue for much preaching about families. It will be best preserved from mawkishness if the sermon will be for the entire congregation and motherhood will serve for incidental application or illustration.

The family is the simplest means by which the church reminds itself that it exists not just on Sunday mornings but always and wherever Christians are. That means that the church's families are the concern of all its people. The preacher can sharpen this concern and implement it by his Word of the Cross, from the pulpit and in the homes.

FOR FURTHER THOUGHT

React to this statement: "Preaching to children is chiefly the problem of finding interesting illustrations and demonstrations that will make them interested."

React to this statement: "Real help for family living and diagnosis of family difficulties takes place in counseling and group work; the sermon puts the preaching of the Gospel into it."

How can one Christian family contribute to the life that goes on in another Christian family?

How does the Christian witness of the family differ from the witness of the individual members of the family?

A text for Mother's Day: Matt. 12:47-50, leaning on John 3:5: "When Water Is Thicker than Blood." Good?

For further reading see p. 305.

The Gospel sustains Christians for life in a heavenly citizenship against all obstacles.

Chapter Thirty-Two

PREACHING TO THE GOAL OF HOPE

Ask a child what preaching and religion are for, and he will probably answer: "So that we go to heaven." As the child matures, other goals of life become more significant, and heaven seems less important. For the old folks heaven again looms brightly, and the preacher's references to it are most meaningful. At the death of a Christian the church stands by with sympathy for the bereaved and soberly reminds itself of its destiny.

The preacher has the task of keeping earth-bound mortals aware of life beyond the grave, and heaven-bound mortals aware of immediate callings and unfinished business.

The Hope for Heaven

Not every sermon talks about heaven, even though every Christian sermon contributes to the perseverance of the believer in reaching his heavenly goal. Particularly in the final cycle of the Trinity season and in Advent the Christian year directs to a pondering of the Last Things. Many other areas of Christian preaching, like the motif of the resurrection of the body at Easter, give occasion to speak of the Christian hope.

It is important that Christians understand what this hope is. It looks forward with faith to the attainment of a goal that lies beyond and outside this present world, but it has foretastes and sees guarantees already now. When the Christian uses the word *heaven,* he is speaking of a state which involves him already in this present time, the rule of God which seeks to pervade his heart even now and succeeds to a degree (Matt. 5:16; Phil. 3:20, 21; Col. 3:1-4). The heaven to which he looks forward is that rule in its perfection, the place where every obstacle is defeated (1 John 3:1-3; Matt. 25:34). His hope for heaven is not just a wish for it, a self-hypnosis that it may come and usher in a time better than the present; but it is of the essence of faith, the hold on an unseen gift with the clutch born of the Spirit of God at work through God's redeeming plan (1 Peter 1:3-5). That Spirit, already at work in the Christian heart, is the Guarantee of God's ultimate perfect rule in heaven. (Eph. 1:14; 2 Cor. 5:5-10)

The Trials of Hope

The preacher holds the hope of heaven before his hearers because they have trouble doing it themselves. The New Testament gives glowing words for it, almost always coupled with the reminder that its readers have to purify themselves from obstacles (1 Peter 1:22; 1 John 3:3). Jesus' parable of the Rich Man and Lazarus (Luke 16:19 ff.) suggests that the ample supply of present joys makes man oblivious of heaven; and the parable of the sower similarly lists concern for the present life as a hindrance for eternal fruit. (Luke 8:14)

Under the guidance of God physical pain and disaster may strike in order to remind of the importance of His grace. The Book of Job describes how adversity can help God's man acknowledge His supremacy, and it warns against false or heartless counsel in time of trouble. The precious case history of St. Paul's thorn of the flesh (2 Cor. 12:1 ff.) does not aim at perseverance for heaven specifically but at the victory of faith which is its obverse. Christian preaching can similarly analyze the plans of God in adversity as intentions of His grace, especially in time of bereavement and disaster.

Folk religion loves to call any sort of suffering "the cross" and to remind that it is imposed by God for spiritual health. The thought is pious even though the use of the term is not exactly Biblical. The New Testament reserves it for trial and persecution for the sake of faith in Christ, the special lot of the believer who is at one and the same time being tried for his faith, improved in his hope, and found worthy to witness (Matt. 16:24; Mark 8:34; 10:21). Especially 1 Peter portrays the significance of suffering for the sake of the Gospel (1:5-9; 2:20 ff.; 3:13-17; 4:12-19), and Psalm 119 praises the Word of God as the believer's resource for sustaining the burden.

The Motives for Going to Heaven

Why does a person want to go to heaven? The question is important for the nature of the Christian's hope. The simplest answer comes from pagans and from some Christians: Heaven is beautiful, earth is hard. Heaven is bliss, earth is hardship, and the alternative to heaven is pain.

The preacher should forestall Mohammedan motivations. The essence of heaven is the place with God, the essence of hell is to be severed forever from God (Matt. 8:12). The New Testament refuses to construct a consistent topography or physiology of the afterlife (cf. Luke 16:19-31; 1 Cor. 15:35-50). Rom. 8:18 also needs careful exposition:

> I reckon that the sufferings of this present time are not worthy to be compared with the glory which shall be revealed in us.

Far from briefing a heaven of self-indulgence and ease, these lines summon to recognize heaven as a place where the life and purpose of God will be displayed to others — the robust prospect which underlies St. Paul's themes of the resurrected life as the full exercise of the Spirit of God (1 Cor. 15:42-44) and Christian love as care for others also in the life beyond the grave (1 Cor. 13:8-13). Jesus affirms the responsibility and the activity of the future life. (Matt. 19:28, 29; 24:44-51; Luke 17:7-10)

The preacher must help his people to yearn for heaven with the hope and will of rich Christian faith and participation in the life of God now. But that means a growing sense of duty toward the current obligations of the Christian calling. St. Paul displayed this dual grasp well (Phil. 1:20-24), and our Lord used his prediction of the last Judgment as a potent reminder that Christians have to be responsible for the care of their fellow Christians now. (Matt. 25:31-46)

Hence the valid motivation for going to heaven must be the desire to be with Christ and God. Jesus (Luke 23:43) and the apostle (Phil. 1:20-26) make this explicit; and the Seer marshals every resource of picture language to write it into the Christian hope:

> For the Lamb which is in the midst of the throne shall feed them and shall lead them unto living fountains of waters, and God shall wipe away all tears from their eyes. . . . I saw no temple therein; for the Lord God Almighty and the Lamb are the temple of it. And the city had no need of the sun, neither of the moon, to shine in it; for the glory of God did lighten it, and the Lamb is the Light thereof. (Rev. 7:17; 21:22, 23)

The Gospel of Hope

The true hope of heaven is a desire: the desire to possess God. Hope is a sign of life — life as it seizes upon the inner impulses and sets up the great priorities of living, life not just for a time but forever. What does the preacher do to give his hearer this high desire and sustain this radical life in God?

He preaches the Word of the redeeming love of God in Christ Jesus, the Word of God's self-giving in grace because of the atoning work of Jesus Christ. St. Paul reviews the Christian's hope of heaven and of the final redemption of his body. He confronts the fact that the Christian's motives for desiring this redemption may be mixed and his hope tainted by the desires of the flesh, and then he draws the reader's mind toward God by one of his most magnificent portrayals of God's love in Christ (Rom. 8:18-39). St. Paul steadies the Thessalonians in their hours of bereavement with the reminder of death and rising being "in Christ," according to a Gospel which was still clear in their minds from his mouth (1 Thes. 4:13-18; cf. 2:8-16; 5:9-11). The Seer puts the Lamb into the heart of his readers' thinking about heaven (cf. the quotations above from Rev. 7:17 and 21:22, 23), and that is an unambiguous picture of the redemptive meaning of Jesus Christ. Jesus Himself summons a grieving sister to faith in the new life that is His gift through His own life and resurrection. (John 11:24-26)

The preacher must couple with his preaching of hope a patient unraveling of human motives. Many a listener feels that he is doing the church and the preacher a favor by thinking of heaven at all. He is willing to be lulled into a sense of security for himself or his dear ones by any means whatever. Hence the preacher must preach his Gospel against the foil of analysis and diagnosis of fleshly motivation, in order to rouse the hearer's best thinking on the grace of God in Christ Jesus. A stab aimed at the self-hypnosis of men in every age is the counsel of the "parable" of the Rich Man and Lazarus: "If they hear not Moses and the prophets, neither will they be persuaded though one rose from the dead." (Luke 16:31)

Many Christian denominations make no attempt at formal preaching at funerals. This custom has its points, especially if the rite of Christian burial amply restates the great Biblical affirmations concerning the life after death, in Christ. Where preaching is the order, (1) let it be brief; (2) let it be optimistic enough that it does not descend to tear jerking, realistic enough that it affirms the grace of God in Christ Jesus as the Christian's only hope; (3) let it bring the Gospel of redemption to the living, in such a way that they listen; (4) let it speak the hope of the church concerning its dead in Christ and the thanks of the church for those who have deserved its thanks; (5) let it say nothing about the dead which the Christian Church cannot hope for them. The tone of the preaching has to be supported by the firmness and objectivity of the service and rite and ultimately by the customs and decorum of the worshiping congregation; otherwise the clearest Gospel will sound cheap or achieve exactly no penetration.

The Christian Church is a band of pilgrims seeking a city which is to come. They speak encouragement to each other on the way. The journey is worth nothing without the destination; hence their mutual reminders are insistent. Their spokesman shares the hardships of their journey, and with them he rejoices over everyone who has traversed the last dread defile before the city. He has one sure word to steady his companions. "Look," he says, "the One who has gone ahead that we all might forever be with the Father — look, He is there, and soon He will take us all to Himself. Let us remember what He did to bring us where He is."

FOR FURTHER THOUGHT

What are your associations with the term "river of Thy pleasures" in Psalm 36 and the General Prayer?

What should the preacher do as he is preaching a funeral sermon and feels like weeping?

How often do you preach, at times other than Easter, on the resurrection of Jesus Christ and the resurrection of the body? How often, in seasons other than Lent, on Jesus and the Thief on the Cross?

What is the malady apposite to the goal of Phil. 1:20b: "Let us magnify Christ by living or by dying"?

What is the origin of the assumption that there will be no work in heaven?

For further reading see p. 305.

Christians seek God in prayer. Preaching helps them both seek and find Him through the Spirit of Jesus.

Chapter Thirty-Three

PREACHING TO THE GOAL OF PRAYER

The most ordinary exercise of worship is prayer. Many Christians feel that they can pray better in private devotions than in the service with fellow Christians. All of them find that their praying becomes listless when all is well and self-centered when they are in trouble.

One species of preaching which is in this domain is termed "devotional." It simply underscores and grooves a mood of prayer and devotion which is already there. It comprises the addresses, full-length or brief, which accompany worship of the Christian congregation or its groups at unique moments — after meetings of fellowship, at nightfall in the open air composing the Christian company for sleep, in an institution of learning or welfare.

The Meaning of Prayer

Common as prayer is, misunderstanding and false motivations often disfigure it. The preacher must diagnose them as he prepares the hearer for the Gospel, which will stimulate him to true prayer.

Most common is the assumption of natural religion that prayer in some mysterious way changes the mind of God, that God stands by with any gift for flesh or spirit, simply waiting for the trap of his bounty to be sprung through prayer. Even Scripture gets quoted for this, notably "Ask, and it shall be given you" (Luke 11:9) and "Whatsoever . . . believing" (Matt. 21:22). But our Lord says that it is the heathen who "think that they shall be heard for their much speaking" —

> Be not ye therefore like unto them, for your Father knoweth what things ye have need of, before ye ask Him. (Matt. 6:7, 8)

St. James echoes His thought:

> Ye lust, and have not; ye kill and desire to have and cannot obtain; ye fight and war, yet ye have not, because ye ask not. Ye ask, and receive not, because ye ask amiss, that ye may consume it upon your lusts. (4:2, 3)

St. Paul kept account of the number of times his prayer that God might remove the thorn in the flesh remained unanswered. (2 Cor. 12:1 ff.)

Another faulty assumption is that prayer is a means by which the will of the pray-er is bent in the direction of the will of God — a means of grace. Prayer is indeed a spectacle of the heart that is in the process of being bent to God's will. But the one source of man's new heart and mind is God's Word to man, and the believer's speech to God should certainly not be confused with it.

These misunderstandings of prayer testify to the obtuseness of the human mind and the power of the flesh even in Christians. For instruction concerning prayer is so ample. Our Lord made clear exactly what to do, and He listed the demands and priorities that go together to make up every act of prayer (Matt. 6:6-15, 24-34; Luke 11:1-13). Worshipers often reduce His words to a mumbled formula; He intended them to describe the concerns and anxieties that go through the pray-er's mind and will in every petition to God, whether for a major spiritual goal or a minor craving of the body. The pray-er is to go to the Father for his brother too. His first demand is that all that he knows about God be used in the service of God Himself and not of his own flesh. He pleads that the rule of God and His Spirit take over the inner life of himself and his associates more and more —

"keep the Kingdom coming!" He asks that he and his people may become instruments on earth for the will of God and that the demands of his flesh be supplanted by utter confidence in the daily provision of God. He pleads for God's forgiveness and couples therewith the plea that he might forgive others. He asks for protection under every trial and ultimate victory over the Evil One.

The Demand of Prayer

Prayer must be viewed as a demand of the heart. It is not an idle exercise of piety but an act of seeking, seeking God Himself. That is the climax of Jesus' description Luke 11:5-13. Thus the psalmist sings:

> Hear, O Lord, when I cry with my voice; have mercy also upon me and answer me.
> When thou saidst, Seek ye My face, my heart said unto Thee, Thy face, Lord, will I seek. (Ps. 27:7, 8; note the entire psalm)

This urgent demand and plea is in first place, that God will shape and change the pray-er's heart to conform to God's. "Delight thyself in the Lord, and He shall give thee the desires of thine heart" — that means not simply the things that were desired but the desires themselves, the desiring! (Ps. 37:4) In the little and the great objectives of living, God's plan for his man on earth is at stake; prayer is the urgent plea that God's man fulfill the plan.

This plea is so important, for it constantly clashes with the cravings of the flesh. They are likely to be desires for things and comfort (Matt. 6:19-34), so insistent and fatiguing that ultimately the desire for God stops altogether (1 John 2:15-18). Hence Jesus puts a premium on persistence in prayer (Luke 18:1-8), which is simply a persistence in faithful desire for God.

At bottom the real thrust for the search and demand of prayer is the Holy Spirit Himself (Luke 11:13); hence the first plea of prayer must be for the Spirit's presence and guidance even in the most physical or elementary prayer (Rom. 8:11-17, 26-28). It is hard for Christians to realize that when they want shoes, they must pray first for the Holy Spirit to shape their want and purpose. Hence the preacher must preach the judgment of God upon the apathy toward God's best gifts and Gift of Himself, and he must preach the Gospel to make God Himself the priceless Treasure.

Preaching the Gospel to Prayer

Preaching about prayer is ultimately preaching to the goals of the church. For in such a sermon a body of hearers are helping one another refine the objectives and desires of prayer; they are dropping or postponing lesser aims while they resolve to seek the Spirit of God Himself, the Spirit who acts on the heart. It is in that sense that "believing" becomes the preacher's goal for his people; not believing in prayer, or that the prayer will come true, but believing and reaching out for the love and power of God (note the shaping of this goal in Mark 9:23-29).

Especially in a materialistic and comfort-ridden world the preacher will work hard to bring the judgment of God to bear upon false objectives of prayer. Matthew 6 shows Jesus stabbing at the chief distortions of prayer: the unforgiving spirit, the thoughtlessness of religious formalism, and the surrender to material things. This is a hard saying:

> Take no thought, saying, What shall we eat? Or, what shall we drink? Or, wherewithal shall we be clothed? (For after all these things do the Gentiles seek.) For your heavenly Father knoweth that ye have need of all these things. (Matt. 6:31, 32)

The preacher must patiently and sympathetically probe to the heart of the hearer's resistance to this program.

The finest art of the preacher must then be directed toward bringing the redemptive work of Christ into play as the corrective both for the false objectives and for the faulty pressure for true prayer. Jesus implies His justifying work in the prescription "Seek ye first the kingdom of God and His righteousness" (Matt. 6:33); first have His Spirit in the heart, first rejoice in His favor and mercy, postpone every other demand. That method of first pondering the redemptive grace of God is echoed in the Word of God to St. Paul, who had first wanted a thing short of God: "My grace is sufficient for thee, for My strength is made perfect in weakness" (2 Cor. 12:9). Jesus is even more explicit in the remarkable saying of John 15:7: "If ye abide in Me, and My words abide in you, ye shall ask what ye will, and it shall be done unto you." His "words" are not His teachings in general but the specific message which He had been seeking to impress in the Upper Room, that He is the Way, the Truth, and the Life through His going to the Father in the redeeming act on the cross and that they could have life only through being attached to Him. St. Paul expressly links the atonement to the life of prayer in Rom. 8:29 ff.

Common in the literature of preaching is a distortion of the Gospel which regards it as "Gospel" to say, "Pray to Jesus, bring all your wants to Him," etc., and which assumes that because He is mentioned, the imperative becomes Gospel. Even the aim in that saying is inexact, and the preacher will do well to ponder frequently:

> I say not unto you that I will pray the Father for you; for the Father Himself loveth you because ye have loved Me and have believed that I come out from God . . . and go to the Father. (John 16:26-28)

The Gospel is a drama of the Father redeeming the world through the Son and therefore sending the Spirit to give life to men. The drama is not improved by abridging its cast of characters.

Particularly as he preaches to and for the church, the preacher-pastor will counsel to ongoing support of prayer through the disciplines of mutual aid and thanksgiving in worship. Interesting are the imperatives in the epistles to "thanksgiving" (thus Phil. 4:6; Eph. 5:20; Col. 3:17; 1 Thess. 5:18). They do not suggest merely that people should have the feeling of gratitude. Gratitude comes not by an imperative but as an inner response to the thankworthy thing. "Thanksgiving" is the disciplined act of worshipers by which they hold up in their own minds and before one another the great thankworthy acts of God, always climaxing with the review of the atonement itself. (Cf. 1 Peter 2:9)

The New Testament does not identify prayer with thanksgiving, for it normally discusses by it the search and petition of the heart for the gift of God. But it does suggest that thanksgiving and prayer be closely coupled. For thanksgiving is an inner and a mutual speaking of the Word of God to the praying person, the Word of God's forgiving grace (cf. Ps. 103:1-6). The church very early called the Last Supper the *eucharistia,* or thanksgiving, a mutual discipline for showing forth the Lord's death and God's forgiveness (1 Cor. 11:26). Hence as the preacher guides and stimulates the prayers of his people, he himself must help them review the grace of God in Christ Jesus out of which their cleansed will and purified desires can adore the Giver and bring petition. (Note the process in James 1:14-27)

It is a great thing when Christians seek God in prayer. When they do it together, they are the church in that place. Their pastor leads them in the process. Through the Sacrament and through his preached Gospel he feeds them for it and sends them home to do the Father's will in their respective callings.

FOR FURTHER THOUGHT

What does the context of Luke 11:9 suggest that Jesus wanted His disciples to pray for?

Is the Lord's Prayer a list of petitions from which the pray-er lifts one or two in a given act of prayer, or is it the structure of every prayer for whatever gift is desired?

Look again at Mark 9:23-29. What does v. 29 have to do with v. 23?

What is the force of "daily" in the Fourth Petition?

How do Psalm 103 and Holy Communion focus upon the same objective of Christian thanksgiving?

In what way does the traditional collect incorporate means of grace?

SECTION NINE

Routines of Preaching

The pastor-preacher is a craftsman. He does similar things over and over. This means that he should develop the ability to do them well. But it also means that he has to safeguard himself against staleness, idle repetition, and the pressure of competing duties.

Basic to such growth and skill is planning. Far from feeling his way through his task week by week, the wise preacher plans the program of his preaching well in advance and correlates it with the other functions of his pastorate.

Coupled with the planning is the execution. This implies habits of work and management of time, so that among the many important tasks of the pastorate preaching still gets the attention it deserves.

*To envision the total task and to
save time when most needed, the
preacher plans well in advance.*

Chapter Thirty-Four

ANNUAL PLANNING

The preacher should thoroughly enjoy the preparation of a sermon. He should thrill to the message of a great text and the challenge of bringing it to his people.

Yet the thrill can lose its edge. The pressure of producing sermons regularly and of fulfilling other pastoral duties brings on the shadows of fatigue and sameness. Some preachers find their words with ease, but gradually they penetrate the Scriptures or organize and speak their message shabbily. Others make the disquieting discovery that they are not taking the time for preparing their sermons that they should — and that they don't seem to have the time. One answer to this problem is planning.

The Scope of Planning

The average pastor can arrange his planning for a period of the year when the pace of administrative and group work in the parish is relatively relaxed. In most cases this is in the summer season. Some

217

pastors take the task of planning along on their vacations; we have found this to be hard both on the planning and on the vacation. How many weeks are to be allotted to the planning depends on how heavy a program of parish work goes on alongside. We have found it possible to plan about a hundred sermons in sixty hours spread over two weeks; if extended over more, the total process will require more time for each sermon.

The program of preaching for the coming year should be built against the setting of the program of the parish. Some denominations suggest monthly emphases or causes clustering about a major accent for the year. These emphases are helpful for suggesting contrast and for keeping the preaching related to practical concerns. The pastor will find it useful early in the summer to meet with the leaders of his church and its groups to evaluate achievements of the past season, think about general improvements, and chart special activities for a new year of church work. At that time he will enlist the counsel of his people for the worship and preaching which is his unique responsibility. He will review his own plans for the past year, see where they came short or were shabbily executed, and try to learn from the experience.

In addition to objectives gained from such review, the pastor will approach his planning for the next year's preaching with a series of routine questions. How can the morning sermons be integrated with the order of worship without losing definition and freshness? How can the secondary and evening sermons of a given week be made to contrast with the morning sermons sufficiently that pastor and people can remember them? In view of the rich resources of Scripture, is the congregation receiving a sufficiently diversified diet of preaching? Are there special needs of the congregation which preaching should aim to serve?

Planning the Morning Service

As the pastor begins to make plans for a new year of preaching, he probably has a number of themes and courses in mind which he is anxious to try. He will do well, however, to make the first approach from the vantage point of the most easily plotted area. That is the morning service. Where his congregation employs an order of worship which incorporates traditional lessons and responses, the basic themes of the services are predictable. He then has the alternative of employing a pericopic system correlated with these themes or of devising a program of free texts. These can be discovered topically or drawn from certain Biblical books in particular. A pericopic system has the advantage of supplying texts about which the preacher has no presuppositions and in which the textual method can be put to work. Especially where the preacher conducts regular secondary services in addition to Sunday mornings, he will find pericopic texts for the major service stimulating for himself and his people. He will choose Sunday morning texts for the sake of contrast with the preceding year, alternating between Gospel, Epistle, and Old Testament selections. Some preachers like to shift from one Biblical area to another at the six-month mark or more frequently. Considerable time saving results, however, when the Sunday morning texts for the year are from the same area of Scripture.

As soon as the texts are chosen, the preacher scans each sufficiently to proceed through the first two stages of preparation and into a major division. The latter is normally essential in order to discern whether the central thought is workable. The first texts will take a great deal of time, since each stage moves over new ground and the skills of outlining in the given area are weak. As the days of planning move on, however, the studies on one text contribute to insights into others, and outlining becomes much easier. Texts are mutually helpful in the study of the general setting and immediate context, common lexicographical and doctrinal themes, and application to needs and objectives of the parish.

Preachers vary as to the amount of notes that they enter into the planbook for the year. Under no circumstances should planning move into the preparation of entire sermons in advance; they should come out of the heat of the given week's ministry. Each month and week bring a quick review of the entire text and preparation, and hence many of the advance operations may be left unnoted. The minimum for good planning is the statement of text, major division, and central thought, expressed in nonrhetorical and unambiguous terms, for each Sunday and festival. We found it useful to indicate the whole morning sequence on one sheet, a day to a line. Other pastors like to set up a file folder for each Sunday of the church year. Into this they put the jottings noted at first planning, to be retraced subsequently; skeleton outlines where they offered themselves quickly while planning; and the standard liturgical correlations and options to be used from year to year. For quick reference on the desk we suggest compiling a prospectus or syllabus in table-of-contents form in addition to these folders.

Planning the Secondary Services

Some pastors take a dim view of secondary services, partly because the people sparsely attend the few that are attempted and partly because the effort of the extra preparation seems out of proportion to the yield. Yet many of the objectives of the parish can be fostered by regular Sunday or weekday evening services. The more regularly they are conducted throughout the year, the easier it is for the people to gain the habit of attendance. Such services may frequently be attached to group work which trains for or carries out phases of the parish program.

After the morning services have been planned, the preacher is ready to fit plans for the secondary services into the perspective. Again principles of contrast and progression apply: What did we do last year? What have we not done for several years? What will duly contrast with the respective morning services? What will pertain to the parish objectives for the given week or season? Many of the places to be filled on the calendar of preaching assemble into courses ranging from three to nine units.

If the morning sermons are based on epistle texts, the Lenten course for the year can take up the Gospel narrative or sayings of Jesus; the Advent series may take up Old Testament forecasts and expectations. The autumn courses will meet basic objectives of the parish in religious education, worship, or stewardship; a major doctrinal series may deal with the legacy of the Reformation. Epiphany-tide suggests evening courses in the Christian witness, or Christian callings such as the family or citizenship; contrast with morning themes and texts must be maintained. If the morning sermons are based on Gospel texts, the Lenten series will pursue epistle themes;

one course of the year will concern itself with one of the epistles in an expository fashion; the Book of Acts can provide accents, buttressed by epistle texts, for preaching to parish concerns.

Good planning provides for reasonable alternation between substantial doctrinal accents and the more recreative courses dealing with hymnody or Christian art. But always the preacher will remember that every Christian sermon is "doctrine," the teaching of the Gospel of God.

Limitations of Planning

Doesn't advance planning handcuff the pastor, so that he cannot meet the needs of his parish as they arise? Isn't he going to stand in the pulpit looking as if he is trying to remember what he planned many months before?

That can happen; and when it does, it means that the purpose of planning was lost and that it went over into preparation. Annual planning gets the preacher ready to prepare his sermon each week. If he doesn't plan, he may not find himself ready to prepare until the week is over, and emergencies force him to improvise or plagiarize. We repeat: Planning is not preparation. It is programming, getting the overview and forecast of what has to be done, and when.

The texts and central thoughts which are set up for each sermon are not in themselves, except in rare instances, a statement of application to particular needs of the parish. Like the basic themes of Sunday morning services they are areas of thought and teaching out of which the specific applications grow. After they are ready, the preacher must still make the specific application. The more immediate that is in terms of the congregation's need, the better the sermon.

An annual plan is not a law of the Medes and Persians. It is a device for getting a head start on the week's work and for entering upon a year's preaching program with a sense of craftsmanship and management rather than the feeling of groping from week to week. As the demands of the year assume shape, an entire course of sermons may have to be postponed and replaced by another. Sometimes a text which provides a variety of goals may be utilized in a way other than planned. But the total plan will offer the preacher the assurance of competence and steady ministry.

A very able preacher said recently: "No preacher can prepare even one good sermon a week alongside the full ministry." Right? Half-right? What can you do about it?

Is it possible to co-ordinate a national calendar of monthly parish accents with the church year and pericopic system? Is it necessary that every morning sermon of a given month correlate with the national accent?

If the texts of a Lenten series are chosen from the Passion narrative, should they synchronize with the readings for the service?

Suppose a bad case of gossip has arisen in the congregation and planning has no sermon on it for weeks to come. What do you do?

For further reading see p. 305.

Chapter Thirty-Five

YEAR-ROUND ROUTINES

The preacher will find it a joyful and stimulating task to plan the program of preaching for the following year. As the years march on and the ministry enlarges, skills improve, and the joy increases. But planning the work is idle without working the plan. Planning is only a starter for the real job of the actual preparation and the final preaching.

The Month

In our experience each month called for a closer review of the plan and a more careful shaping of each sermon than initial planning could provide. We published a little parish magazine or house organ which went into the homes of the parish and of others who had shown interest in the church or were without a church home. The paper carried a display of sermon themes and texts and of the new courses of sermons with the projects to which they were customarily attached. Wherever we could find it possible, we printed not only themes but one-sentence digests of the sermons. The special programs of the parish for the coming month and the editorials and articles inviting to them naturally reinforced the announcements of the preaching.

This meant that during the third week of any month we had to scrutinize the plans that had been made for the sermons of the following month. We looked at the prospectus and reviewed the texts, themes, and divisions of sermons in the next period. This was the time to improve a unit that had received insufficient study in the planning stage or was unfortunate in theme or major division. The aim at planning time had been central thoughts phrased precisely or unambiguously rather than interestingly; now we could work out memorable titles, and they had to be brief to fit into a display page. Now the program of preaching underwent final check with regard to the activities of the parish, its projects and events, its emerging needs and experiences, especially where they had changed since the planning season. And always came the question: "Will these sermons be easy to keep apart? Will each be useful?"

Some preachers plan the hymns for a year's services in advance. In some years we tried to set up a reasonably accurate forecast of the contributions to worship of the choirs and children's groups. But we found it useful to select the hymns for the services at the monthly stage. Particularly in extended seasons which dealt with the same theme, like Advent, Christmas, Epiphanytide, Lent, and Easter with its subsequent Sundays, several hours with the hymnal made possible a wider and more thoughtful choice in advance than the hasty moments before the deadline for the Sunday bulletin.

In our experience this monthly routine for defining and advertising the preaching of the church consumed a half day. This put a strain on the other demands of the church office. But the time was well spent, for it made some of the final weekly operations less hectic and crowded; and it helped to give preaching the stature in the minds of the congregation and community which pastor and people intended it to have.

The Week

Most congregations publish a bulletin or announcement sheet for a given Sunday morning which is prepared the previous Friday. It will list the sermons to be preached during the following Sunday and weekdays and sometimes publish a synopsis or outline of the Sunday's sermon with its text and theme. The preacher will find it useful to plot these statements in advance so that he can avoid repetitiousness and prepare helpful forecasts. The monthly planning stage provides copy for these announcements; the weekly stage puts them into print.

The real preparation of a Sunday's sermon begins during the preceding week. The preacher finds it ideal not to make any detailed preparation of one sermon until the preceding one has been delivered. This is obviously impossible where he preaches two different sermons on the same Sunday. If he is planning to preach on a Wednesday evening, he will usually want to begin some preparation before then on the sermon for the following Sunday. How will he arrange his time?

Let him plan backward from what is perhaps the most crucial point of preparation — to clear away every preoccupation for the Seventh Stage discussed in Chapter 20 above. With experience this stage becomes brief, but it should mean concentrating on only one sermon at a time! With these hours plotted for the given sermon, the preacher can then plan how each previous stage will be ready for the next. Obviously each pastor has a different total program, and no one man can plan for another. The chart (page 226) illustrates some combinations.

Behind these suggestions are several common sense principles: Write out at least one sermon a week, preferably the longer one; spend the hours of the day which are most suitable for creative work, namely, mornings, at the desk. These suggestions do not imply that entire mornings are spent on preaching or the same amount each morning.

Special and Guest Sermons

Often during the year the preacher must prepare sermons which he had not foreseen in his annual planning. Most of these involve guest appearances in other pulpits — anniversaries, dedications, mission Sundays, group rallies. These impose a considerable burden in excess of an already tight schedule.

Fortunately the preacher finds these invitations increasing only after he has accumulated some skills and experience. Several years

Schedules for Preparing One or More Sermons Weekly

Day	Weekly One Sermon	Two Sunday Sermons x A.M. y P.M.	Two Sermons Weekly x Sun. A.M. y Wed. z Wed. next Plan A	Plan B
Monday A. M.	Stage 1	x Stage 1	x Stage 1 y Stage 4	y Stage 1, 2, 3
Tuesday A. M.	Stage 2, 3	x Stage 2, 3 y Stage 1	x Stage 2, 3 y Stage 5 *or 7	y Stage 4
Wednesday A. M. P. M.	Stage 4	x Stage 4 y Stage 2, 3	y Stage 6, *7 y Stage 7, Preach	y Stage 5, *7 y Stage 7, Preach
Thursday A. M.	Stage 5	x Stage 5	x Stage 4 z Stage 1	x Stage 1, 2, 3
Friday A. M.	Stage 6	x Stage 6 y Stage 4	x Stage 5 z Stage 2, 3	x Stage 4
Saturday A. M. P. M.	Stage 7 Stage 7	y Stage 5 *7 x Stage 7	x Stage 6 x Stage 7	x Stage 5 x Stage 6, 7
Sunday A. M. P. M.	Stage 7, Preach	x Stage 7, Preach y Stage 7, Preach	x Stage 7, Preach	x Stage 7, Preach

* Where writing stages for a sermon in a secondary service are omitted, Seventh Stage follows immediately on construction of working brief.

of parish concern in morning and evening preaching, in addition to work with the Bible privately and in his Bible classes, make him sensitive to Biblical texts which lend themselves to the occasion and which suggest their material with a minimum of delay.

What of reusing previously preached sermons? There is certainly no law against it. Preachers differ, and some find themselves at their worst when they try to repeat "old" sermons. If the preacher is going to employ one, let him go through the entire process of preparation, refreshing every stage, rewriting limp paragraphs or sections demanding new applications, working out some changes perhaps for the simple purpose of keeping himself alert and of incorporating signs of his own growth, and giving himself time for a patient Seventh Stage.

Filing

Twice in these paragraphs we have drawn attention to the need of filing, and the reader has been aware of many more. The preacher must store up in a manner that makes any given item accessible to him at a moment's notice: materials for coming sermons; illustrations and incidental quotations; past sermons and sermon studies, classified both by text and by subject. What process of filing will be used depends to a great extent upon the individual. Some men have a memory that stores pertinent anecdotes for instant use, the way Lincoln's did. Others find so much concrete and vivid material as they apply goal and Gospel to the parish that they find little occasion for an apparatus of quotations. Some preserve their previous sermon manuscripts and studies for the sake of record, with no intention to use them again. At the opposite extreme are the men for whom office system and filing are a hobby. As everywhere the golden mean is the best. The hobbyists need to remember that files need annual cleaning out and adequate cross-indexing to serve their purpose; and the bigger the files are, the more tedious the housecleaning. The memory experts have to make sure that their disdain of filing isn't a bit of undercover laziness.

The simplest method of filing sermons is by number, in boxes or folders; these can then be indexed by number in card catalogs of subjects or texts, or noted in the file folders that carry the other materials on file, or listed in the old-fashioned bound index volumes. Many pastors prefer to keep two separate sets of file folders: one of books of the Bible broken into portions depending on the amplitude of the material; the other of topics. Some preachers like to open a third file — sermon illustrations. For all files new subtopics and classifications can be set up as the material expands. Good cross-filing takes care of the problem of classification set up by courses.

General principles of good filing apply: Keep files useful both for preaching and for other phases of pastoral work and study; keep them

clean and current; keep them simple; where you have to be your own
secretary, hold clipping and filing to a minimum.

Whether the preacher will use routines of his craft like those in
this section or not, he will have to develop some. Let him take pride
in his craftsmanship and exercise it for the sake of husbanding his
time to best advantage so that he will be a faithful minister of the
Gospel to his people.

FOR FURTHER THOUGHT

Preaching more than one sermon a week confronts the preacher
with the situation that he cannot write a second draft for every
sermon. Can you develop the skill of following the Fourth Stage
with the Seventh? Does it help to extemporize a trial sermon on the
basis of the working brief on tape?

What portions of the hymnal provide selections for a Lenten series
of services?

Have you ever tried publishing theme and major divisions of the
sermon in your parish bulletin? in advance or in a bulletin distributed
after the service? How ample did the statements of the divisions
have to be in order to be helpful?

For further reading see p. 305.

*The preaching ministry requires
knowing what things come first —
and how to keep them first.*

Chapter Thirty-Six

CO-ORDINATING PRIORITIES

Preaching is important business. Congregations, fellow pastors, theologians, church administrators — all agree with the preacher that his preaching is of top importance.

In actual practice, however, he has trouble keeping it at the top. The trouble strikes from many sides. In addition to preaching he has to bring the Word of God to people by means of many other activities — educational classes and programs, group work, pastoral care. The pulpit is not the only post for his preaching. As the preacher administrates the business activities of his congregation, he finds that they foster the Word only indirectly, but they are concrete and time-consuming, and they allow no delay. But he can postpone the preparation of his preaching, and when its zero hour comes, he can talk vigorously with surprisingly little effort. He finds some phases of his ministry more congenial to his temperament than preaching, yet they are rich in human values and are good for the church. Before he knows it, preaching no longer has top priority in his work.

Competing Priorities

Perhaps we are unwise in trying to assign top priority to preaching and make the other activities of the pastorate secondary. Many of them are so closely interwoven with the Word of God and with preaching that they share its priority. This chapter tries to appraise them and to suggest modes by which the pastor can discipline himself, manage his time and effort, and properly relate his tasks to one another. As we review them, we should be asking: "What time of day or week is best adapted for this work? Which requires daily care? Which can receive less frequent though regular attention?"

Pastoral care takes the Gospel to the sick, the shut-ins, and the aged. It speaks the Gospel to the perplexed at deskside. It pursues the straying and rallies to the emergencies of human collapse.

Evangelistic outreach travels into the homes of the community with the Christian Word. It reinforces the individual invitation with publicity in print and evangelism by radio. It promotes the approach of the parish to its community through organized or intangible witness.

Christian education devotes patient hours to the indoctrination of children and adults in preparation for membership in the church. It trains members of the parish to teach in the church's schools; it equips parents to nurture their families in Christ.

The administration of the parish supervises the church office and the activities of volunteer church workers. It trains members of the congregation for mutual service by means of regular and special groups recruited for Christian edification and fellowship. It interprets the activities and causes of the church's denomination and enlists support of time and money.

The pastor has to keep the skills of his calling fresh. He needs to grow as a professional interpreter of Scripture and spokesman of its theology and that of his church. He needs deepening insight into human nature and ability to guide people. He must develop and maintain a cultural level equivalent to that of the educated people of his community. He must stay abreast of community and national affairs.

The pastor is a citizen who owes time and counsel to selected community concerns, chiefly in the fields of education and welfare.

He must preserve a contagious concern for people and a clear track of communication to as many of them as possible.

In most instances the pastor has a family. This is a calling under God, and it involves responsibility for the total life of wife and children. The pastor's relation to his family is a primary ingredient in his total influence and witness toward his congregation and community.

Multifarious activities demand an alert mind and a functioning body. The pastor must take time for constructive recreation. He should not be neurotic about his health, neither should he be a bad steward.

Co-ordinating Priorities

Not one of the above tasks is unimportant. If the preacher is going to do the job for which he is called, he has to decide not what to omit but how to do everything at peak efficiency. This is not a hopeless ideal. The activities of the parish ministry support one another and facilitate preaching when they are properly done. Certain hours and situations are of special value for certain tasks.

The graduate of the seminary has not had too much experience in managing his own time; he has worked with bells and assignments imposed by others. Most men under that routine learn to dislike mornings, for they are spent in classrooms after a short night's rest. These men do their most zestful reading or writing late at night. Many parish pastors take these habits out into the ministry — at least until the babies arrive and get them out of bed early. Even then they keep late hours with the good conscience that the parish makes them necessary, but they view their desk each morning through a fog of fatigue. These are the habits that make vital and sustained preparation for preaching impossible. Rather must the pastor-preacher learn to get his seven or eight hours of rest at night and to be fresh in the morning. A rested mind is essential for the mechanisms of good preparation — concentration, quick logical thinking, ready association of ideas and words, patient Biblical and doctrinal exploration, the optimistic and good-tempered outlook on people. When the pastor has his skills in shape and his program functioning, he may need no more than one hour on some mornings of the week for his preaching, and the other time can be devoted to other study. At least one morning a week, of course, he will need the connected hours of writing or rethinking which his plan demands.

The work with individuals and with groups can go on efficiently after the fine edge is off the power of concentration. Yet all of that work is valuable for preaching also (cf. Section Twelve below). We do not believe that the average pastor-preacher should devote twenty hours in a given week to a single sermon. He does not have the time if he is reaching people individually and in groups as much as he should. He has a hold on his hearers through his basic message, which does not become more powerful through time-consuming literary operations. In a well-planned year he invests much more time on any one sermon than the hours between Monday and Sunday of a given week. However, the preacher gives proper priority to his preaching when he uses for preparation not just the amount but the kind of time which is best suited to it and when he properly discerns and utilizes the contributions that all of his pastorate makes to his preaching.

The Daily Plan

It is sheer presumption for any writer to tell a pastor what his daily program ought to be. Even the standard formula — mornings desk, afternoons calls, evenings meetings — needs a great deal of improvement and elasticity, especially in the matter of calling on men. Our suggestion about the early hours of the day for preparing sermons derives from the fact that a man does his best mental work when he is fresh. Top tasks lose priority not because some over-all formula breaks down but because random tasks that could wait for less important moments encroach on the ones that are good for preaching.

This does not alter the fact that the preacher should plan each day. One or two tasks can be predicted by the month; a larger number by the week. During the last minutes of each day the business of tomorrow will be pretty clear. It will help one feel like getting to work the next day and also will help one go to sleep quickly, putting tomorrow into the hands of God, to sketch out the details of the program. It should have gaps in it for leeway. It will not be a fetish but a piece of job engineering. People come first, and it will yield to emergencies.

The morning hours should be planned for mental work. Time with the family for chat about the day and morning prayer will come first and then the desk, and the family and parish can learn to respect those hours for their purpose. If the pastor can do his morning work away from the parsonage, well; but he can set up an orderly field for concentration in a one-room apartment. Typewriter, paper, books, notes, files in progress, have to be set up to be as accessible and inviting as possible. Where the pastor works with a staff, he will want a period of worship and conference as early in the day as possible. This will contribute to the theological task as well as parish business. When the time is at hand for the desk, the preacher will begin with prayer and the Word for himself.

The sermon does not have to be the very first item on the agenda. The set for sermon preparation doesn't come just by saying, "Begin!" Perhaps the daily scientific study of Scripture, or the careful reading of a theological monograph or professional journal, will be a good "warm-up" — provided that the book won't be a temptation to stall. The textual preacher usually finds the First Stage exciting and needs little inner prodding to get at it. Normally the set for each subsequent stage will come as the discoveries or the unfinished problems of the previous ones are briefly retraced. In our observation the first draft is often a chore that tempts to procrastination. The resolve to write in one not too extensive sitting, on the basis of an ample working brief, will usually serve to get things started.

Every pastor has his own particular handicaps for working out the plan for the day, and we do not intend to dictate ingredients even by way of suggestion. Some men carry a reflex of procrastination into their ministries. Others have strong bias in favor of office routines or legwork in the community or endless chat or theological study. The stress of this chapter is: the preacher need not have a bad conscience about any of his predilections or specialties. He need not make preaching important by rendering his other activities null. But the Holy Spirit has given him resources of intelligence, family, congregation, prayer, and spiritual life that he may be a good steward of his time. The time spent for preaching is of a special kind — when the mind is fresh and ready to grapple with the Word of God for the sake of people. Good stewardship of time means investing the right kind of time on the job. Nothing else need be done shabbily. The best engineering is only good enough for the task of sounding God's call to men in such a way that they hear.

FOR FURTHER THOUGHT

Do you understand the concept of "kind of time"? The slang phrase "I don't have that kind of time" usually means, "I don't have the time." Do you understand how different hours of the day are suitable for different kinds of work?

In terms of mental alertness, which hours of the day are most essential for (1) playing with your children, (2) watching television, (3) studying a new commentary on Romans, (4) mimeographing Sunday's bulletin, (5) calling on a kindly and alert shut-in, (6) working on a paper for a pastoral conference?

How do you handle this inner voice: "It's time to work on the sermon, but I don't feel like it; and it will be stale if I work on it?"

SECTION TEN

Self-Criticism

The preacher sows the seed of the Word. It is the seed of the Spirit, who alone can make it grow. But the preacher has to get the seed into the ground. Is he doing it?

This inquiry is termed self-criticism. Criticism does not mean reproach, although it may uncover deficiencies that are to be remedied. If the preacher is putting himself to work for God and growing in that service, he wants to know what he is doing.

Criticism asks what the hearer is getting from preaching. The preacher himself can estimate this to a degree, as he reviews his manuscripts and especially his recordings. Competent hearers are able to tell him ever better. If he is wise, he will accept their help.

The preacher should want to know whether his message actually reaches his hearer with the Gospel.

Chapter Thirty-Seven

THE PLACE OF CRITICISM

The preacher has accepted the mandate from God to bring the Word of reconciliation to people. God is concerned that he carry out his assignment. Therefore he should be concerned too.

Only God can tell whether the preacher seeks to carry out his task for the sake of God rather than himself or the approval of people. Hence the preacher rests his case on God's judgment rather than man's.

> With me it is a very small thing that I should be judged of you or of man's judgment; yea, I judge not mine own self. For I know nothing by myself, yet am I not hereby justified; but he that judgeth me is the Lord. (1 Cor. 4:3, 4)

The preacher must through Word and Sacrament keep on refreshing his faith in God and his dependence on God's grace (cf. Section Twelve below) and must disregard every human condemnation thereafter.

In an altogether different domain, however, is the preacher's concern whether he is actually getting his message to his hearer. That is his job, the purpose of his skill. To that end he needs to scrutinize what he is doing and to enlist the aid of helpers.

Blocks to Self-Criticism

Many a preacher finds himself quite unready to scrutinize his own work. In most of the pastor's communication to his people they show him whether they are listening and understanding by some variety of "feedback." They converse, ask questions, react unpleasantly or with cheer, attempt to carry out his counsel or remain apparently apathetic. But preaching seems immune to these tests. The pulpit often symbolizes not merely dignity but remoteness. In many congregations the accepted decorum is that the hearer during the sermon look passive and barely conscious. Preaching makes high demands on people, but the actual results seem to come quite generally from the reinforcement of parish administration and counseling and religious education. Hence the preacher is apt to expect few direct results from his preaching and is reluctant to gauge its effectiveness.

Coupled with this situation is a reflex which many a preacher carries with him from school days. In college and seminary the student faced a constant barrage of criticism by instructors and fellow classmen. Schoolboy mores put student and instructor into opposing camps. Criticism was viewed as one episode of this battle.

A final block to self-criticism is that the preacher is overbusy and tired. He does not take time for patient preparation. A sense of imperfection lurks right under the threshold of consciousness. He gets along with his own conscience by means of the formula "What I have written, that have I written." When unpleasant criticism reaches him, he protects himself inwardly by saying: "If I preach the truth, that is all that I can do; the results are not my business but God's."

Like all rationalizations this assumption is a half-truth. God does indeed produce all the results that His Word achieves, just as the harvest is due wholly to seed. But just as it is the sower's business to get the seed into the ground, so it is the preacher's business to get the Word where it will produce results. The preacher does not play God, but he is God's workman to reach men with the Word. Hence it is part of his business to ask the question without flinching: "Am I reaching the people? Is my Gospel hid from my hearers because of their lack of faith which God alone can penetrate or because of my poor preaching, which is my responsibility and which keeps them from hearing the Word?"

More Than Faultfinding

Preachers and theological students frequently react against criticism because they identify it with faultfinding. This is due to the fact that criticism does not concern itself with intentions but with performance. Nor does it concern itself with generalities. It is really criticism as it analyzes specific components of the total task and seeks to recognize where these components have served well or failed. Unfortunately — and this is part of the schoolboy reflex previously discussed — the negative is more dramatic and memorable than the positive or the neutral. The preacher hates to face criticism or exercise it upon himself because he fears the discomfort.

Hence the first thing for the preacher to remember is the purpose of his preaching. It is not to enhance his self-esteem but to give God's life to people. Hence if criticism links in the preacher's mind with the enjoyment or discomfort which he feels at his work, it fails of its purpose. As the preacher confronts the criticism of his own judgment or that of others, his question should not be, "Can I take it?" but "Can I afford to remain in the dark about what I'm doing?" On the rifle range the sergeant announces the score of his trainees. His language may even be rather pungent as he comments on some unmarked targets. But he announces the score for one purpose: to correct faulty procedures on the firing line and to produce better marksmen.

The preacher should beware of a faulty reaction to criticism, the sense of wearing the hair shirt. He should criticize his own preaching and encourage others to do so not just so that he can sigh, "I am an unprofitable servant." He is not to become conscious of his frailties to the point of forgetting his people and his service to them. Exactly the opposite end is the purpose of criticism. St. Paul mercilessly held up to view the unsophisticated and hampered qualities of his own preaching, yet wholly for the sake of what it accomplished for people:

> I was with you in weakness and in fear and in much trembling, and my speech and my preaching was not with enticing words of man's wisdom, but in demonstration of the Spirit and of power, that your faith should not stand in the wisdom of men but in the power of God. (1 Cor. 2:3-5)

He viewed his preaching as a channel for the Gospel of God and at times spoke almost cockily of its merits. Yet underneath it all was the one passion that through him people might actually hear the Gospel.

> Our mouth is open to you, Corinthians; our heart is wide. You are not restricted by us, but you are restricted in your own affections. In return — I speak as to children — widen your hearts also. (2 Cor. 6:11-13 RSV)
>
> I thank God that I speak in tongues more than you all; nevertheless in church I would rather speak five words with my mind in order to instruct others than ten thousand words in a tongue. (1 Cor. 14:18 RSV)

Perhaps the analogy of Law and Gospel applies to the preacher's self-criticism. As he confronts his own shortcomings, he is not to brood over them or despair about them or wish that he could think of something else, but he is to apply the remedy. When he confronts his competence, he is not to gloat or strut but to place it in the service of God and his people.

The Purpose of Criticism

Criticism is not being hypercritical about one's own preaching. But it asks about the preacher's methods: Are they serving their purpose? Are they bringing the Word to the hearer?

This does not mean that criticism operates by trying to measure the results of preaching in the growing faith or the new life of the hearers. That would indeed be measuring something for which God alone is responsible. That sort of measurement is difficult, if not impossible, for it has to discern inner operations which hearers can fake. Furthermore the pastorate applies the Word of God to people by so many different operations other than preaching that the hearer's growth can hardly be ascribed to a single one of them. But criticism ceaselessly inquires concerning preaching: Is it getting the Word to the hearer? Look again at the purpose of preaching set up in Chapter 8 above. Are the preacher's words making sense to the hearer? More, are they meaning to him what they should?

One reason why this program of criticism is so necessary for every preacher is that he is inclined to measure his performance by his intentions. He wants to preach the Gospel, and therefore he thinks he does. He has the Gospel of God in his mind and acknowledges it as the dynamic of God, and yet he speaks it perfunctorily or neglects to link it to the goal of his sermon as its major impulse. He wants to speak clearly, and he says facts that mean much to him and uses words which are clear to him — and yet the people may be sitting there as spectators of an alien show. Good preparation said every inch of the way: "What do the people think? How can I reach them?" Criticism says: "Did you?"

As the preacher trains selected hearers to help him in this process, he has to fight the impulse of the flesh to organize compliments. The self-esteem that feeds on praise is not to be confused with the new man that feeds on the Word of God. But the preacher should try to be a craftsman who brings about spiritual goals through technical means. If he takes his work seriously, he has to know whether he is using his techniques effectively. The golfer measures the worth of his methods by distance posts and greens. The preacher's measurements are more difficult. He is reaching ears and hearts simultaneously. He can't be satisfied with saying, "I didn't forget," or "I felt good in there," or "I imagine it went badly." In fact, many preachers discover that when they feel most self-assured about a message, it may be making the poorest impact.

After the service hearers often speak a polite and sometimes fervent word of appreciation to the preacher. He should not belittle these comments, for they are part of the relation between pastor and people. But they themselves need investigation, nor do they always indicate thoughtful reaction to the sermon. Sermons are supposed to change people for the better. That change runs counter to the flesh, and its dynamic is a Gospel which is an offense for that flesh. If the hearer has really listened, he may want to get home and think the matter through again; he may want to see the preacher for more help. Hence the preacher must look for more than indications that the hearers are pleased.

The preacher should have a good conscience about testing his own job. But he should know what he is testing. He wants to make sure that he has amply preached the Gospel of God. He wants to know if his message made sense and meaning. He wants to forestall or remedy bad habits of writing or speech that distort his purpose. He wants to know whether people have listened in order to stay awake, or to be entertained, or to be changed. He is sowing seed, and he wants to make sure that the grains are not blowing over the highway — and that they are really seed.

FOR FURTHER THOUGHT

What is the difference between the judgment of men of 1 Cor. 4:3 and the hearer's criticism of the pastor's sermon?

Do you ever have the feeling that you preach the Gospel more aptly in some field of the pastorate other than preaching — catechetical instruction or bedside, for example? What can you do about it?

Do you ever attempt to measure the spiritual growth resulting from the Gospel spoken in the nonpulpit preaching activities of the ministry? the sense and meaning of the words spoken in them?

Why do a few words at the sickbed seem to do more for hearers sometimes than the many words of a sermon from the pulpit?

*Critical review of his own written
or recorded sermons will help the
preacher to improve.*

Chapter Thirty-Eight

METHODS OF CRITICISM

Criticism begins before the product is finished. During the entire process of preparing a sermon the preacher is asking these questions: "Which alternative shall I employ in order to reach the hearer best? What have I learned from the past to suggest how to do this better?"

Also while preaching to the audience, the preacher will try to improve the effectiveness of his planned message and will sometimes reshape an expression or a paragraph or an illustration in order to meet the hearer more adequately. Sometimes the puzzled or lethargic expression on the face of a hearer will cue the attempt. Most of the time he will not wait for such signals but will anticipate the hearer's need and make the improvements that occur to him, now that he has the hearer before his eyes.

Is Self-Criticism Possible?

But now suppose that the sermon is over and the people have gone home. Shall there be any self-criticism at this point?

Some blocks against the process will probably emerge in the preacher's thinking and mood. But now suppose that he has properly dealt with them and knows that he should do his best. Can he do it? Can a preacher really judge his own performance so far as its impact on others is concerned? Must it not be left up to the judgment of hearers altogether?

The preacher will want to make the effort to do so himself; for not all hearers are always able to analyze the components of the sermon and its delivery or of the impact which it has made upon them. And the preacher himself is not utterly helpless. His whole ministry teaches him to try to put himself in the place of the hearer, throughout the entire process of preparation and preaching. Why should he suddenly halt that effort as he reviews the sermon after it has been preached?

Two types of self-criticism make the process easier. The one is to allow some time to elapse before returning to the critique of a given sermon. Days and weeks between the preaching and the critique help to weaken the rationalization "What I have written, that have I written." The other method of self-criticism is to review a sermon for the sake of appraising only one facet of preaching; or to compare a number of recent sermons with reference to a narrow sector of the whole range of preaching — introductions, Law and Gospel, summary and applications, inflection, rate and perspective, style and variety. This method will dilute the pessimism engendered by too unhappy a performance in a given instance, the critical faculty will be sharper and more objective, and accent will be thrown on growth through experience rather than faultfinding.

Reviewing the Manuscript

Not every sermon manuscript serves equally well for critique of a past performance in the pulpit. Inflection, facial expression, total delivery, had much to do with the actual yield for the hearer. The preacher often used words in the pulpit which were different from, and usually better than, those on the manuscript. The Seventh Stage may take the preacher beyond the Sixth, at least in certain areas of the sermon. Nevertheless some sermon manuscripts will serve well for postcriticism. Shortly after preaching and before undertaking a fuller critique the preacher will note on the manuscript or the working brief where he departed from the plan, where he elided or amended. Important will be the signals that he altered the outline, or introduced a new strategy for introduction or conclusion, or devised other illustrations.

Now a number of criteria for criticism can be applied. They pertain also to the review of a recorded sermon and hence are sketched here in detail. The preacher had been thinking about them during his preparation, for the sake of reaching hearers; now comes the test whether they actually came through in the finished product.

Language and Style. — Are the sentences clear? subjects and predicates close together? few pendent and rambling constructions? few passives? Are the subjects concrete and personal? Do the verbs suggest movement? Do we see pictures when we think about the doctrinal concepts?

Are the paragraphs unified? Does the topic of each one stand out clearly near its beginning? Are the summaries adequate so that the hearer will consciously move on to the next idea? Does each paragraph have data that are sufficiently visual and applied? Is the introduction engaging and simple? Does it put the purpose and goal of the sermon on the table and invite the hearer to pick it up? Does the conclusion summon to resolution as well as to thought? Is the hearer left with a clear reminder of the goal and a clear application of the Gospel as power?

Do the ideas march on promptly without too much backtracking? Are new ideas introduced slowly enough for the hearer to catch them? Are the definitions clear in terms of the preacher or in terms of the hearer? How many people in the audience will find the sermon easy to listen to?

Doctrine and Fact. — Is the hearer made to confront his relation to God promptly? Is the goal of the sermon interpreted to the hearer as a plan and design that God has for him? Is he led to confront God's judgments over his failure to meet that plan? Does the hearer meet God in terms of his own daily experience? Is a sufficiently wide net thrown out over the audience so that people of various ages, economic levels, and Christian experience are helped to think the sermon through together?

Does the sermon take pains to preach the Gospel? Does its complex of the Gospel mesh with the mode of exploring the hearer's malady and preaching the Law? Are the descriptions of Law and Gospel phrased in terms of the hearer's language and experience?

Is the text quoted sufficiently to become memorable to the hearer? Is it used to help the hearer focus on the goal, or does it merely get in the way of the sermon? Are the personal and concrete implications of the text adequately exploited? Does the total sermon reflect God, who is concerned for His people and reaches out to them in grace? Does it sound like the conversation of a man of the church working for the people of the church that all might be edified? Does the concern that every Christian should have for the erring and straying as well as the safe sheep properly come to the surface? Is the tone of the sermon equally kind and firm? Does the preacher avoid riding hobbies?

Reviewing the Recording

Where no recording of the sermon is available, the review of the manuscript will prove helpful, and it will stimulate to improvement of subsequent sermons. Ideal, however, is the method of criticism by a recording. Its advantage lies, obviously, in the opportunity to hear what the people heard and not just what the preacher intended to say. It shows what the delivery of the sermon did to interpret the material and to give it meaning. If the parish does not own a recording machine, the preacher will find it useful to rent or borrow one from time to time to see what he has been doing. He will discover where he has been inclined to view himself too favorably or too harshly.

All of the criteria of judgment indicated in the previous paragraphs apply to the recorded sermon too. The criticism will be more adequate if the preacher will listen for just a few factors at one time.

Delivery tends to introduce complications in content and style that may not appear on the manuscript. Hence these criteria should be added to the above: Is there a tendency to clutter the grammar?

to multiply the number of predicates attached to a single subject? Are the transitions clear, or do they become obscure or wordy? The portions that adhere to the manuscript and the improvised additions should have the same level of style; do they? Is the style sufficiently "spoken"? Are new ideas introduced slowly enough to be understood, rapidly enough to keep interest? Did the entire sermon set up a goal and lead the hearer to it without derailing or taking too much for granted?

A recording gives the opportunity to test criteria of speech. Here are some of the deficiencies that are most common:

Voice. — Is it ample? Does it sound strained? Does it have the wheezy or squeezed sound due to improper stress and breathing? Does it sound "nasal"? If so, is it due to a cold or sinusitis, or is it the mark of self-conscious tightening at the velum? Does the speaker's voice seem unexpectedly high? low? Is the speaker (often the case with tenors) unduly depressing the key of his voice so that it gets windy and unresonating? Is he using one level of key too constantly? Is he playing over enough keys on his instrument? Can you hear him inhale?

Inflection. — Is the same pattern stamped on most of the sentences? Do they all begin on a high key and end low? Are any notes on the musical scale repeated very frequently? Are the chief accents of the sentence (at the beginning and toward the end) properly indicated by upward stabs of the voice? Instead of upward flicks of the voice does the speaker employ little loud thrusts of sound? Do the main ideas of the paragraph stand out poorly in inflection? Does the voice insufficiently show climaxes?

Rate. — Does the sermon have "one speed forward"? Is the speech too slow? too fast? Are accelerations and decelerations appropriate to the idea and the mood, or are they artificial? Are tiny pauses introduced at easy spots of the sentence and between words that belong together? (This indicates that the speaker is trying to remember how he phrased the sentence on his manuscript and is getting his mind off the hearer and the subject.) Does the whole sermon have a relentless and breathless quality instead of using pauses at peaks of the persuasion to let the material "sink in"? Is the rate jumpy and tumbling, indicating that the preacher is not thinking of the capacity of the hearer to stay with him?

In General. — Is the delivery suited to the material, or is it inappropriate and absent-minded, at least at spots?

Appendix IV gives a chart which we have found useful for checking recordings. The preacher will find it helpful to listen to a sermon for the sake of only one area at a time; and he may wish to set out some criteria in more detail as he works over an extended period of time in improving selected areas.

Always let the preacher remember, however, that he is going to the trouble of criticism so that he will improve. The criticism does not make the improvement; it alerts to its need. The improvement comes by regrooving the process of preparation and in the total growth of the preacher.

FOR FURTHER THOUGHT

Have people ever told you, "You speak too fast" (or slow)? Did they perhaps mean: too steadily, with too little attention to meaning?

Which of the recording criteria deal with clergyman's throat? with pulpit tone?

What difference would a hearer find between a sermon delivered in a monotone and one in which each sentence has the same inflection pattern?

Do you have a tendency to speak in long sentences? Have you fooled yourself about this by using periods in your manuscripts which did not set off sentences but phrases (incomplete sentences)?

For further reading see p. 306.

*Certain listeners will be. of service
to the preacher in helping him
estimate his effectiveness.*

Chapter Thirty-Nine

USING CRITICS

The maturing preacher does not look for people to compliment his sermons. But he does look for reactions. The proof of the pudding is in the eating, and the eater is in the best position to describe the pudding.

Learning to Use Critics

The preacher has to know whether he has succeeded in putting himself into the place of the hearer. He has to find out whether his speech and demeanor actually reveal his inner concern for the hearer and his intention to say the helpful and meaningful word. He has to find out whether the impression that he gives as a speaker is unified, whether face and gesture and voice and inflection and message and plan blend into a working whole, or whether some elements obtrude themselves and something is still awkward or even disturbing.

The preacher tried, but other people have to tell him whether he succeeded or not. Not all of his hearers can do so; fewer will. Not all of them should. Many of them have an inner image of what a preacher should be which they have gained from childhood and which has little to do with the craftsmanship of persuasion. Many of them view criticism simply as faultfinding, others as paying compliments. The preacher has to find those who can help him most, and he may have to train them what to look for and how to put their findings into words.

Having done this, the preacher now has to train himself to listen to this criticism and to put it to best use. Some of the most useful reactions come immediately after listening; others take shape in conference that looks back over many months of preaching. In every case the preacher has to remember the purpose of the criticism, the means at hand for improvement, and the process of laying aside whatever impedes or disfigures the saving message. Normally a random or total judgment about a sermon, good or bad, is not as useful as a conference in which the critic can focus on a practical observation or two and outline definite areas for improvement.

Wife and Family

Many a preacher calls his wife his best critic. It isn't safe to generalize. Some well-meaning and zealous women plan to recast their preacher-husband in a mental image of their own and distort the unhampered quality of his witness. Others comment so incessantly that they insert symptoms of self-consciousness into his delivery and speech. Certainly the first purpose for wife and family to listen to the preacher's sermons is personal worship and intake of the Word, and any critique of his performance should be strictly a by-product.

The calling of the pastor's wife is primarily not that of a critic or homiletical technician but that of steadying the man, of bringing him up out of his pessimisms, and of gently ignoring the heady moments of pride. Some women who are highly trained as speakers and writers interpret their calling as pastors' wives in those terms, and well. The glow that is better than words will tell the preacher that he broke through; the silence where he is soliciting compliments will remind him that he is too anxious and his calling may derail.

A great source of helpful criticism, however, is the Sunday noon chatter about the sermon that goes on in the parsonage council. Some of the great compensations for having a family, the preacher will agree, come then as he finds out whether the basic goal and doctrine came through, also in terms of the children; whether diagnosis of malady was pertinent and penetrating; whether basic Gospel was ample, visual, and fresh enough; whether the text became at least in part as dear to this circle of hearers as it was to the preacher. After all, similar conversations are going on over all the dinner tables of the congregation. In this and other conversations the pastor's household can give the first indication that the preacher is preaching for the church and not just to it. As the pastor's children grow to maturity and he senses their changing response to his preaching, whole new ingredients of proportion, common denominators, and vitality of style enter into his thinking and planning.

Training Critics

Where the congregation includes teachers of speech or literature, personnel in radio or television, they are a resource for criticism which the pastor will wish to exploit at least occasionally. Radio preaching is more akin to communication with the small group than to pulpit delivery. But it does have in common with parish preaching the need for directness and apt approach, speech with realistic inflection and pace, over-all human interest and applied quality. Hence broadcasting people can offer useful judgments, especially in view of their overview of standards and tastes of the community. The judgment of teachers is valuable if it is not colored by too narrow a field of interest. We have no experience with using journalists or lawyers as critics; in theory they should be important.

Normally the most important critics will be the very limited number of men in the church who have the chief responsibility for the congregation's worship and preaching — its board of elders or deacons. Even when they have no advance technical training, they will have promise for the task. Occasionally others will prove important: teachers in the parish schools, staff persons, such as organists or chief ushers or choral directors, who are closely associated with

the worship of the church. Obviously the basic interests of these
people vary. If the pastor directly encourages them to help toward
the improvement of his preaching, he may lead to their improved
devotion and concentration in worship rather than gain remarkably
from their criticism. Sometimes useful critics turn up in unexpected
quarters. Thus a housewife with no special training, but with a family
representing most of the age levels and widely respected and acquainted in the congregation, was a most useful sounding board for
parish reactions to preaching. We found it useful annually to have
a brief discussion with women's, youth, and men's groups about
preaching; how to listen to sermons, what to look for, how to discuss
them helpfully with others, how to enhance the hearing of a sermon
through reviewing text and theme. Often helpful comments emerged
in the group and privately concerning level of language, applicability
of illustration, adequacy or tedium of the preaching, mannerisms in
delivery.

To help a board of elders function in ongoing critique of preaching, the preacher should discuss the purpose of his preaching, the
problems that he has to keep in mind, and the goals that the board
itself has for him. Detailed check lists, such as are set up in the
preceding chapter, are probably of little value in this regard. But
as the preacher occasionally talks to the group about the process and
program of his sermon and shows his sincere concern to improve and
to make the best use of criticism, he will develop helpful reactions
which will become more skillful as time goes on.

Conference with Professionals

Fellow pastors should be especially valuable critics. They have
the same concern to grow in their skills, they are honest about facing
their handicaps, they can pool their judgments for mutual profit.
Individual conversations and larger conferences will alike serve for
stimulus and criticism.

In the custom of a former generation a pastoral conference would
hear one of its number deliver the sermon which he had preached
to his parish most recently, whereupon the group voiced its favorable

or unfavorable criticisms. This arrangement was not ideal. The message was not pitched to the group but was an imitation of a previous address with its own goal and setting, and hence the version in the conference probably suffered from self-consciousness. Where the sermon was simply read from manuscript, the situation was even less favorable for balanced criticism. The general plan was valuable, nevertheless, for a review of basic theology, approach, and preaching style.

Tape recordings played back from a previous Sunday's actual preaching should offer a considerable improvement over the direct repetition. Here the total operation, with the exception of actual appearance, is on view. Perhaps kinescopes will become so common in several years of television that the replay of the preacher's total performance will be available. One or more critics may lead the discussion on the basis of a chart like that in Appendix IV. Similar portions of several recordings by various members of the conference may be played back for comparative purposes, and the group can become a workshop on a phase of preaching. Or a member of the conference can offer a description of his maturation over a period of several years by means of recorded excerpts.

Unusually useful for mutual criticism is a multiple ministry within the same congregation. Again the recordings can serve as a basis for discussion. Small segments of the total process can be reviewed, and the results ploughed into the preparation for forthcoming sermons. Pastors appreciate the contributions of their student vicars with their recent classroom experience and bibliographies, the vicars profit from the pastoral sense and the direct application to concrete situations, and both gain much from review of each other's preaching. Where teachers are on the staff, conferences on speech performance and method will serve to improve not merely the pulpit but also the classroom.

In this entire program of criticism the first and last word must be: the preacher is not looking for praise or blame but for ways of improvement. He wants to help people. He is not trying to find a message that will be more powerful than the Gospel; it can do more than he or any man. But he is trying to find out whether he is giving the Gospel to people, whether they are hearing it, wanting to pay attention to it, or discovering that it pertains to them. His job is to throw God's own lifeline out to men. Let him be willing to ask whether his cast is reaching the mark.

FOR FURTHER THOUGHT

Do you become embarrassed when someone compliments you about your sermon? Do you become nettled when they give an adverse criticism? Do you try to defend your performance? apologize for it? What else?

Try a simple check sheet on preaching, in a youth group: Do you like sermons on stories or on texts from the letters? Do you pay attention to the text? Can you mention the subject of last Sunday's sermon? Do illustrations help you? Do you like them from Scripture?

Suppose somebody says: "Pastor, last Sunday you preached too much Law." What is the best answer: (1) That's just what you folks need; (2) You misunderstood me; (3) You don't know what Law is; (4) What was the section that made this impression on you? (5) Did you hear my Gospel?

What do you do when a radio man says: "You read script poorly"?

SECTION ELEVEN

___

Growing as a Preacher

The preacher must grow. Year by year his preaching should improve. God gives him His Spirit so that he may mature as God's man. The Spirit works on him through the very Word which he preaches to others.

The preacher is conscious of barriers to this growth. At times he feels stale, harried, ill-prepared, discouraged by lack of results.

The preacher can safeguard his growth. He can practice several means for it simultaneously. He must begin with maturation in Christ. He must continue by deepening his insights into the Bible and God's plan for men in Christ as it is set forth there. He must use the techniques at his disposal for broadening and deepening the skills of the preacher.

*The preacher must keep on turn-
ing to the Sacred Scriptures for
personal refreshing and maturing.*

Chapter Forty

SAFEGUARDING SPIRITUAL GROWTH

The alert preacher tests himself and his preaching by means of
various devices of criticism. Repeatedly he discovers room for improvement. He becomes aware not simply of occasional lapses, of
fatigue or preoccupation which kept him from doing his best, but
he finds how certain attitudes and practices are beginning habitually
to block the best outreach of the Gospel to his hearers. He realizes
that some of his handicaps lie in the area of output to people; others
concern intake of essential power.

When the preacher discovers these deficiencies, he should remedy
them. But more: he should make the direct attempt to grow out of
them. It is bad to play the game of preaching at less than the
preacher's par for the course. But it is equally bad to play the same
par year after year. "I never was good at this in the seminary," "Some
other parts of my ministry work better than this" — these assumptions
should not mask lethargy that blocks growth. For the Lord did more
than put us into our callings; He planned that we should grow in them,

257

Spiritual Growth

Growth starts with faith and life. St. Paul has hard words for the preacher who summons others to this growth and himself becomes guilty of collapse (1 Cor. 9:19-27). It is easy to verbalize the marks of growth in Christians: firmer faith in God through Christ; increasing trust and confidence in God's fatherly guidance; progressively warmer love toward people; new victories over the lusts and selfishnesses of the flesh; growing joy at the prospect of the ultimate life when Christ comes again. It is not so easy to stake out advance or retreat in one's own inner maturation. The preacher is a frontman, and that means that he can assay the richness of his spiritual life so exclusively in terms of what he accomplishes in others that he does not remember how the life of God has to keep on growing in his own inner self.

Preachers have various ways of describing their inner standstill when they become conscious of it. One word for it is *professionalism*. The preacher goes about his daily tasks for the purpose of finishing them. He manipulates the people for the job rather than the job for the people. He meets his deadlines and runs through the routines of his ministry so that he won't be embarrassed by faulty or postponed preparation. The surface symptoms of professionalism are haste, clichés, masklike smiles, and false bravado. The underlying sensations are manifold: fatigue from doing disliked tasks; the feeling of playing at a nonessential game rather than distributing the Bread of Life; a bad conscience from posing as a man enthusiastic about something that bores him, from summoning others to action when he is standing still.

Another description for inner standstill is the special bane of the preacher, staleness. He has to speak words to people not just "when the Spirit moves him" but when a stated and regular hour arrives. They must be words that people understand, and those words are few. Every message has to convey the same basic truth and apply it to a relatively small list of human goals. The preacher begins to resent his own work because it gives him so few chances for novelty. He begins to feel more ill at ease with the people who hear him regularly, his own sheep, than with strangers whose curiosity he can still pique. He says that his message is the dynamite of God, but he is disgusted with its package. All this ultimately adds up to littleness of faith.

The Task as a Resource

Many routines of spiritual growth are at the preacher's disposal. Let us begin with the one that he may most easily overlook. That is the preaching itself, its preparation, and the worship with his people. The moment that the preacher fails to find means of grace right there, he imperils any other devices for growth which he wants to employ.

Herein lies one of the finest recommendations for textual preaching. As the preacher honestly turns to the Scriptures to have them supply insight into the Word of God and the heart of people, they turn their power upon him. If the preacher's own sermon should do for him what it is supposed to do for the people, he has to practice exactly the same mental and spiritual self-discipline that he recommends to them when he tells them how to study the Bible or how to listen to sermons helpfully. If the people expect no fresh power from the Word as they turn to it, they won't find it. Neither will the preacher.

The inner thrust that stirs both people and preacher, as they turn to the Bible to get God's own new and strong Word, we call prayer. Let us not be too glib with the phrase; let us think it through in its most radical dimension. "I must pray," says the preacher as he begins to prepare a sermon. Perhaps he is saying: "God, help me get this sermon ready; help me to be on time; help that it will help the people." That isn't bad praying; but the first prayer ought to be: "God, speak to me in this text, grasp my heart, confront me with a goal for my life and faith, clamp Thy judgment upon my own deficiency first, throw the power of Thy redemptive plan in Christ behind my own growth and action." God wants to be wanted, His Word comes to them who seek Him. Hence our first and last inner bent as preachers must be to want God Himself for our own faith and life; and, finding this desire weak and flabby, our first prayer must be the desire to have the desire! What we viewed as one of the accents of preaching (cf. Chapter 33 above) pertains to the preacher himself as he grows through his preaching. All the resources of God's redeeming grace stand by him to throb with the desire for God and to regain God and His Spirit as the end and goal of that desire.

Likewise the entire service of worship — its hymns and prayers, its lessons and responses — becomes a continuing source of spiritual supply and growth for the preacher. He is not a puppet wired for sound. He is a human being who conveys God's life to the church while the church is conveying God's life to him. As he worships, his personal prayer will be that God make good to him, too, His promise that His Word does not return to Him void. This is obviously true also of sharing in the Holy Communion. In many parishes the pastor seldom receives the Communion which he distributes. These parishes will do well, in keeping with their own liturgical practice or polity, to work out ways by which he can join them in this safeguard for growth.

Pastoral care sets up many occasions when the preacher prays with the members of the parish and shares the Scriptural word that conveys power to him as well as to them. Many pastors can tell much about the spiritual refreshment that they carry away for themselves from bedridden or shut-in Christians. Religious instruction in its many forms also gives the preacher an ongoing resource of spiritual growth. A knot of lively children at prayer, the earnest discussion of inquiring young people, the members of the parish bent over perplexities of their work in their callings, are a continually strengthened set for the hearing of the Word, which helps the preacher as well as the people.

Special Sources

The preacher gladly uses Word and prayer shared with his people as a resource for his own spiritual growth. But he must also become a man of much Word and prayer in solitude. Many busy pastors excuse themselves from this on the assumption that they do not have the "gift of contemplation" or perhaps the time. Or they reckon the fragments of thought tossed Godward while driving from call to call or walking up to doorbells as their personal devotions. True, all our life is "worship" in the sense of being service to God; but the preacher needs the discipline of moments when nothing else intervenes, when he confronts God not in the comfortable anonymity of piety in the church but naked and alone; when he faces his own handicaps and weaknesses, his stunting growth and his sin, confesses them, and listens for himself again to God's Word of forgiveness. Where the personal devotions languish, there professional lusts of pride and self-esteem, of fatigue and busy-ness, begin to flourish unhindered. And then the seed of the Word begins to be choked out of the preacher who forgets that he is not only its sower but its field.

The pastor should view his devotional life with his family as a source of growth. There are people who are also growing. He shares with them their stresses and growing pains, their moments of high happiness and special thanksgiving, their need of constant prayer. Into that prayerful set can be dropped the great words of God, read from Scripture or thought through in paraphrase by the preacher or his family or a devotional manual; and the net result is a revival of growth.

Especially helpful are the devotions with fellow members of the church staff — secretary, sexton, teachers, organist, vicar, associate pastor, volunteer workers. Let the preacher share in them, not just to set a good example or cement good relations but to consume food. Many preachers have profited from a brother pastor who served as a father confessor. Such an arrangement is not congenial to every temperament. It is useful when it is regular and systematic and more than just an hour of shoptalk. Let each confess his sin and lay his littleness of faith before God and the brother; let each speak words of absolution from God; let each joy in the sense of closing doors on the past and opening them to the future.

On the borderline between the domains of the spiritual, theological, and professional are occasional monographs or articles in the professional journals which stimulate to spiritual growth. They will usually do so because they are marked by ample Biblical concern, by a note of reverence for God and gladness to function under His calling, and by aptness for humble sharing. The preacher will profit most from such print if he has plenty of moments to look away from it and think or if he has the opportunity to converse with a brother preacher or worker about its spiritual purpose and supply. For spiritual growth is a matter not just of and for the individual but of and for the church. Hence we should be ready to accept the food of life from every member who can reach us; and our best eating for growth comes as we share the bread.

FOR FURTHER THOUGHT

On the basis of this chapter, what kind of Bible reading would be for spiritual rather than for theological or professional growth?

What must happen in a period of family worship if it should provide spiritual growth for all concerned, including the preacher?

What does 1 Cor. 10:16, 17 suggest about the pastor's participation in Communion with his congregation?

Does preaching set up any goals which the preacher does not share? any maladies? any Gospel?

Try to conduct a diary of prayer for one day — fragments, full-dress devotionals alone, periods with family and staff, bedside and counseling, parish services.

For further reading see p. 306.

*The preacher must constantly re-
fresh the ideas and words that help
his message be God's Word to
men.*

Chapter Forty-One

SAFEGUARDING THEOLOGICAL GROWTH

The preacher grows and matures in his preaching as he grows and matures in the life of God. He has to keep on taking the food and medicine which he gives to his people — and for the same purpose.

But the preacher is a craftsman. He is not simply the layman busy at his witness to the Lord. He is chosen as a man who is "apt to teach" others and as a man who is the trainer of others in their task. The power of the Word of God at work in him must be ample not just for his personal relation to God but for his equipping others. In addition to his own hold on God through Christ he has to help others to that hold by speaking to them. This means that he must want to speak, he must know how to speak, and he must know what to say.

Theology and the Bible

This chapter deals with growing in the knowledge of what to say. That means knowing what the Bible says. This is not to discount the contribution of human experience and science to insight into human nature (of that more in the next chapter). Here we are speaking of theology, the understanding of God. To know what to say theologically means more than having labels for the commonplaces of religion — love of God, need of man, beauty of love, hope of heaven, peace of mind. But it means to be able to discover, envision, and articulate the truths of the Christian revelation in concepts that hearers can take and ponder, that hang together in the minds of people, and that grow as an organism in their hearts. That discovery, articulation, and weaving into a meaningful whole is theology. It centers in competence in the Bible.

Most sectors and persuasions of Christendom agree that this is true. The performance has trouble keeping up with the theory. We reproach major trends in Protestantism for missing the mark. Confessional and fundamentalist varieties have always paid lip service to the Bible as "sole source and norm" of doctrine, but they have often allowed a total theology to thin out into special enthusiasms, or they have vigorously quoted proof passages rather than listen to them or search them. Liberal and even humanistic wings of Protestantism show a noteworthy deference to the Bible and make this a good time to be alive in Biblical studies; yet their critical presuppositions are no guarantee of permanence to this trend. Let the preacher indulge in no idle finger pointing but begin with himself. How disastrously many a parish pastor of whatever trend has let himself be caught up in the clatter of his job and allowed theology to wait for another day! But this means that his growth is stunted. His power in preaching can grow only as the Bible speaks to him more and more, as he improves in the skills of apprehending its message, as he finds it speaking to the human situation in the days of its origin as well as today.

"My ideas are getting stale," says the preacher as he finds himself using the same words for the same concepts. He should have said: "My ideas are getting pale." He isn't thinking about the ideas as he should. Freshness comes not just with finding new words and formulations. The real excitement of new lexicons and translations and Biblical studies comes not from their novelty but from the deepening and refreshed meanings which they convey. New portions of the

Biblical message become uncovered which had been unproductive for preaching because they had not really been a message of God's work among men. The preacher discovers new depths in concepts which he thought he had plumbed. These discoveries may come through spiritual search in a moment of need. But they also arrive as the preacher disciplines himself to regular exploration and study of the Bible as a professional theologian.

Every man has to devise the methods of this study for himself, and perhaps he must alternate between several. One will simply continue routines which he began during seminary days under instructors. Another will invest scheduled moments each month or week in ploughing with Testament or lexicon in hand through a new commentary or monograph or technical article. The high discoveries of these hours will reflect themselves in preaching. In our experience the best Biblical study goes on where plenty of mechanisms help to share the gains with others — people in the pews or in Bible classes, brother ministers in conferences tiny or large, study routines in postgraduate programs in schools in the area or by correspondence.

Theology as a System

The preacher grows as a theologian not simply through apprehending excerpts of Scripture but through putting them together. We do not believe that theology improves as it becomes abstracted from life or rarefied into indigestible propositions. Such procedures have little to do with the growth of the preacher. But the preacher grows theologically as he becomes more and more at home with more and more of the Bible; as he sees the whole panorama of the Christian revelation and discerns God at work with the same plan which He had from before the foundation of the world, which came true in Christ the Truth, and which is now preached that it may come true in men everywhere.

The preacher grows as a theologian, furthermore, as he is able to articulate this plan and to find words for describing and interpreting it. Professional theologians have sometimes been given the right to speak obscurely. But the preacher grows theologically as his preaching simultaneously incorporates more of the Bible and as it affirms and interprets its total meaning with joyful simplicity. That simplicity is not a matter of barren imagination or threadbare word forms but of the clear unified picture of the one God at work in Christ. Our Lord, as reported by the synoptists, spoke repeatedly of the Kingdom or, as reported by John, of life and truth, and Paul recurred again and again to the themes of righteousness and grace. But this does not suggest that they suffered from a poverty of imagination but that they played the role of mature theologians who organized God's Word around central themes.

The preacher will continue to read theology, therefore, not for the sake of complicating his speech or obscuring his vision of people but for mastering the facts of his message. This mastery shows in unity and simplicity. This means that he will constantly search for the theologians who can put the Cross into the center of their system and make the Bible speak it for men in our time. It means that he will read theology like a preacher; and that does not mean on the scent for "preaching angles" but with the will to hear and speak the Word of God.

Nor should the preacher avoid reading on the periphery of theological interest, provided that it does not tip over into speculation. The preacher will be able to give more vitality to the central message of the Cross as the subordinate areas come into life — the creation and God in nature, the Spirit and the vocation, the civil orders and the divine providence, and many more. Monographs and articles in the technical journals prod the preacher's mind into action and help him to walk safely, rather than limp or dodge, through the multiplicity of Biblical suggestion. For the preacher who is training himself in the textual method the literature that is frankly Biblical in method will be most fruitful for growth.

Theology and the Church

The preacher has a calling. This means that his theology must always concern people. Much of his finest growth comes therefore as he becomes increasingly aware of the church, absorbs and digests the contributions that come from fellow Christians in the parish and in the profession, and converses with fellow Christians. Nothing is so deadly to growth as theology for the sake of hobby! Rather must the preacher sit at his theology like a switchboard, drawing a message from the whole Scripture to distribute it over a whole people. Every pastor makes awesome discoveries of the competence that some quite inarticulate laymen develop in the primary theological skills of interpreting and systematizing Biblical truth.

Some of his most notable theological growth occurs as the preacher seeks to interpret the church to those who are entering it. In ways that are intelligible to the uninitiate he has to verbalize the outstanding teachings of the Bible concerning its most difficult and heavenly truths — the wrath and grace of God, the relation of time to eternity, Father and Son and Spirit, the battle of flesh and spirit. This implies the simultaneous grappling with Scripture, the human mind, and the resources of language, which is always good for the maturation of preaching.

As the preacher keeps abreast of Christian theology enunciated also by leaders of Christian thought outside his own denomination, his maturation enters into an especially fruitful phase. On the one hand he is grateful for every insight into the Word and from the Word of God, even when couched in forms of language and modes of thought which had not been his custom. He learns to be a learner. On the other hand he discovers how to discriminate. He learns to hold up the criteria of basic Gospel against the work of interpreters, inclusive of the theologians of his own denomination, in order to appraise both the aptness of Biblical footing and the effectiveness of the language that seeks to interpret.

Ultimately the preacher's task is the same as the theologian's. Each observes the data of Scripture, ponders the situation in the life of people past and present who came under the thrust of the Word of God, envisions an audience with certain common denominators of ability and concern, and transmits his data and understanding for the sake of enlarging the spiritual life of reader or hearer. The preacher aims at a wider but not less respectable target than the theologian. The preacher is concerned that theology apply to life and edify the church. This means that he wants to put to use every contribution that the theologian can give him of Biblical competence and insight. Men of God have spoken His Word for a long time. The preacher is glad for their help to frame his message to his people now.

How does exegesis differ from systematic theology? What have both to give to the preacher?

List the last five books that you have read on theology (whether they are seminary textbooks reviewed or new). What is their span of subject matter? How many of them have a basically Biblical method?

When reading a monograph or article with extensive Biblical references — like the early chapters of this book — do you have the habit of referring to the Bible at once to identify them?

How do Karl Barth, Paul Tillich, Francis Pieper, and Martin Luther differ in theological method?

Which is the most "systematic" book of the New Testament?

For further reading see pp. 306, 307.

The growing preacher deepens his insight into human beings and improves his communication with them.

Chapter Forty-Two

SAFEGUARDING PROFESSIONAL GROWTH

If the preacher should truly grow, he has to do it in a total and balanced way. If he excels as a man of prayer but is tongue-tied in communicating with people, if he is stirred as a theologian but cares little about stirring others, he is a kind of awkward adolescent who is all legs and no voice. Hence to his personal growth as a Christian and his increasing competence as a theologian the preacher must join an ever finer skill as a craftsman. His craft is to preach to people.

Knowing the People

The final section of this book observes the relation between the pastorate and preaching. At this point we note simply that as the skills of the pastorate grow and increase, the preacher and his message mature. These skills improve as the pastor endeavors not to practice his own mistakes and as he keeps abreast of the devices and the counsel by which his skills are refreshed and enhanced. This

269

is not the place to review developments in the field of pastoral care or to recommend its literature in general. Here we wish to note that every improvement in understanding people and communicating with them individually and by groups directly pertains to improvement in preaching.

The preacher preaches Law and Gospel. This is not an option which he exercises in certain sermons only, but it is of the essence of every sermon. Staleness sets in not just with the feeling that the words are too limited and stereotyped. But it enshrouds the preacher as he admits to himself that he is not reaching people or talking to them about themselves or summoning them to the correction of difficulties which they actually face. The gravest handicap of much pulpit preaching is that it doesn't matter. It does not concern primary damage, it is no life-or-death enterprise. The preacher matures as with horror and concern but also with pity and the will to help he learns to gaze right into the thick of human need. A basic theology of preaching helps, but the preacher must also be the right sort of professional workman.

Obviously all this means that the preacher actually deals with need and doesn't merely read about doing it. But the reading supports the doing. It sorts out the impressions of the ministry and indicates where the preacher has been refusing to function. It cuts away the dangerous assumption that human need just happens and becomes an impervious mass too formidable to touch. It helps to ask questions about origins and sources, describes human beings as organisms thrust about by environment, defines where the Word of God takes hold and what expedients in church and community are important to keep the seed of the Word growing.

Important as reading is for this maturation of the pastor's insight into human need, even more important is the support which he gets from people. His own deacons and staff will have much to share with him from the daily routines of visitation. Neighboring pastors will be tight-lipped about individuals and cases but vocal about insights and principles. They will do much for the will to look at need and to find the resources for help. Outstanding helpers in every community for meeting the problems of families and children, of aged and abnormal, are its social workers. Usually they welcome even the most amateur concerns of an alert pastor. They share their insights and methods of arriving at them and help the preacher to recognize the interaction of forces in his community which produce the human cases of misfortune or difficulty to which the preacher must respond. All of this is especially useful for erasing the boundary between the needy and the untroubled and for helping the preacher to construct the "fellowship of the concerned," which is the great contribution of his Gospel to the relief of human need.

Growing as a Communicator

Preaching always involves language — the language of the hearer. Knowing the people — what words they use, what they think about, what their goals and interests are — makes for better communication.

Some of this can be gleaned from simple conversation. More massive is the preacher's problem of understanding the thought forms and the basic logic of his people. The phenomena of our time — mass man, suburbia, the machine, the amusement and advertising industries — influence not only the content but the very mechanism of thought. What makes much of the published sermon literature of a previous age only indirectly exemplary for our time is not simply the changes in language, or the way people's minds are crowded with new and different pictures, but the changes in their minds. People do not react to language in the same way as in the past. The preacher must discover this for himself. He must face the situation that preaching is foolishness to many potential listeners of our own time not just because it is supernatural or because it offends innate self-righteousness as in 1 Corinthians 1, but because it is said in words, subjects and predicates. Obviously the preacher can't give up the attempt to preach and look for something other than words. But he can see how people communicate with one another. He will closely observe the language mechanisms of the men who have the ear of his community, especially its journalists and politicians, the entertainers, and perhaps even some preachers. He will carefully appraise what supports are at hand for the words — methods of mass conditioning, obvious and transparent concern for people, the exhibit of convinced and listening groups, and the timeless routine of painting pictures in terms of the people's own experience.

Much of this the preacher can learn from the members of his own church. They are people of the community who have found the capacity to pay attention to words and to discern their meaning. Part of the new priceless ingredient is, certainly, the presence of the Spirit. But they will be able to describe how they have been able to make use of unaccustomed mechanisms of language in personal conversations, in the family circle, in the religious training of children. The next section will discuss the basic factor of rapport. Here we want to remind the preacher that he must learn ever better to sense how he and the church can set up language mechanisms that the people otherwise use but rarely.

Self-criticism every six months or so unearths a habit of speech or verbalization which needs improvement. Maturation implies that the preacher goes to work on it, without too much disgust or pessimism but with the same self-evident care with which he washes his face or brushes his teeth. He will do so whether the problem is mechanical in the domain of voice or articulation or whether it is semantic and relates to putting words together so that people will act. Occasional books or articles will alert to the problem and suggest modes of improvement. At the same time the preacher will realize that he is not alone in the difficulty and that the defect is not simply an unalterable peculiarity.

Sermons and Growth

Preaching is more than the sum total of individual sermons. It is always the preaching of Jesus Christ, and it is always the witness of a man who loves men. What place will the preacher find in his maturation for reading sermons by preachers other than himself?

He will read sermons not simply for his own spiritual growth and comfort, although some will provide them. He will read them not primarily for rich and new theological insights, although a few giants of the pulpit have been able to use the pulpit to communicate creative theology. But he will read sermons usually for the purpose of growing as a preacher of sermons.

This means that he must never let his reading stunt growth rather than contribute to it. If he substitutes the sermon of another for one or more stages of his own preparation of a given sermon, that stunting sets in. Even the so-called emergency should not cause the preacher to borrow. For no matter how good the net results will be, judged by the individual words, the incident will mark a lull, if not a decline, in the process by which the preacher grows as communicator and witness. Although they are customary in printed sermons, even only quotations of paragraphs or sentences from another man's sermons break the attention of the hearer or insert a different kind of attention; and certainly they break the pressure of the preacher, so that their use except in rare instances is questionable. This obviously does not apply to quotations of phrases, memorable ejaculations, or arrow insights that have gone over into the blood stream of the preacher.

All this does not imply that the preacher should not read sermons. He should read many of them, and a book or two of them should be on hand all the time. He should read them not in the preparation of a sermon on that theme or text, but for the sake of satisfying the interest of the craftsman in the labors of his fellows and for the sake of discerning how colleagues of his calling measure up to their task.

The preacher will read sermons rapidly, at times, for getting the total one-time impact that the original hearers received, and he will read portions aloud to himself. Others he may read critically in order to analyze individual components. Sometimes he may scan a half-dozen sermons in a given volume to judge their effectiveness or practice in one given field, and the questions set out in Chapter 38 may serve. He is bound to discover favorites. It will be good to ask why. Specializing in the publications of one preacher may be a way of practicing a skill that does not grow. If he can ascertain the chronology of a published output, he may find it instructive to observe changes in method over the years.

The tremendous literature on preaching, in books and magazines, occasionally provides professional guidance of high order. The pastor will find it useful to circulate such items among the members of his conference, discuss them, try out their suggestions, "prove all things, hold fast that which is good." No preacher who truly speaks for God and His church has ever finished improving or has ever lost the will to grow as a Christian man, as a theologian, as a preacher.

FOR FURTHER THOUGHT

Have you found it useful to read sermons for the sake of more than "quotable quotes"?

Have you read some of the current literature on ways of thought of contemporary man (David Riesman, Karen Horney, Erich Fromm, etc.)?

Have you read a book or article recently on pastoral care, the sociology of the church, pastoral psychology, or parish administration, that you found helpful for preaching? Did you discuss it with a member of your parish? with another pastor?

How recently have you had professional judgment on your speech? Any problems? Do you know how to proceed with improvement?

Are you acquainted with professional caseworkers who serve your community?

For further reading see pp. 307, 308.

SECTION TWELVE

_____

Preaching and the Ministry

Most preaching is done by pastors in congregations. It is a part of their total ministry. This circumstance seems to rob preaching of its prophetic or dramatic qualities.

To the contrary, the total ministry makes contributions to preaching. The pastor's relation to individuals in his care makes his message to the whole congregation memorable and heeded. His labors with small groups give practical significance to the address to the parish.

Conversely preaching contributes to the total ministry. For it is the witness of the entire congregation to the power of the Word in the very moment that the preacher speaks. It is a crucial part of the process by which he equips his people for their calling in Christ.

Chapter Forty-Three

THE INDIVIDUAL

Some preachers have been prophets who burst on their age with fury and excitement. Others have been evangelists who enthralled the masses and gave prestige to the Christian religion and its preaching. The pastor is apt to view these heroic figures wistfully. He labors in the plodding routine of the daily pastorate. He influences relatively few people. Compared with these great preachers, isn't he of a minor order?

Quite the opposite is true. His work with people outside the pulpit makes a vital contribution to his preaching and to the attention which his people give it. This does not suggest that the total ministry is simply an expedient for giving power to sermons. The pulpit is only one of many platforms from which the Word is launched. As the preacher recognizes the intimate relation between the pulpit and the other phases of his ministry, he will stop playing favorites between them, and he will be grateful for the resources that strengthen and refresh his preaching day by day.

277

Pastoral Care and Preaching

A major part of the pastor's ministry is his care of the individual. He is likely to think of it as far removed from the techniques of the pulpit. It usually deals with emergencies and special problems. It plunges him into unexpected situations and forces him to improvise his methods.

Yet the routines of pastoral care make a huge contribution to the pulpit preaching. The latter also addresses individuals. No hearer benefits from preaching except through his own act of hearing and thinking. Pastoral care ceaselessly practices asking the same two questions that the pulpit preacher must ask: "What is the specific thing that I can do for this person?" and "How can I get this person to listen to me?" True, pastoral care involves more than speaking to people, and sometimes less; yet its true help ultimately reaches the client as the pastor speaks the Word of God, and all the other elements of care contribute simply to the channeling of the Word to the heart. Pastoral care, finally, illuminates the paradox that is the dismay and the challenge of the pulpit preacher: human need is infinitely varied; yet human need is strangely similar under the surface. As the pastor trudges from case to case and bedside to bedside, as he counsels in home and at the desk, as he intervenes in the multifarious problems of family and marriage, as he explores human nature in endless profusion, he is practicing the same skill which gives penetration to the Word from the pulpit.

Thus the most direct contribution of pastoral care to the ministry and to preaching is that the human being whom the pastor reads about in the Bible and in his books on pastoral care and preaching becomes real. Human life is complex, the variation wide between children and adults, literate and illiterate, dependable and wayward, fortunate and unfortunate, privileged and underprivileged, veteran and neophyte in the faith. But the preacher does not deal with statistical tables or sociological abstractions, but with human beings, out of whom life is made. His preaching becomes direct and personal, not as he imitates great speakers or struggles for novel words but as he sees people for what they are and finds it in his heart to help them. Like God he calls people by name.

Preaching requires a technique, of course, which the individual case of pastoral care does not demand: the discerning of common denominators of need. Yet the sermon to the group must not address abstract or total problems. It must still explore how sin and flesh ravage genuinely human people, and its language has to set up applications that make men in groups feel struck as directly as men one by one.

Pastoral care adds a note to preaching which it can hardly get anywhere else. That is one of personal pity. The preacher may affirm with fervor that he is concerned. But the concern rings true not just in the sound of the voice or the apt words. It takes insight into the human situation and the sense of being personally involved (cp. Saint Paul in 2 Cor. 11:29 or Gal. 4:18-20). This mirrors itself in preaching through a spoken line that is much simpler, quieter in the presence of need, and more beset by the pain and reality of human care than the language of the preacher who is only making words.

Rapport

One person cannot help another unless he can communicate with him. But the communication needs to be more than audible; it has to be acceptable. If the preacher should help a hearer, *he* has to be accepted before his help is accepted. This set for acceptance is called rapport, the magic word in human relations. Where shall the preacher go for it? The answer is pastoral care.

The pulpit is a high moment in a service of worship. To its meaning contribute the encounter of God and man displayed in the text and all the Scriptures basic to the message, and the thousands of years of the church here coming to their focus in the group in that room. But still more contributes! For the people listening to the preacher's words are individuals who have been led through their personal encounter with God by the ministry of that preacher. They have put his witness to the test. They have discovered that he speaks not just for the sake of drawing his salary or securing their approval but for God and the church. He is their servant for Jesus' sake. In times of personal crisis or in disciplined moments of search for Bible truth he has been imparting to their minds a vision of Father and Son and Spirit which they have found to be worth more to them than anything else in their lives. Hence they listen as he speaks. They are *en rapport*.

If a preacher is to speak effectively, he must know his message, mean it from the heart, and have a genuine sympathy for his hearers. In the experience of his congregation this comes true already before he gets into the pulpit and after he leaves. Certainly the people of the congregation are not to think of the preacher as less sincere in the pulpit than out of it, although he may have to fight with himself, as he begins to speak, not to revert to schoolboy showing off or fright. But through the ministry to individuals the pulpit becomes tightly interwoven with the whole meaning of pastor and pastorate. The warp is not a misguided habit of telling stories out of his ministry but the evident consistency of his sympathy and of the unwavering thrust of his message of Christ, relentlessly applied, always the same, in the care of the individual and in the address to the congregation.

The House-going Preacher

The apostles prayed that their people might have knowledge of God and grow in it (cf. Phil. 1:9 or 2 Peter 3:18). This means experience and recognition that God is at work in them. The preacher's entire ministry supplies him with such knowledge. God has promised it to the believers of all ages in the pages of Scripture, to his predecessors in the ministry of the Word and to him. In the life-and-death situations of his pastoral care the promise comes true; he sees God at work before his very eyes. Preaching announces the discoveries and repeats the promises. For this reason preaching may sound more final and superior, more serene and victorious, than the patient conversations at sickbed or deskside. But the experiences deepen and multiply particularly in the latter. Hence the preacher-pastor labors to make the service of worship and the moments of preaching a piece of the same companionship which he shares week-round with his people in Christ. The church is no place for Olympian detachment but a place where worshipers share with one another words of forgiveness and life and where the servant of the Word is extending their daily conversations into the mutual speech and song of God's people together.

The house-going preacher is not dismayed by the panorama of pain which his parish unfolds before his eyes, for he knows that it is God's opportunity. He is impressed by the nearness of God's action in Christ, the action of love as well as the action of judgment. Each new application of the grace of God in Christ helps the preacher to a stronger will to help — psalm and prayer at bedside, absolution spoken to the guilty heart, the summons to the straying underscored with the plea of Jesus' own "come." This will to help is not a slogging sense of duty but the response to God's own presence in the heart; hence it feeds on every demonstration of God at work among his people. The preacher speaks the Word to the individual and to the church always "from grace to grace," for that Word is caught up in the chain reaction of God's own answer to each Christian's prayer, including the preacher's.

Hence every sermon that the pastor preaches is pastoral. He cannot belie his calling. He cannot mask his concern for people and his love for them. He is shamelessly anxious that people should hear him preach. He advertises his sermons and promotes attendance at his services and quotes himself in hundreds of calls and anticipates future sermons as he counsels people in need. In all of that he is not yielding to some theatrical complex — or he need not be. But it is just the symptom of tremendous pastoral concern, in "season and out of season," for the individual and for the crowd, person to person, over radio and in letters, in chance encounters on the sidewalk, or in the conduct of the most formal service of worship.

Preaching can actually become a tool of the flesh. The safe rampart of the pulpit may seem a shield against the anxiety of hearers, the unexpectedness of emergencies, or the shabby attention of drooping plants in God's garden. From the pulpit so construed come no words of life, for it enshrines a puppet rather than a preacher. It is pastoral care and the pastoral concern which will transform the pulpit from a barricade to a vantage point from which the beams of the grace of God will seek out needy men with healing and fellowship, to a launching platform sending no missile of destruction but God's own mighty rescue from sin and death. This it will be, provided that its light and its explosive will always be the Word of God's redeeming grace in Christ.

> *Father in heaven, make Thy preachers men who carry the pains of Thy people in their hearts and speak Thy words of healing by all means and in all places. Amen.*

FOR FURTHER THOUGHT

Thurneysen says that a pastor's visit in pastoral care is a "conversation" — both he and the client are talking. What sort of client must this be? what sort of pastor? What are the implications for preaching?

Does the doctrine of rapport infringe on the doctrine of conversion and involve synergism? Note also Chapter 7 above.

Would you call "sin" or "need" a common denominator of people in preaching? Why must the preacher be more specific?

What use in pastoral care do you make of previously preached sermons?

For further reading see p. 308.

The preacher speaks to groups,
and his preaching profits from each
discussion and concern.

Chapter Forty-Four

THE GROUP

Some pastors in our time become neurotic under the manifold demands of their callings, and they fear that they are not giving attention to those which are most important and spiritual. The fatal split seems most cruel between preaching and parish administration. This chapter purposes to review the pastor's work with Christian groups. The pastor should make the attempt to weld a bond between group work and preaching. They need not clash.

Obviously such an attempt involves a careful understanding of parish administration or any work with groups. That parish administration in which the pastor is a solo operator, addressing himself to others only for the sake of gaining organizational consent to private objectives, has little in common with the calling of the pastor-preacher set out in Chapter 2 above. But the pastor is a trainer of people. As he administrates his parish, he devises individual and group situations in which people learn better to take up their tasks of edification and witness.

The Group in the Church

The church in the place is itself a group, two or three gathered in the name of Jesus (Matt. 18:20), practicing the business of speaking the truth of Christ to one another for their growth (Eph. 4:1-16). The preacher operates with the total group of his church in the services of its common worship, and there his preaching has a major function to and for the group.

Such a group of Christians functions never only in the total but divides into interrelated cells. Even in the most elementary situation the basic cell of the church is there — the Christian family, the church in the house (e. g., Rom. 16:5). Much of the most strenuous labor of the congregation and its pastor seeks to enhance family life and to help it focus on the Word of God.

Other cells soon appear. Some center in common interests, such as the youth, men's, and women's groups, parents' and couples' clubs, for the simple aims of acquaintance, fellowship, and exchanging of experience; the parish seeks to direct the capacities of these groups into service. Other groups are summoned because a special service is required. Here function the administrative bodies and committees, the boards charged with spiritual guidance, business and finance, maintenance and public relations, evangelism, and other services. Still others are educational in nature: classes of children and adults organized for Bible study in the church schools or for preparation for church membership, teachers in preparation or training. Other groups work together for special services involving worship: choirs, ushers, altar guilds.

As a congregation grows in numbers and experience, these groups multiply and exert more demands upon the pastor's time. He spends most evenings in meetings, few in calls or with his family. He gets too tired to prepare his sermons carefully. He sees groups and preaching in competition for the attention of his people. Much of his most tangible ministry is exerted in these groups, and they slowly begin to seem more essential than the preaching. Under these terms how can he expect his ministry toward groups to contribute to his preaching?

The congregation and its groups can make no such contribution at all unless they do the work of the church. Hence the pastor will steadily hold before them their purpose: to edify the members of the church so that it is a mutually helpful and Spirit-filled body of Christ and to foster Christian witness toward those who are outside. With some this is easy, for they concern themselves directly with discussion of the Bible or with worship. He must write into the consciousness of all of them what they have to do for the church, that they are the church; and he will do so through periods of worship related to their activities and through explicit descriptions of their functions.

The pastor should see to it that his service to groups is really ministry of the Word. As he associates with groups, he has a chance to confirm his relation to their members as individuals, to discern their needs and strengthen acquaintance, and to observe their Christian gifts and abilities at work for one another. These experiences contribute to the human note, the practical quality, and the spiritual optimism which preaching needs. The group, furthermore, is the training ground for the pastor's business of equipping his saints for their ministry. He does not counsel how carpenters ply their hammers or finance committees slit open collection envelopes or members of the women's guild cook or sew. But he does empower people through the Gospel of Christ to bring this Gospel into the hearts of others. He does not tell them to stop driving nails or opening envelopes or cooking or sewing. But he does help them to use every activity of their group as a setting and matrix for calling God's call. As the preacher accumulates precision and skill at this business, his preaching to the entire congregation gathers momentum.

The Contribution of Group Work

If the pastor truly ministers to his Christian groups, he will find that his preaching gains. But there are even more obvious contributions. In the groups are the people whom the pastor enlists for the vital role of criticism. But more: here are the people who are putting the preaching to work. Every group, down to the smallest, is engaged in trying out the recommendations that preaching gives. They are applying themselves to its goals and harnessing its Gospel to their tasks.

In the activities of Christian groups the preacher gains insight into the handicaps which beset people in their relations to one another. Here he sees the most potent exhibits of the interaction between world and church, of the fluctuating battle line between the two. Here he can observe the pitiful capitulation of even the most dependable church workers to self-righteousness and religious formalism. Here, right in people who are God's saints, he can see the flesh driving to gossip and partisanship. Here comes the sad discovery that much church work stems from a motive little better than escape from loneliness or tedium.

But group work gives the preacher the opportunity also to see that the Word of the Gospel is a power. As he administrates the parish, he tries to match people and their gifts of the Spirit to their respective labors, to find use for their gifts, and to gain their will to work. The Spirit's work is always a surprise. His Word does not return to Him void. The preacher is a husbandman trying to raise a harvest for God, and sometimes he imagines the clods are too dry. But out at the grass roots where people are actually growing in the life of their family and community, it becomes apparent that the Christian Gospel is not just idle mysticism but a practical power. As they labor together in the organism of the congregation, the preacher can really see the contributions of the Spirit to Christian leadership, to clear judgment, to the ability to talk and admonish, to growth in love and self-sacrifice and energy, to insight into the meaning of the Bible and of worship. All this is exactly what Christian preaching talks about and tries to foster.

Preachers grumble about the low level of love among the people. Yet a growth in that love is always apparent. Group work gives a chance to see it and to encourage it. The group has to realize not simply that it should raise money for other people's projects but that they are right now at the business of loving one another God's way.

The Relation to Preaching

Does this add up to saying that some Sundays a sermon should be to the young people and another to Sunday school teachers and a third to the altar guild? If two factions of the ladies' aid are embroiled in a quarrel, should there be a sermon on it? Doesn't that wreck the plans that have been constructed in advance or invalidate the rather general goals and objectives of pericopic preaching?

Certainly there should be sermons specifically to the young people; let them be preached when the young people are there, at one of their meetings, in the church. In the regular parish sermon the young people take home their application, more or less explicitly made, as do the other hearers to whom that subject applied on that day. Perhaps the ladies' aid should get a sermon, but then it shouldn't be at a time when three quarters of the congregation sit in church mentally pointing fingers at them. It should be in one of their meetings or a special rally, in the church building, with all the reinforcement of worship. The entire congregation frequently hears sermons on the Christian life. When they direct an admonition against gossip, .it aims at all the hearers present. Obviously any special address, in the church building or anywhere else, directed to just one group of Christians will preach Law and Gospel as scrupulously as the parish sermon.

Preaching can serve to keep the true purpose and mechanism of the Christian group clear. Whenever the love of Christians to one another in the church is the burden of preaching, the concrete self-sacrifice of Christians in the family and community and group is illustrative. As the Gospel of God is sounded as the one source of power, the sermon will indicate that it pertains to every group relation.

The sermon frequently gives the opportunity to share the gains of a group with the entire congregation. The parish service has been likened to the assembly period of a school, at which all classes gather; the sermon is the assembly address. That analogy does too little for the meaning of the common worship of Christians or of the mutual word of admonition and Gospel which they speak during the week. But it does suggest that the common service gives the Christians of the parish the chance to see that they are all working on one great task. The parish sermon can give that interpretation, alert to the discoveries and gifts of some for the benefit of all, and invite all to share in the gains of some for the sake of the good of the body.

The competition between group and preaching can be allayed in the preacher's mind as he remembers the "kind of time" principle of

Chapter 36 above and as he keeps group work as much a ministry of the Gospel as is his preaching. Then he will be always preacher, always pastor.

Father in heaven, make Thy preachers men who shepherd groups both large and small, so that they feed men for Thy life and lead them in the ways of Thy plan in Christ. Amen.

FOR FURTHER THOUGHT

Run a diary on your work with your organizations for one week. How much time is devoted to (1) plans for their projects? (2) preparation for the Gospel to enable the projects? (3) recruitment of workers and leaders?

A good means of integrating Gospel with an organization's program is a period of explicit worship and Word before or after the meeting. In your experience, how well does this work with (1) youth groups? (2) men's groups? (3) women's groups? Do you have "fellowship" groups that avoid worship programs?

Do the discussion programs in your parish groups give time for explicit discussion of Gospel? do administrative boards?

Preacher and people pray and work to the end that God's own Spirit press him to preach Christ Crucified.

Chapter Forty-Five

THE PRESSURE

Where does the preacher get the continued will to preach? What moves him to have his sermon ready whether he feels like preparing it or not? What prompts him to do his best each time, to find new resources of zest and skill, to have an energy that is unflagging and yet genuine?

Counterfeits

The Sunday morning service is usually the week's largest gathering of the congregation. This means that then the preacher does some of his loudest talking. With the effort to be heard may merge other demands for force: the desire to impress, the tensions of anxiety about himself or his people. Perhaps the preacher is tired and preoccupied and unpleasantly stirred up through the midsection; but the show must go on, and he shouts.

Obviously these pressures for preaching are not all salutary. Some belong on the stage rather than in the pulpit. Some come from the flesh rather than the Spirit of God. In order to counteract them, some pastors are studiously limp and relaxed while preaching. That doesn't help. For after we have said everything about the preacher's techniques of preparation and the interrelation of his preaching with all his ministry, we want him to sense an urgency and a thrust that forbids him to keep silent, that makes the moment of preaching a peak experience of life, and that shows.

Where shall he get the right kind of pressure for preaching? And how shall he get it every time that he needs it?

The Plan of God

The first answer is: The preacher has a mandate from God. He plays a part in the plan which God devised from before the foundation of the world to reconcile men to Himself. The plan was carried out in Christ, who was made sin that men might be made the righteousness of God. The plan is brought to the person in the preacher, who accepts the Word of reconciliation in trust and brings it to people with the pressure of God's own plea and Christ's own desire.

Just to read the words of 2 Corinthians 5 which give this orientation may not generate much pressure. But God, who gave Christ and gives the Gospel, gives the pressure. The Christ who was sent by God and who thus sends men to bring others to faith gives the pressure. As a man ponders his own poverty of expression or his own fatigue, or as he seeks a faked pressure in his own exhibitionism or his desire to cover up his apathy, God is not speaking to him and Christ is not setting him apart to be His spokesman. But as the preacher keeps on confronting God's design in Christ by which God redeemed him and appointed him to speak and plead for Him, God will give him the pressure for preaching.

This pressure can be refreshed. Many a preacher has found an hour of preaching to be so exhilarating that it blasted fatigue or a respiratory infection or a migraine headache. But suppose that he still felt bad; what counts is that he could not but speak. St. Paul discussed his own vitality for preaching not as something that replaced fear and trembling but as something that led him to preach in spite of it. His very disabilities gave him the opportunity to make clear that preaching is God at work and not just a man. The will to preach comes from confronting the will of God, not the euphoria of the preacher. Throughout the Book of Acts and in the epistles the term "boldness" denotes about what we mean by pressure for preaching (Acts 4:3, 31; 9:29; 14:3; 19:8; 28:3; 2 Cor. 7:4; Eph. 3:12; Phil. 1:14). As we scan these passages, we find that boldness indeed involved a contagious courage under obstacles and that it always concerned speaking the message of God's grace for men in Christ. It is the mark of the man who is saving men with God's great rescue and is himself saved in the process. (1 Tim. 4:16)

The Love from God

Another facet to God's pressure for the preacher is that He gives him love for people. His pleading with and for people is to come from a heart that yearns for the people and seeks to help them with the help that comes from God.

Again we must guard against thinking about something visceral or sentimental. The preacher with at least average success and rapport in his parish feels very good indeed in the midst of his people on a Sunday morning. Most of them love him and his family. Many are loyal to his projects and share his judgments. As he says "dear friends" or "beloved," he actually means it with a sense of much kindliness and joy of companionship.

But the pressure for preaching must come from more than that. For the pastor is there to help men in need. Many of his people are lovely folk, but the unlovely have an equal claim on his concern, and the lovely have no guarantee that they will not soon be tested by weakness and trial. The preacher's diagnosis of his people's ills will have to cut with the judgment of God into unpleasant facets of character and hidden recesses of the flesh that are seemingly best covered up; but the preacher is there to bring help and to guide his people to carry one another's burdens and not just to rejoice in perfection or the comfort of being undisturbed. The preacher's Gospel is always the Gospel of the forgiveness of sins. Like his Lord the preacher comes to call sinners to repentance, and he agonizes in heart over those who are so obtuse as to imagine that they need no repentance.

The pressure of this love can be replenished too. True, the preacher has his days when he wants to shake the dust of the parish from his feet for more grateful fields of labor. He wishes that God would remove some of his cases and sift the shabby hearers from good or that some church board could cancel out completely those who don't come to church; and he begins to find fault with the parable of the tares. But then — and it can happen while he is preparing a sermon — the Lord tells him where he can find the power to keep on loving, not just in word but in deed and in truth, as an instrument by which the love of God reaches men. He is to find it by continuing to look at God's love to him in giving up His Son for him. Let the preacher keep on looking, and find it the power for just him and his need. For then he is hearing the Word of God, which is the power for life and love.

The Servant of the Church

Finally let the preacher replenish the pressure for his preaching by remembering who he is: the servant of the church. He is a preacher to the church and for the church.

The word *minister* has an aura of dignity and reputation, and that it should have. But too frequently the mental picture has to do with black broadcloth, the mellow oak of the pulpit, the demeanor of a man set apart from other people. When Paul and Peter called themselves servants, they meant workingmen, helpers, and often they equated the word with slave. The people that knew Paul remembered him as a man in prison, beaten, shipwrecked, dying and yet alive. For our Lord the servant is the opposite of a ruler.

In Chapter 2 above we reviewed the contrast between the ruling and serving conceptions of the pastor. In the thinking of Jesus the will to rule for the sake of exercising power is the mark of the mind that has not found God (Matt. 20:25-28). Even the finest pastor will find his will to serve befouled by the desire to be over and ahead of people and to shape their minds by force rather than by the Word of God. That temptation struck Jesus, and the disciple is not above his master. But the moment that it takes hold, a false pressure invades the ministry and the preaching of the pastor. His governing is to be like the helmsman's who guides the ship so that the wind fills its sails (1 Cor. 12:28). That means that the wind moves the helmsman too. The preacher's business is to direct the Spirit of God into the hearts of the church's people. But he has only one means by which he can convey Him — by reminding them of Christ Himself.

The preacher is a helper of his people. They share good things with him in return (Gal. 6:6), but that does not make his work less a help. He helps them to be helpers; his word and guidance builds them up for the business of building one another up. The pressure for this task comes not from the prestige of position, or the excitement of able verbalizing or the experience in handling people, but from what builds up and what the church gives to the preacher as well as expects from him: the truth of God in Christ (Eph. 4:15). Hence his preaching will not be blatant with personal demands or whining with complaint at not getting his way. But it will be one of many ways by which he can help his people confront the redeeming act of God in Christ, receive the forgiveness of their sins, and be charged with the life to serve one another. He shares that life with the people. They speak it to him, for his speech is their mandate. He is their servant bringing their admonition to one another, and therefore he stands before them as a servant who eats the same food which he serves.

That same pressure to speak for the church moves through the speech of the preacher to the community around the church. He is a fellow witness with the witnesses whom he is training. His behavior and his life in and with his family is a calling with which he reaches out, along with his fellow Christians, to his neighborhood so that men might find Jesus Christ. As he speaks from pulpit or radio, his people pray for him, and his words are consistent with the witness which he displays, together with his people, in love.

Preaching is itself ministry, a serving. It serves God, who gives the mandate. It serves the Christians who commission the preacher to do it. It serves the hearer as it leads him to repentance and offers the forgiveness of sins and holds him on the track of faith till our Lord's return. Like the Good Samaritan the preacher has to do the

laborious thing of loving the needy man at all costs. Like the Good
Shepherd he, too, is ready to give his life for the sheep. The will
to that love is God's own gift to him, for he becomes a tool in the
hand of God by which God Himself loves people. "When the Chief
Shepherd shall appear, ye shall receive a crown of glory that fadeth
not away." (1 Peter 5:4)

*Father in heaven, lift thy preachers from weariness, live in them with
Thy Spirit, that they speak Thy Word with joy and represent Thy Son
as men who cannot keep silent. Amen.*

FOR FURTHER THOUGHT

What does fatigue do to your willingness to preach? Does it
really make a difference? What are other blocks to your will to preach?

Can you tell your particular way of compensating for a sense of
flabbiness or apathy in the pulpit? Do you get loud? bright? wordy?

What spiritual discipline do you find most helpful just before
entering the pulpit? just before beginning to prepare a sermon?

Have you found a work on pastoral theology or the ministry helpful for refreshing your sense of ministry?

For further reading see p. 308; also 306.

FOR FURTHER READING

The next pages are not a documentation of the whole science of homiletics. They supply rather a means for extending the thinking of the sections of this book, whether for quick refreshment or for serious study.

The effort has been made to incorporate materials which are still available to the average reader. Hence many of the older handbooks are not mentioned.

Publisher and year are entered at first listing of the respective volume; the section of the first listing is thereafter indicated by (I).

FOR FURTHER READING

Section One

The chief tract on preaching in the Scriptures is 2 Corinthians 1—7 (1 Corinthians 1 and 2 supplement); in the sayings of Jesus, John 17; in the Old Testament, Isaiah, especially Chapters 40 and 52. Paul's principle of Law and Gospel is summarized Galatians 3 and 4.

The classic review of all factors of the preaching process is John A. Broadus, *On the Preparation and Delivery of Sermons,* 1870 (reprinted New York: R. R. Smith, Inc., 1930; rev. ed. J. B. Weatherspoon, New York: Harper and Bros., 1942). A useful overview in this pattern is Andrew W. Blackwood, *The Preparation of Sermons* (New York: Abingdon, 1948). Phillips Brooks, *Lectures on Preaching,* 1877 (reprinted, Grand Rapids: Zondervan), is still valuable. Most useful in this writer's judgment for total survey, theological accent, and focus on the place of preaching in the church, though hampered by original German language and method, is still M. Reu, *Homiletics* (Columbus: Wartburg, 1924, trans. Albert Steinhaeuser; reprint 1950, Minneapolis: Augsburg). Current volumes with a basic theological concern are: very thorough and with comprehensive bibliographies, Ilion T. Jones, *Principles and Practice of Preaching* (New York: Abingdon, 1956); less detailed but refreshing, Walter Russell Bowie, *Preaching* (New York: Abingdon, 1954). Brief lectures on the whole field are W. Harry Krieger, *Angels Having the Gospel to Preach* (St. Louis: Concordia Publishing House, 1957). Valuable for integrating the entire process with the basic theology is Wolfgang Trillhaas, *Evangelische Predigtlehre* (Munich: Kaiser, 1948).

The current revival in the theology of preaching is due to Biblical studies in general and the investigation of the meaning of the Word of God and the church in particular. Ahead of his time, amazing in style and in his grasp of Word and church, is P. T. Forsyth, *Positive Preaching and the Modern Mind* (London: Independent Press, 1907 and 1953). Still important for pastorate and preaching is C. F. W. Walther, *Die rechte Unterscheidung von Gesetz und Evangelium* (St. Louis: Concordia Publishing House, 1901; trans. W. H. T. Dau, *The Proper Distinction Between Law and Gospel*). Martin Luther's dynamic concept of the Word of God is well set forth in his *Sermons on the Gospel of St. John,* Chapters 1—4 (from 1537, trans. Martin H. Bertram in *Luther's Works,* American Edition, Vol. 22, St. Louis: Concordia Publishing House, 1957). The Biblical data are summarized by the present writer in "Concordance Study of the Concept 'Word of God' " in *Concordia Theological Monthly* (St. Louis: Concordia Publishing House), XXII (March 1951), 170—185.

Current works of importance in the theology of preaching are: C. H. Dodd, *The Apostolic Preaching and Its Developments* (New York: Harper, 1944; 2d ed., 1951), which does not put *kerygma* and *didache* into the bald contrast of Dodd's imitators; Archibald M. Hunter, *The Message of the New Testament* (Philadelphia: Westminster, 1944; in England, *The Unity of the New Testament,* SCM Press), brief but valuable; Jesse B. Weatherspoon, *Sent Forth to Preach* (New York: Harper, 1954); and Leon Morris, *The Apostolic Preaching of the Cross* (Grand Rapids: Eerdmans, 1956), a painstaking exploration of the basic theological concepts of the message itself. On the process of preaching viewed theologically, Gustav Wingren, *Die Predigt,* trans. Egon Franz, of *Predikan* (Göttingen: Vandenhoeck u. Ruprecht, 1955), illustrates the motif theology, in English: *The Living Word,* trans. V. C. Pogue (Philadelphia: Muhlenberg, 1960); James S. Stewart, *A Faith to Proclaim* (New York: Scribner's, 1953), is helpful; Herbert H. Farmer, *A Servant of the Word* (New York: Scribner's, 1942), has existential accents; Karl Barth, in the revised *Kirchliche Dogmatik,* Part I, Vol. 1 (Zuerich: Zollikon, 1944), amply portrays the meaning of the Word (this edition is not translated); early lectures of Barth under the title *The Preaching of the Gospel* are less valuable; Henry Sloan Coffin, *Communion Through Preaching* (New York: Scribner's, 1952), describes the sermon as "the monstrance of the Gospel"; Theodore O. Wedel, *The Pulpit Rediscovers Theology* (Greenwich: Seabury, 1957), analyzes the theological revival; Max Warren, *The Christian Imperative* (New York: Scribner's, 1955), reflects the missionary insight; T. A. Kantonen in *The Theology of Evangelism* (Philadelphia: Muhlenberg, 1954) draws upon the Apostolic Creed for his method; and D. T. Niles portrays approach and the preacher's character in *The Preacher's Task and the Stone of Stumbling* and *The Preacher's Calling to Be Servant* (New York: Harper, 1957, 1959).

Section Two

Still quoted in works on public address is Aristotle's *Rhetoric* (a convenient edition is Loeb Classical Library, No. 193, Cambridge: Harvard Univ. Press, 1939); the quotation on p. 38 above is from I, ii, 3—6, p. 17. A basic modern work is H. L. Hollingsworth, *The Psychology of the Audience* (New York: American Book Co., 1935); more popular, Robert Oliver, *The Psychology of Persuasive Speech* (New York: Longmans, 1942 and later rev. ed.). A useful textbook on the rhetoric and speech basic also to preaching is Lew Sarett and William T. Foster, *Basic Principles of Speech* (Boston: Houghton Mifflin, 1936; rev. 1946). Direct application of psychological principles to preaching are Webb B. Garrison, *The Preacher and His Audience* (Westwood, N. J.: Fleming H. Revell, 1954), and Edgar N. Jackson, *A Psychology for Preaching* (Great Neck: Channel Press, 1961); William Muehl, *The Road to Persuasion* (New York: Oxford University Press, 1956), is a good non-technical discussion. Carl Jung's theory of the mass unconscious is applied to preaching by Otto Haendler in *Die Predigt* (Berlin: Toepelmann, 1960); the relation of theology to speech is set forth by Hans-Rudolf Müller-Schwefe in *Die Sprache und Das Wort* (Hamburg: Furche, 1961). The basic question of communication, considered by F. W. Dillistone in *Christianity and Communication* (New York: Scribner's, 1956) or Hendrik Kraemer in *The Communication of the Christian Faith* (Philadelphia: Westminster, 1956) is given special scrutiny by Harry A. DeWire in *The Christian as Communicator* (Philadelphia: Westminster, 1961) or Reuel Howe in *The Miracle of Dialogue* (Greenwich, Conn.: Seabury Press, 1963). The philosophical questions are brought into relation with the theological in Jules L. Moreau, *Language and Religious Language* (Philadelphia: Westminster, 1961); Frederick Ferre, *Language, Logic, and God* (New York: Harper, 1961); and John A. Hutchison, *Language and Faith* (Philadelphia: Westminster, 1963), to mention a few. *The Gospel in a Strange New World* by Theodore O. Wedel (Philadelphia: Westminster, 1963) and Merrill R. Abbey, *Preaching to the Contemporary Mind*

(New York: Abingdon, 1963), try to render this material assimilable for the pastor-preacher.

The magazine *Pastoral Psychology* along with materials on pastoral care, guidance, and counseling, provides helpful articles and bibliographies for preaching to people. Edgar N. Jackson in *How to Preach to People's Needs* (New York: Abingdon, 1956) and Charles F. Kemp in *Life-Situation Preaching* (St. Louis: Bethany, 1956) and subsequent volumes discuss their subject and illustrate with sermons. The sermons of David Roberts, *The Grandeur and Misery of Man* (New York: Oxford Univ. Press, 1955), display a penetrating concern with human need.

Section Three

Luther D. Reed, *The Lutheran Liturgy* (Philadelphia: Muhlenberg, 1947), gives a useful analysis of the propers for each day, with some suggestions for unifying service themes (pp. 438—514). This writer offers themes for each day in Appendix II below; others are given in the lectionary of the Swedish Church (see Paul Nesper, *Biblical Texts* [Columbus: Wartburg Press, 1952], or A. G. Herbert, *The Parish Communion* [London: S. P. C. K.; New York: Macmillan, 1937, rev. 1944]). Useful is *The Sermon and the Propers* by Fred H. Lindemann (four volumes, St. Louis: Concordia Publishing House, 1958—1959). The Episcopal point of view toward preaching in worship and·its church year is reflected in *The Anglican Pulpit Today,* ed. Frank Dean Gifford (New York: Morehouse-Gorham, 1953), in 42 sermons and a useful introduction; the Roman Catholic, in *Die Predigt* by Anselm Guenther, O. S. B. (Freiburg: Herder, 1963). Suggestions for texts and treatment for the major seasons of the church year and other days customary in Protestant churches is *Resources for Sermon Preparation* by David A. MacLennan (Philadelphia: Westminster, 1957); in anthology style is *Worship Resources for the Christian Year* by Charles L. Wallis (New York: Harper, 1954). Andrew Blackwood presents 38 *Special-Day Sermons for Evangelicals* with annotations (Great Neck: Channel Press, 1961). He has published a similar anthology, *Evangelical Sermons of Our Day* (New York: Harper, 1959).

On Biblical method, Ronald E. Sleeth, *Proclaiming the Word* (New York: Abingdon, 1964), has sensible comments on the preacher's alternatives. Chalmer Faw gives a wealth of hints in *Biblical Preaching* (Nashville: Broadman, 1962). D. W. Cleverly Ford in *An Expository Preacher's Notebook* (New York: Harper, 1960) illustrates some of the preacher's primary concerns as he works with texts. In *Encounter with Spurgeon* John W. Doberstein brings together the essay of that title by Helmut Thielicke, plus selections from Spurgeon's "Lectures to My Students" and several of his sermons (Philadelphia: Fortress Press, 1963).

On evangelism Bryan Green's *The Practice of Evangelism* (New York: Scribner's, 1951) is outstanding for its account of the meaning of the church; the suggestions on preaching are general. In *Stir Up the Gift* (Grand Rapids: Zondervan, 1951) Paul S. Rees offers a study book for parish groups and includes a good discussion of the evangelistic sermon. Charles B. Templeton in *Evangelism for Tomorrow* (New York: Harper, 1957) makes useful suggestions for evangelistic preaching; he has an aversion to the theology of the atonement. E. C. Parker, Elinor Inman, and Ross Snyder in *Religious Radio* (New York: Harper, 1948) give valuable suggestions for the radio sermon; the subsequent book by Parker et al. on *The Television-Radio Audience and Religion* (New York: Harper, 1955) is a study of the New Haven survey and includes interesting analyses of Fulton Sheen, Ralph W. Sockman, Charles E. Fuller, and Norman Vincent Peale.

On methods of preparation Donald MacLeod, in *Here Is My Method* (New York: Revell, 1952), presents sermons by thirteen noted preachers, each prefaced by his description of his method. Clarence S. Roddy in *We Prepare and Preach* (Chicago: Moody Press, 1959) presents sermons and preaching method of eleven evangelical preachers; the variety is amazing. For examples of sermons without texts see Harry Emerson Fosdick, *What Is Vital in Religion* (New York: Harper, 1955); Robert J. McCracken, *Questions People Ask* (New York: Harper, 1951). For textual and nontextual approaches in the same volume cf. Ralph W. Loew, *The Hinges of Destiny* (Philadelphia: Muhlenberg, 1955). Interesting are the many sermons published by Clarence Macartney (New York: Abingdon), which consistently post texts but employ them only in part. Contrary to the theory that radio preaching does better without texts than does parish preaching are the radio sermons of Edmund Steimle, *Are You Looking for God?* (Philadelphia: Muhlenberg, 1957), with ample texts.

In two small but important volumes Donald G. Miller stresses the importance of Biblical preaching and pleads for using texts as they are originally intended in Scripture: *Fire in Thy Mouth* (New York: Abingdon, 1954) and *The Way to Biblical Preaching* (New York: Abingdon, 1957). These books are a landmark in their field and deserve the most serious attention. Miller publishes an exemplary sermon in *Interpretation*, XI (April 1957).

In *Heralds of the Gospel* H. T. Lehmann (Philadelphia: Muhlenberg, 1953) discusses the theology of the kerygma and defines Luther's preaching method as the homily; Vol. 22 of the American Edition of *Luther's Works* (I) gives newly translated illustrations. Calvin's method is briefly discussed by Leroy Nixon in *John Calvin, Expository Preacher* (Grand Rapids: Eerdmans, 1950). Andrew W. Blackwood in *Preaching from the Bible* (New York: Abingdon, 1941) gives numerous methods for preaching from texts; his *Expository Preaching for Today* (New York: Abingdon, 1953) carries on the theme, with a definition of "expository" as a sermon from a Bible passage longer than two or three consecutive verses. Faris D. Whitesell and Lloyd M. Perry, in *Variety in Your Preaching* (Westwood: Revell, 1954), do a similar job. The classic concept of expository preaching is developed by F. B. Meyer in *Expository Preaching* (Hodder and Stoughton reprint, Grand Rapids: Zondervan, 1954). Dwight E. Stevenson, *Preaching on the Books of the New Testament* (New York: Harper, 1956), and *Preaching on the Books of the Old Testament* (1961), uses whole books as texts.

Paul W. Nesper gives rich compilations of both free and pericopic texts in *Biblical Texts* (Columbus: Wartburg, 1952).

Section Four

Luke 4:16-20 gives an interesting account of Jesus' preaching from the synagog lesson for the day as a text.

Donald G. Miller's *The Way to Biblical Preaching* (III) eloquently stresses the importance of using the text as originally intended, and he provides ample illustrative material to point up the process. In *Expository Preaching for Today*

(III) Andrew W. Blackwood properly stresses the importance of focusing on a unified truth in a textual sermon. The recently completed *Interpreter's Bible* (New York: Abingdon, 12 volumes) makes an interesting difference between its exegetical interpretations of the text and its "exposition" of the respective book or section; similar aids are provided by older commentaries devised for the preacher's use. Important for preaching are lexicographical studies like Leon Morris (I), translations from G. Kittel's *Theologisches Wörterbuch* (six volumes of *Bible Key Words* have been published by Adam and Charles Black of London, 1952 ff.); or Alan Richardson, *A Theological Word Book of the Bible* (New York: Macmillan, 1950). The New Testament scholars are especially active in recapturing the living background of the original writings; useful reviews and bibliographies are available in *Interpretation* (a quarterly, Richmond, Va.).

Useful volumes employing the textual approach to sermons directed to days of the church year are *Sermonic Studies*, on the "standard epistles" of the liturgical year of the Lutheran Church (two volumes, St. Louis: Concordia Publishing House, 1957, 1963); on the *Thomasius Old Testament Selections* cf. M. Reu, trans. Max L. Steuer (Columbus: Wartburg Press, 1959), written in 1899.

Brief as it is, W. E. Sangster, *The Craft of Sermon Illustration* (Philadelphia: Westminster, 1950) is superior. Books of illustrations are useful chiefly for alerting the reader to sources and methods of discovering them. Charles L. Wallis is an able compiler; cf. *A Treasury of Sermon Illustrations* (New York: Abingdon, 1950) or *Speakers' Illustrations for Special Days* (New York; Abingdon, 1956). F. F. Selle and Ewald Plass have gathered many, chiefly from Luther and Maclaren, in *Quotations and Illustrations for Sermons* (St. Louis: Concordia Publishing House, 1935 and 1951).

Outstanding annual volumes on preaching are the published Beecher Lectures on preaching at Yale University Divinity School. B. B. Baxter has digested all up to 1944 that are concerned with technique rather than content or theology in *The Heart of the Yale Lectures* (New York: Macmillan, 1947).

The preacher will do well to reread his college handbooks on composition and rhetoric to improve his style and discrimination. On clear and direct communication Rudolf Flesch has published a number of books which should prove helpful (e. g., *How to Make Sense*, New York: Harper, 1954). Useful on current usage is the handbook by Bergen and Cornelia Evans, *A Dictionary of Contemporary American Usage* (New York: Random House, 1957). Even more important than the use of handbooks is the careful reading of writers who have the skill of interpreting religious truth to the nonprofessional reader. C. S. Lewis is still significant in this area; his introduction to J. B. Phillips, *Letters to Young Churches* (New York: Macmillan Company, 1952), though on principles of Bible translation, is important for every preacher. American writers of comparable stature are Chad Walsh, Alexander Miller, and Bishop James Pike. Tremendously useful is *Design for Preaching* (Philadelphia: Muhlenberg, 1958), in which H. Grady Davis, in a highly original and painstaking fashion, offers guidance to the processes of developing a textual idea in appropriate forms of thought and language; nothing in the literature of preaching is comparable to this book.

As a good contemporary display of preaching to the standard epistle pericopes note O. A. Geiseman, *Old Truths for a New Day* (St. Louis: Concordia Publishing House, 1949, 2 vols.); he replaces texts for Christmas and Easter. A German collection on the Gospels is C. C. Schmidt, *Glaube und Liebe* (St. Louis: Louis Lange, 1911), at the peak of simplicity, careful exposition, and practical application.

Section Five

Ordinarily the Scriptures give no special attention to the speech of the preacher separated from what he says. Our Lord was acceptable to the common people not because of a domineering manner but through the ability to bring His hearers into freedom (Matt. 7:28, 29). St. Paul contrasts the speech of the preacher of the Gospel with the finesse of the rhetors of his day and pleads an essential self-effacement. (1 Cor. 1:23—2:13)

Preaching shares with all persuasive speech its theory and best mechanisms; hence any good book on speech will serve for instruction and refreshment. A good current volume is A. Craig Baird and Franklin H. Knower, *Essentials of General Speech* (New York: McGraw-Hill). It would be well if the book for teachers, *The Teacher's Speech* by Wayland Maxfield Parrish (New York: Harper, 1939), had a counterpart for preachers; it offers a basic theory of phonetics and oral interpretation and supplies exercises. Sarett and Foster (II) is especially valuable for stressing the entire organism in speech and breaking up patterns of self-consciousness; it discards the traditional concept of gesture. Muehl (II) gives good general advice on how to read a manuscript on radio; he thinks that it is satisfactory to read the manuscript from the pulpit. Especially prepared for preachers is *The Preacher's Voice*, by William C. Craig and Ralph R. Sokolowsky (Columbus: Wartburg, 1945). It is especially concerned about preventing nodules on the vocal tract, but it also gives general suggestions on preparation before delivery. The paragraph on radio articulation may be misleading. Grant Fairbanks, *Voice and Articulation Drillbook* (New York: Harper, 1940 and rev.), gives suggestions for measuring optimum pitch, for rate and phrasing, as well as basic phonetics.

The conscious and practiced mechanisms of oral reading are useful for setting up reflexes valuable in preaching. Good for the entire field is Ben Graf Henneke, *Reading Aloud Effectively* (New York: Rinehart and Co., 1954); for the oral reading of Scripture in particular Nedra Newkirk Lamar's *How to Speak the Written Word* (New York: Revell, 1949) is especially good, with exercises and an "answer book." No attention is given to the reflection of mood.

Robert White Kirkpatrick, *The Creative Delivery of Sermons* (New York: Macmillan, 1944), develops a complex theory but is suggestive. Few books on preaching have other than common-sense things to say on "memorizing" or preparation before delivery. The psychological theory of functional memorizing is set down by Bess Sondel, *Are You Telling Them?* (New York: Prentice-Hall, 1947). Dwight E. Stevenson and Charles F. Diehl, *Reaching People from the Pulpit* (New York: Harper, 1958), is a useful work and includes helpful self-survey material.

Section Six

The method of choosing a theme or topic first and thereupon correlating a text with it is described by Andrew W. Blackwood in *The Preparation of Sermons* (I). He gives suggestions for special fields of this process in *Biographical Preaching for Today* (New York: Abingdon, 1944), *Preaching from Prophetic Books* (New York: Abingdon, 1951), and *Doctrinal Preaching for Today* (New York: Abingdon, 1956); his suggestions for major divisions are not always fortunate.

Hillyer H. Straton publishes useful volumes on miracles and parables of Jesus: *Preaching on the Miracles of Jesus* (New York: Abingdon, 1950) and *A Guide to the Parables of Jesus* (Grand Rapids: Eerdmans, 1959). A similar duo is by Ronald Wallace, *The Gospel Miracles* (Grand Rapids: Eerdmans, 1961), and *Many Things in Parables* (New York: Harper, 1955). Splendid sermons on the parables are Helmut Thielicke's volume *The Waiting Father*, trans. John W. Doberstein (New York: Harper, 1959).

Ideas for preparing sermons related to great pictures are gathered in *Preaching from Pictures* by Kenneth W. Sollitt (Boston: W. A. Wilde Company, 1938). *Christ and the Fine Arts* (New York: Harper, 1938) by Cynthia Maus has studies of pictures, poems, and hymns; *The Old Testament and the Fine Arts* (1954) is less useful in the field of art. Though less accessible, *Great Painters and Their Famous Bible Pictures* (New York: Wm. H. Wise and Co., 1925) by William Griffith is quite useful. Erik Routley, *Hymns and the Faith* (Greenwich: Seabury, 1956), suggests a method for bringing the theology of great hymns to the surface.

David A. MacLennan gives good suggestions on gathering materials, in *Pastoral Preaching* (Philadelphia: Westminster, 1955), and displays the process at work in *Resources for Sermon Preparation* (III).

Collections of readings and illustrations sometimes provide good material for sermons textual or topical. They are usually better for displaying one man's method of gathering findings which appeal to him than for offering items for direct use. In addition to the collections of Wallis (IV), Gerald Kennedy's *A Reader's Notebook* (New York: Harper, 1953) will be found useful in this respect.

Section Seven

As an illustration of the expository method, with much additional material and topical flavor, note Donald G. Barnhouse's sermons on Romans, *Man's Ruin* and *God's Wrath* (Wheaton, Ill.: Van Kampen, 1952 ff., the first two chapters). Some have used *Expository Outlines on the Whole Bible* by Charles Simeon (Funk and Wagnalls, New York, 21 volumes, reprinting the original *Horae Homileticae* of 1819—20). Useful for method in preparing Lenten preaching is Leon Morris, *The Story of the Cross* (Grand Rapids: Eerdmans, 1957), devotional studies of Matthew 26—28 worked into seven units, including the story of the resurrection.

Harold A. Bosley's *Preaching on Controversial Issues* (New York: Harper, 1953) is a good illustration of topical sermons, several of them in courses, with very brief textual concern. A contrasting method by the same author is *Sermons on the Psalms* (New York: Harper, 1956), 20 sermons which were delivered over a period of three years.

The course on hymns is illustrated by W. G. Polack in *The Seven Ways of Sorrow* (St. Louis: Concordia Publishing House, 1948), with sermonic studies of eight hymns for Passiontide; the other unit in the same volume, by Alvin E. Wagner, is biographical in method. For preaching on hymns note Routley (VI).

For sermon courses correlated with pictures (cf. Sollitt in VI) note the Lenten series by W. F. Bruening in *God Goes to Golgotha* (St. Louis: Concordia Publishing House, 1948), with six pictures for distribution to the audience (the series by W. A. Poehler in the same volume is topical); and by Erich H. Heintzen, *Were You There?* (St. Louis: Concordia Publishing House, 1958) with eight pictures, each with a section of the Passion history printed on the reverse side; the sermons are a direct review of the Passion story.

A huge literature of Lenten preaching is available. Stanley D. Schneider and others furnish 14 series of sermons in synopsis in *Facing the Cross* (Columbus: Wartburg, 1955). Spare in expression, but warm and theologically precise are Andrew W. Blackwood, Jr., *The Voice from the Cross* (Grand Rapids: Baker, 1955); Ralph G. Turnbull, *The Seven Words from the Cross* (Grand Rapids: Baker, 1956). Interesting without becoming obscure are G. S. Thompson, *The Cross Is Urgent* (Minneapolis: Augsburg, 1952), chiefly topical in method; A. Reuben Gornitzka, *Seriously, Now* (Minneapolis: Augsburg, 1956). In high literary style are the sermons of Robert D. Hershey, *The Secret of God* (Philadelphia: Muhlenberg, 1951). Unusually warm and Biblical in method, in the opinion of this writer, is *King Ever Glorious* (St. Louis: Concordia Publishing House, 1955), by Paul W. Streufert. Recent volumes of Passiontide preaching are: Karl A. Olsson, *Passion* (New York: Harper and Row, 1963); William A. Buege, *The Cross of Christ* (St. Louis: Concordia Publishing House, 1963).

Section Eight

The theological study basic to preaching toward special accents is well exemplified in Leon Morris, The *Apostolic Preaching of the Cross* (I); note also Kittel and Richardson (IV).

The preaching classically termed "evangelistic" and directed to those outside the church is well represented in the anthology, *Great Gospel Sermons* (New York: Revell, 1949). Vol. 1 brings sermons by evangelists from Finney to Truett; Vol. 2 the contemporary, including Walter A. Maier and Billy Graham.

An anthology of 30 sermons for special occasions is edited by William H. Eifert, *In Season — Out of Season* (St. Louis: Concordia Publishing House, 1944), by 23 pastors of The Lutheran Church — Missouri Synod.

Interesting approaches to a Christian college and the goal of fellowship in the church are to be found in *The Chapel Hour* (St. Louis: Concordia Publishing House, 1955) by Thomas Coates; *The Classic Christian Faith*, Chapel Meditations Based on Luther's Small Catechism, by Edgar M. Carlson (Rock Island: Augustana Press, 1959); and *Chapel Time* (Minneapolis: Augsburg, 1956) by G. L. Belgum and G. E. Frost. Substantial theological material pervades some of the 30 sermons and six articles of *Successful Fund-Raising Sermons*, ed. Julius King (New York: Funk and Wagnalls, 1953). Twenty pastors of the Evangelical Lutheran Church publish *20 Stewardship Sermons* (Minneapolis: Augsburg, 1954).

The same publisher issues *20 Confirmation Sermons* (1951), with accents shared by motifs of youth and of the church.

In Time . . . For Eternity, Sermons for the Church Year Based on the Eisenach Epistles, by G. W. Hoyer and J. P. Kretzmann (St. Louis: Concordia Publishing House, 1963), reflect the concern of parish preachers to reach familywide interests. John Charles Wynn, *Pastoral Ministry to Families* (Philadelphia: The Westminster Press, 1957), includes helpful reflections also on the function of preaching. Edgar N. Jackson (II) describes preaching to problems of family and the aged. J. W. Acker edits *Wedding Addresses* (St. Louis: Concordia Publishing House, 1955), some of which stress the theology of the family. Suggestions for preaching specifically to children are given by Theo. W. Schroeder, *49 Worship Stories for Children* (St. Louis: Concordia Publishing House, 1957), and C. L. Wallis, *A Treasury of Story Sermons for Children* (New York: Harper, 1957).

Collections of funeral sermons are published by Augsburg at Minneapolis (*20 Funeral Sermons,* 1952) and Concordia Publishing House in St. Louis (*The Life That Never Ends,* 1949, ed. William H. Eifert. It contains 30 addresses). Interesting are the chapters on preaching the resurrection and the last things to contemporary science-minded audiences, in A. C. Craig, *Preaching in a Scientific Age* (New York: Scribner's, 1954).

Section Nine

The best recent book on planning recommends the accents of the church year but incorporates customary Protestant accents in addition. It is George Miles Gibson, *Planned Preaching* (Philadelphia: Westminster, 1954). Among the handbooks on preaching Ilion T. Jones (I) has a very good section on planning.

John P. Milton, *Preaching from Isaiah* (Minneapolis: Augsburg, 1953), publishes a remarkable effort to distribute useful texts from Isaiah over a whole year's preaching adjusted to the liturgical year. The themes for the day are taken from the Swedish Lectionary. Additional listings place texts under 25 topics and a miscellaneous assortment of "great texts." The method of this book suggests planning of other Biblical areas in relation to the propers of the church's service book.

Among suggestions for filing, those of Ilion T. Jones seem most sensible (I). For pastors interested in setting up a comprehensive program of filing covering all of their work, *Practical Study Methods for Student and Pastor* by Donald F. Rossin and Palmer Ruschke (Minneapolis: D. F. Rossin Co.) will be helpful; the Rossin Company supplies materials for sermon-building and filing systems.

Denominational offices provide planning suggestions to congregations and ministers in order to expedite national as well as local projects. Materials for the congregations and their officers as well as pastors, built around annual and monthly themes, established by the Co-ordinating Council of The Lutheran Church — Missouri Synod, can be procured from Elmer A. Kettner, editor of *Advance* and of the *Workbook and Manual for Planning Parish Programs,* 210 N. Broadway, St. Louis 2, Mo.

Section Ten

In his anthology, *The Protestant Pulpit* (New York: Abingdon, 1947), Andrew W. Blackwood publishes a work sheet (p. 305) on "How to Study a Sermon." While adapted especially to the review of published literature, it will be serviceable also for phases of original sermons.

Charles F. Kemp (II), p. 28, gives a guide for studying a life-situation sermon. Parker et al. in *Religious Radio* (III) gives a very good guide for the evaluation of a radio sermon (p. 125). Kirkpatrick (V) gives a useful chart for the critique of delivery. It presupposes that the preacher holds the attention of the hearer. The chart used by the present writer for critique of the content and delivery of a recorded sermon is Appendix IV below.

Fairbanks (V) gives helpful suggestions for self-check concerning articulation.

Section Eleven

We do not propose to furnish bibliographies for refreshment in all of the fields cognate to preaching. Books aiming at the enhancement of the total ministry, with preaching as one phase, are always helpful. Note Anders Nygren, *The Gospel of God*, trans. L. J. Trinterud, an episcopal letter of 1949 (Philadelphia: Westminster, 1949); Raymond Calkins, *The Romance of the Ministry* (Boston: Pilgrim Press, 1944); Ian Macpherson, *The Burden of the Lord* (New York: Abingdon, 1955), with a splendid description of growth. Items in Section Twelve pertain here. On the basic will of the preacher to speak note lectures of the Wenchel Foundation at Concordia Seminary in St. Louis: Oswald G. L. Riess, *Nothing and All* (St. Louis: Concordia Publishing House, 1954), noteworthy for a glowing style, and William A. Buege, *Preaching with Power* (St. Louis: Concordia Publishing House, 1956). A constant stream of monographs on preaching is available, and most of them will provide new stimulus; for basic spiritual and theological growth items noted in Section I bear rereading frequently. In addition we may suggest on the preaching of St. Paul A. M. Hunter, *Interpreting Paul's Gospel* (London: SCM Press, 1954); Paul Scherer, *For We Have This Treasure* (New York: Harper, 1944); Eric Wahlstrom, *The New Life in Christ* (Philadelphia: Muhlenberg, 1950), a careful study of Pauline metaphors for the atonement; hopeful and positive, *The Audacity of Preaching*, by Gene E. Bartlett (New York: Harper, 1962); *The Ministry of Preaching*, by Roy Pearson (New York: Harper, 1959). Theologically refreshing and a contribution to the preacher's thinking concerning the church year is *Preaching the Christian Year* (New York: Scribner's, 1957), ed. Howard A. Johnson, comprising eight major articles on phases of the Christian year and its message. Periodicals are important for continuing professional growth. Useful for all theological fields, with a direct contribution to preaching in each issue, is the quarterly *Interpretation* (Richmond, Va.); *Concordia Theological Monthly* (St. Louis: Concordia Publishing House) plans accents in all fields and gives attention to pericopic preaching. Among the magazines of preaching the *Pulpit* (Chicago: The Christian Century Foundation) is a useful monthly.

Concerning phases of technique, attention to speech is essential. An occasional review of a book like Sarett and Foster (II) is helpful when supplemented by technical aids like Craig and Sokolowsky (V) or Fairbanks (V). The preacher will refresh articulation in general and pronunciation in particular through area reviews and introductions of a good dictionary. We have found *Webster's New World Dictionary* (Cleveland: World Publishing Company) good. Working through some of the problems of oral interpretation set up in Lamar (V) will stimulate.

For stimulus to better techniques Halford E. Luccock is always good. *Communicating the Gospel* (New York: Harper, 1954) is no better than *In the Minister's Workshop* (New York: Abingdon, 1944). Brief but able and quietly humorous is Robert J. McCracken, *The Making of the Sermon* (New York: Harper, 1956).

The preacher will profit from the study of great preachers. Edwin Charles Dargan, *A History of Preaching* (Boston: Hodder and Stoughton, 1905) gives no American survey but is still helpful; F. R. Webber, *A History of Preaching in Britain and America* (Milwaukee: Northwestern Publishing House, 3 vols., 1952 to 1957), concerns itself also with American preachers in the third volume. The Beecher lecturers through 1949 are interestingly portrayed in Edgar De Witt Jones, *The Royalty of the Pulpit* (New York: Harper, 1951).

Important for reading individual sermons are the suggestions of Andrew W. Blackwood in *The Protestant Pulpit* (X); this volume offers an important anthology of 19 past and 20 current sermons. Another superior anthology is *Master Sermons Through the Ages*, by William Alan Sadler, Jr. (New York: Harper and Row, 1963).

Some sermons will be read chiefly for the sake of basic Gospel content and method. At random we note Dwight L. Moody (many editions; good is *Great Pulpit Masters* [New York: Revell, 1949] Vol. I, intr. by Charles R. Erdman); Arthur James Moore, *The Mighty Saviour* (New York: Abingdon, 1952); of course Charles H. Spurgeon, tediously reported by his editors but remarkable in facility of Gospel expression (a useful single volume is II of *Great Pulpit Masters*, intr. by Andrew W. Blackwood [New York: Revell, 1949], 16 sermons); and Walter A. Maier, whose style, pitched to a national audience, is not suitable to the parish but whose fertility of Gospel variation is Biblical and warm (St. Louis: Concordia Publishing House, many volumes).

We note volumes which combine interesting facets of technique with evangelical warmth and variety. Major theological themes are treated by profound theologians with disarming simplicity in D. M. Baillie, *To Whom Shall We Go?* (New York: Scribner's, 1955); Emil Brunner, *The Great Invitation* (Philadelphia: Westminster, 1955; trans. Harold Knight) and *I Believe in the Living God* (Philadelphia, Westminster, 1961; trans. John Holden); Karl Heim, *The Living Fountain* (Grand Rapids: Zondervan, 1936; trans. John Schmidt). Lucid style supporting explicit Gospel affirmations is at work in Robert E. Luccock, *If God Be for Us* (New York: Harper, 1954); David A. MacLennan, *Joyous Adventure* (New York: Harper, 1952; sermons for the Christian year, with small, sometimes compound, texts); W. G. Polack, *Beside Still Waters* (parish sermons at a lake retreat, with interesting doctrinal materials and applications [St. Louis: Concordia Publishing House, 1950]); Alvin N. Rogness, *Who Shall Be God?* (Minneapolis: Augsburg, 1954), the stylist among current Lutheran preachers in America; and James S. Stewart, *The Strong Name* (New York: Scribner's, 1941), 24 sermons on the Apostolic Benediction, not basically textual in method but with high style. George Arthur Buttrick prefaces *Sermons Preached in a University Church* (New York: Abingdon, 1959) with a useful introduction on sermons in print. A. Leonard Griffith of the City Temple in London is unusually readable, in *Barriers to Christian Belief* (New York: Harper and Row, 1962) and *What Is a Christian?* (New York: Abingdon, 1962). Martin Luther King's volume *Strength to Love* (New York: Harper and Row, 1963) is significant as good preaching and not merely as a social document; interesting is *Preaching on Race* (St. Louis: Bethany Press, 1962) by R. Frederick West. An anthology of sermons, *Preaching on Christian Unity*, is edited by Robert Tobias (St. Louis: Bethany Press, 1958). In the Scottish tradition is *I Am Persuaded*, by David H. C. Read (New York: Scribner's, 1961).

For good insights into good style directed to the hearer situation read J. H. Jowett (a useful edition is Vol. V of *Great Pulpit Masters*, intr. by Elmer G. Homrighausen, 27 sermons; New York: Revell, 1950); Harry Emerson Fosdick (III); Robert J. McCracken (III); *Go Preach*, ed. Theodore O. Wedel and George W. R. MacGrath, 30 sermons for lay readers of the Episcopal Church (Greenwich: Seabury Press, 1954); Melvin E. Wheatley, Jr., *Going His Way* (New York: Revell, 1957); Edmund Steimle (III); and Armin C. Oldsen, *A Message from God*, radio sermons with strong personal quality (St. Louis: Concordia Publishing House, 1953).

The authors noted with reference to changing American reactions to persuasion are David Riesman, *The Lonely Crowd* (New Haven: Yale U. Press, 1950), *Faces in the Crowd* (1952); Karen Horney, *The Neurotic Personality of Our Time* (New York: W. W. Norton and Co., 1937); and Erich Fromm, *The Sane Society* (New York: Rinehart, 1955).

Section Twelve

The problem of the multifarious American ministry is well discussed by H. Richard Niebuhr, *The Purpose of the Church and Its Ministry* (New York: Harper, 1956), and by Dr. Samuel Blizzard in studies soon to appear under the auspices of the Russel Sage Foundation. Niebuhr describes the rallying of the pastor's efforts around his major objectives. Helpful notes in this direction are sounded by W. E. Sangster, *The Approach to Preaching* (Philadelphia: Westminster, 1952), and David A. MacLennan in *Entrusted with the Gospel* (II).

The interrelation of the total ministry and the life of worship of the people is defined by Walter E. Buszin in *The Doctrine of the Universal Priesthood and Its Influence upon the Liturgies and Music of the Lutheran Church* (St. Louis: Concordia Publishing House, n. d.). Pastoral care is treated by Eduard Thurneysen in *Die Lehre von der Seelsorge* (Munich: Chr. Kaiser, 1948), and Wayne Oates, *The Christian Pastor* (Philadelphia: Westminster, 1951). A good illustration of correlating all fields of the ministry in a special area is Edward K. Ziegler, *Rural Preaching* (New York: Revell, 1954); this should be done for city and suburbia likewise. William E. Hulme's *Counseling and Theology* (Philadelphia: Muhlenberg, 1957) is useful.

For sermons with the pastoral note and insight thoroughly evident cf. Geiseman (IV) and Herbert Lindemann, *Dead or Alive* (St. Louis: Concordia Publishing House, 1955).

APPENDIXES

APPENDIX I

Planning and Preparing the Textual Sermon

Section Four describes the routine of preparing for parish worship the sermon which employs a Biblical text. The stages of such preparation are herewith set forth by way of illustration from the author's own recent experience. In actual practice many of these items are not written out; here the effort is made to display the process.

The assignment was to conduct, on a Sunday morning in mid-September, the two services of a parish temporarily without a pastor. The parish has a wide cultural and educational range. It employed the "Order of Morning Service Without Communion" of *The Lutheran Hymnal* (St. Louis: Concordia Publishing House, 1941) for the 14th Sunday after Trinity, omitting the Gradual.

FIRST STAGE

Epistle for the day is Gal. 5:16-24; Gospel, Luke 17:11-19. The Introit stresses faith in the hour of worship; the Collect for the day is a notable plea for God's mercy on the church; the propers as a whole stress the dependence of the Christian on God and His Spirit for mercy and help, a dependence to be revealed in thanksgiving. The Eisenach Epistle for the day seemed promising in its accent on "ministry." It is 1 Tim. 1:12-17.

General Setting. — The Epistle conveys instructions for the ministry of Timothy; not only instructions but heartening and power. 1:18; 2:15, 16; 6:11-16 are summaries; 2 Tim. 3 is parallel.

Immediate Context. — The special charge is to safeguard the church from false teaching, without being caught up into fruitless debate (1:3 ff.). The chief error seemed to be a loss of the understanding of Law and Gospel; the Law should reveal sin (vv. 9, 10), highlighting that which is contrary to the product of the Gospel (v. 11). Paul has a charge for Timothy personally to keep on in faith (vv. 18, 20). The text enters as depiction of the example of St. Paul and the power for faithfulness. (This writer finds assumptions that 1 Timothy is not Pauline less tenable than the traditional judgment and the Epistle therefore a case study of practical concern, for the apostle and his pupil, concerning his calling. N. J. T. White's unit

311

in v. 4, *Expositor's Greek New Testament,* 1917, Hodder & Stoughton, was useful. The text had no radical problems of text transmission.)

The Vernacular. — 12. St. Paul finds enablement (RSV, strength) from Christ, particularly in the act of his call into the apostolate and in Christ's redeeming work (v. 15).

13. Once Paul was a blasphemer; how? "Because ignorantly in unbelief"; does that suggest that the gravity of his unbelief was less and God's mercy greater because he was ignorant?

14. Mercy is equated with grace; does this imply God giving a power of faith and love or God giving Himself? Is "Lord" Christ or God?

15. Why is this introduced? Does it underscore the preceding? The abundant grace of God in Christ hinges on His coming into the world to save sinners. St. Paul calls himself chief of sinners; how does the application extend to the prospective hearer?

16. For this cause — purpose? In Paul, Christ would show His patience and mercy over sin, for the sake of others who would come to faith later; the meaning of "pattern"? RSV, "example."

17. Is the King Christ or God? The former would restate vv. 12, 14, 15, 16; the latter, v. 14, if there "Lord" is Father and the passage Trinitarian. The words are majestic, the adjectives to be explored.

Paul recommends as power for Timothy's ministry the same which Christ gave him, through His mercy and because of His atoning work. Christ's gift and mercy thus has enabling power for the faith and the calling of Christians in the same ministry. Can the application be made to Christians in general or only to pastors and preachers?

The Original. — Lexicon employed: *Bauer-Arndt-Gingrich,* Chicago and Cambridge, 1957. Parallel passages noted, Nestle Text, Stuttgart, 1945.

12. Christ was One strengthening (cf. Acts 9:22).

hoti, because He considered me as faithful (could be also: trusting).

ministry: service; Paul uses it frequently of his apostolate (Acts 20:24).

13. The three adjectives supplement one another. *hybristen,* vio‐lent, insolent.

hoti gives a cause, not for what prompted God to be merciful, but for what necessitated God's act to be merciful (cf. Rom. 5:20); on *hoti* cf. Blass-Debrunner (Göttingen, 1921), "on account of the fact that."

14. with faith and love in Christ — faithfulness and love from Christ or faith in and love toward Christ, as the working of His grace? The latter seems suggested; White: manifestations of grace.

Lord is used of the Father (Rev. 11:15).

15. *sosai:* behind it the phrase of John 3:17; 10:36; cf. Luke 19:10.

16. *dia touto,* coupled with the purpose clause, *hina,* God's grace to Paul has the effect on later believers in view.

hypotyposin: BAG suggests prototype, the demonstration that it can happen.

17. *time,* in Paul only in 1 Tim. 6:16; cf. Rev. 4:9, honor. It would be important to distinguish between it and *doxa,* the self-revelation of God's glory; hence a word applicable to the function of the calling (cf. 1 Peter 4:11).

Other parallels: on Paul (1 Cor. 15:9). On God the Only-wise (cf. Rom. 16:27 and Jude 25).

Doctrinal Study. — The grace of God in Christ, in sending Christ into the world for His redemptive work. The grace of God directed to the establishment of Paul and Timothy in their work of bringing the Gospel to people; directed to the sustaining of Christians in that calling. The preacher as a witness to the redeeming mercy of God; a reminder that he is in the business of having all Christians bring the ministry of that witness (Eph. 4:8 ff.). Special stresses: The superabundance of God's mercy in Christ, functioning under the most unlikely situations. God's mercy to one that many others may be reached and believe.

Central Thought of the Text. — The Gospel enables to the Gospel calling by conveying the grace of God in Christ.

Or: God has grace for the greatest sinner through Christ.

The stress of the day on God's mercy in Christ is equally applicable to either focus of the text. In view of the resumption of the activity of the church at this season and the particular review going on of the function of the ministry, the former area seems pertinent.

The central thought restated in terms of the day: If we are to carry out God's plan for our lives, we must depend utterly on His grace in Christ Jesus.

Abbreviated for publication: "God's Mercy Is Our Only Help."

SECOND STAGE

Revised theme: *"God's Mercy Is Our Only Help for Our Task"*

The goal could be: the Christians of this congregation should carry out their Christian tasks. This would be a life goal.

More central to the text and day: Christians should grasp and use the grace of God in Christ Jesus for their task. This is a faith goal.

Malady: surface symptoms of doubt, self-righteousness, lethargy for worship, or apathy in mutual Christian service can be traced to weak grasp of faith (1 Cor. 11) on mercy and forgiveness.

Means: The text is very rich. The free mercy of God in Christ is the stimulus to faith for all generations who look back to it.

THIRD STAGE

God's Mercy Is Our Only Help for Our Task. Outlined conventionally:

I. Our task

  A. Timothy's: Preach Gospel, reject the false doctrine of the Law.

  B. Ours: Bear witness to Jesus Christ that all mercy is in God and He is Lord; service of the Gospel to one another.

II. Our handicaps

  A. Our birth; our continuing selfishness.

  B. The world in which we live; its repudiation of God's help.

III. Our help

  A. The mercy of God; Gospel: dependence on God the source for wholeness.

  B. The mercy of God, Paul (vv. 12-14; 15).

  C. A mercy to apply to us all (v. 16).

  D. Thus we can glorify God, show Him at work (v. 17); Epistle: fruits.

A reconstruction for achieving more ample Gospel affirmation:,

I. For our task of keeping the faith

A. Timothy: false doctrine; we: a materialistic world; doubt.

B. God's mercy is in Christ; He came to save us. Our sin too great? See St. Paul.

II. For our task of worshiping God

A. We tend to become cold, religion only disputatious.

B. God's mercy is superabundant in Christ; lifts our eyes to v. 17.

III. For our task of service in the church

A. The service: speaking the love of God to one another and to our community; stimulating one another to I and II in love.

B. God Himself must enable us for this service. The Collect.

C. To that end hold before one another the mercy of God in Christ, the enabling. Review it in thanks; in Communion; in speaking the Bible word to one another; in worship services.

FOURTH STAGE

Introd.: What is good about the tenth leper? Faith in mercy of God, betokened by his thanks. The prayer of the Collect.

Revised to be more direct than the liturgical opening: Many responsibilities crowd in upon us during the service: keep strong in God, worship Him, our church work; plus everything else that we are trying to forget. How shall we meet these responsibilities? In text Paul writes to young man having his troubles at his new job. The answer:

God's Mercy Is Our Only Help for Our Task

I. For our task of keeping the faith

A. We live in a world that questions the Christian faith; have our own doubts. The way of morals (vv. 3, 4, 6), and that brings even greater doubt. How can we help one another?

B. God's mercy is our help. The Gospel of forgiveness (v. 15 and parallels).

C. It is sufficient to reach the gravest sin (Paul, v. 16).

D. It is sufficient to reach down even to us who harden against it; let us view it, see it, remember it.

II. For our task of worshiping God

A. At this moment engaged in this worship. But religion often becomes a matter of dispute, denominational competition (v. 4).

B. View the grace of God in Christ (v. 14).

C. Then we shall come under His lordship (v. 17) and bring Him our honor together.

III. For our task of service to one another in the church

A. We are called to serve one another, speaking the love of God to one another and to our community, helping one another against doubt and to worship under God. So Paul (v. 11); Timothy (v. 18); all Christians (Eph. 4:11).

B. God Himself must enable us for this service. Collect. Fruits of the Spirit, Epistle.

C. To that end hold before one another mercy of God in Christ, say our thanks to God before each other (Luke 11); Communion; speak Bible words to one another in Bible class and worship, hymns, family worship. The pastorate which we are thinking of and praying over, to be a service by which we are helped to speak the mercy of God to one another in Christ. Become our "only" help as we crowd every other trust out.

Conclusion may be in III C.

At this stage no illustrative material was at hand beyond human situation of the text and congregational application.

FIFTH STAGE

(The working brief is expanded into a sermon — in one sitting. This version is undersize for full parish use and receives final expansion in subsequent stages. This required about an hour's writing time. The same purpose could be achieved through a tape recording in less time; this writer uses between thirty and forty minutes for a twenty-five minute sermon.)

Sunday is a day of rest, we say. Yet church members feel many responsibilities crowd in upon them, even though they are sitting in a service of worship. We don't have to talk about the ones we are trying to tune out — business worries, problems of health or family. But just what we call church work, especially at this time of year, settles down upon us with strong demands. Worship itself exacts a toll of energy, to keep concentrating, to try to envision the unseen God and consecrate self to Him. Then there are the things that we call church work — our giving to the church's treasury and sharing in the work of the church's tasks in the community through the voters' assembly or through the societies and groups of the congregation or in the church school. When we think about it all, we get a little tired in advance. How shall we keep ourselves at all the responsibilities of life? In the words of Scripture before us St. Paul is writing to a young helper of his who must likewise have been somewhat dismayed at all the tasks before him. He encourages him through a very personal reminder of how he himself had found strength for his own work. That prescription is good for us all, and let's resolve to take it in strongly today as we plan for a new season of church work and ponder the importance of the holy ministry in this congregation. This is the prescription:

God's Mercy Is Our Only Help for Our Task

I. Keeping the Faith

A. We don't have to look long for things to do when we call ourselves members of the Christian Church. For we live in a world that questions our faith, looks down on our church membership, practices ways of living that run quite contrary to our own. And we have our own doubts about Christ's way of living, once in a while. St. Paul told Timothy that he must keep strong in his faith, be able to reprove and correct men who were teaching contrary to it, and be an example of the right faith and way of life to other people. The chief false teachings in Timothy's day sought to turn people simply to give in to the promptings of their baser nature, to forget about God altogether, to live it up; or, quite in the other extreme, they told people that in order to gain the favor of God and ultimately enter heaven they would have to behave themselves not only perfectly but with the keeping of many additional religious observances. Each one of us finds himself, right in our present world, tugged off the track of true faith by one or the other of these extremes: forget about God and do what comes naturally, or make God like you by doing religious things and being perfect in your behavior. The trouble with them is that they bother not only our faith but our conscience. We have built-in reactions that seem to approve of both of them by turns, and then our conscience smites us for giving in to what we can tell is sin or for hoping to be perfect when we can tell very well that we aren't.

B. How wonderful to sound to one another this morning the message of our text: "This is a faithful saying and worthy of all acceptation, that Christ Jesus came into the world to save sinners." It reminds us of Jesus' own words in his meeting with Zacchaeus: "The Son of Man is come to seek and to save that which is lost." There is a thing to set the teeth of faith in, there is help for every need! For there is God's own help for even our gravest sin; St. Paul said that it could reach him even though he was a persecutor of the church. And there is help even for those horrible times when we think we have lost sight of God altogether. It's so easy to get hardened against God, to forget His goodness, to find everything else in life more important than He is. As we ponder it, we must become hot with shame at our own apathy. But the mercy of God in Christ is great enough to reach us. St. Paul remembered what he called his own ignorance, his thoughtlessness about what God was doing for him in Jesus Christ, and his unbelief, and he marveled that God could still have mercy on him. For when God gave His own Son Jesus Christ into the world to share our life and take our sin upon Himself and ultimately to die on the cross forsaken by God, that was the act of God's being merciful to us. And there we see the power, the power of God Himself, to keep us strong in the faith that He is our God and His mercy and forgiveness is the one source of our standing with Him.

II. Worshiping God

A. The second great task that we remind ourselves of is to keep on worshiping God. The Bible calls worship a service; we call this meeting in this building a church service. Where shall we get the power to keep on serving God with our worship — properly, thought-fully, sincerely, regularly? America is seeing a wave of interest in religion, these days, but often it is a sort of disguised selfishness and the attempt to find some quick cures for illnesses without paying doctor bills. For many folks their religion is a means of bolstering their self-approval in arguments and debates. St. Paul warns Timothy against getting involved in bickering about speculations and fables and curious questions rather than actually helping himself and his fellow Christians in their faith.

B. St. Paul tells us where we are going to get the power to worship God. At the end of this text he breaks out with a wonderful hymn of praise and adoration to God: "Now, unto the King eternal, im-mortal, invisible, the only wise God, be honor and glory forever and ever. Amen." That means that he found God ruling and governing his heart. Even though he could not see Him, he was learning that God was in control of His life in the wisest and best way possible; and he couldn't help telling of his adoration. We are reminded of the leper to whom, in this morning's Gospel, Jesus said, "Thy faith hath made thee whole." He glorified God when he had been healed. Where do you get the power for this?

C. You don't get it just through lucky breaks of fortune, fun, and hilarity, through having everything your way. Truly to worship God means to know Him as the Only-wise, and that means to adore Him in days of difficulty as well as times of joy. And St. Paul tells us how to get the power for it: "The grace of our Lord was exceeding abun-dant with faith and love which is in Christ Jesus." Our faith in God and our love for Him, and for one another for that matter, must come from God Himself, from His mercy in Jesus Christ. As we remember God's gift of His Son into death for our sins, we see again the lengths to which God went to love us and make and keep us His and have us be not just physically well and happy but whole, whole in Him. So if you plan to worship God faithfully in your prayers day by day and in your family circle each evening and in your church week in, week out, then turn your eye to Jesus, lift them to His cross, see there God's love for you; and then tell God that He has bought you wholly and all of you and your whole life belongs to Him forever.

III. Serving One Another

A. A final set of responsibilities remain. Paul wrote to Timothy because he wanted him to be a good pastor to his congregation. But this pastorate was simply to help his people be good ministers to one another. For that is what it means to be a member of the church: to help your fellow member, in the family or in the congregation, to remain firm in the faith and rich in love toward one another. The moment that I say this I can imagine you listing your handicaps for it. "I don't have the time to come to services and meetings." "I'm not able to talk about the Christian religion to people." "I'm pretty weak in faith and pretty selfish myself; how am I supposed to be able to help other people be better than I am." "We don't get to talk much religion in our family."

B. In our text St. Paul reminded himself and Timothy how God Himself had helped him for that purpose. "I thank Christ Jesus, our Lord, who hath enabled me, putting me into the ministry." When God sent Jesus Christ into the world and to the cross, He didn't produce merely a story to be read in churches or carved into crucifixes. But He planted power into people. That was God giving Himself back into the hearts of His people, so that they might believe in Him and love one another. What happened to St. Paul, so that he who had been a sinner became a servant of God to bring and keep many in life with God, that has happened to many millions of Christians since that time.

And so from this text we have one great lesson to learn for our church work this morning. And that is to keep on, and help one another keep on, taking hold of the mercy of God in Jesus Christ. We have to plan to keep on speaking that mercy to one another in our worship and our hymns and prayers of thanksgiving. Remember how we prayed in the collect for this morning: "Keep, we beseech Thee, O Lord, Thy church with Thy perpetual mercy; and because the frailty of man without Thee cannot but fail, keep us ever by Thy help from all things hurtful, and lead us to all things profitable to our salvation." In our families parents keep pumping good food and vitamins into the little children. In our motor trips we keep pumping good gasoline and oil into our cars. Very well, in our church life let us be busy keeping at it, pumping the mercy of God through the remembrance of Jesus Christ into one another. As we do so, we grow in the power to keep on doing it. As we pray over the vacant pastorate of this congregation, we can remember that it is simply the system by which we shall be enabled to keep the mercy of God at the peak importance of life for each one of us. And then we shall have the ability for our service to one another in the church, for our sincerity and persistence in worship, for keeping the faith in God pure.

"Keep, we beseech Thee, O Lord, Thy church with Thy perpetual mercy." Amen!

SIXTH STAGE

The first draft is now revised. Most of this revision occurs in the process of rethinking done in the "memorizing," and it continues till the moment of preaching. This sermon was preached to two audiences on the same morning and underwent conscious changes. The chief question at revision was: Do the three major divisions possibly disrupt unity in the minds of the hearers? Should they be brought into one focus of "church work" rather than left as unrelated episodes? Should the goal of apprehending mercy be one describing the joint activities of Christians in the church? This accent, not so apparent in the text, is more amply underscored in Ephesians 4. Other initial judgments:

Introduction: too long; too many challenges before defining the goal.

IA: Is the introduction of "conscience" a hindrance?

IB: Set teeth in — danger of talking goal rather than means? Is this cyclical treatment of the paragraph satisfactory, or should it be sorted out topically?

IIA: Amplify the meaning of "glorify God."

IIB: B and C of the outline were unclear. The first sentence of B on the manuscript belongs to C.

SEVENTH STAGE

This is a written-out example of thinking through the sermon before final delivery. Others follow between writing and speaking.

We call Sunday a day of rest, and we come to church to get relief from the problems and cares of life. Hence it's apt to hit us with

a bit of dismay that just at this time of year in church we talk about
a great deal of work. Worship itself takes energy, to get ready and
to concentrate on what we're doing and to consecrate ourselves to
God. Church work takes energy, and every church service emphasizes
it — giving our offerings and sharing in the church's activities in its
societies and its church school and in the care of property and the outreach to the community. Even talking about it makes us a little tired.
How can we keep ourselves at it? Have you noticed that we often
protect ourselves against the demands of church work by simply not
paying attention to them — right during a sermon? Before us we have
words of St. Paul to a young helper who was probably also somewhat
weary of the tasks before him. The apostle encourages him by telling
him how he himself had found strength for his own work. He found
it in God's mercy, he said. That prescription is good for us all. Let's
resolve right now to take that mercy in strongly and to keep on taking it in as we plan for a new season of church work. This is the
prescription:

God's Mercy Is Our Only Help for Our Task

I

The first job that St. Paul tried to help Timothy with was *keeping
the faith.* That's our first job, too. Let's look at it and then see how
we need God's mercy to do it well.

A. We live in *a world that questions our faith,* looks down on our
church membership or ignores it, and practices ways of life that are
quite contrary to what we want ours to be. In Timothy's day people
were tempted to give in to the promptings of their baser selves, forget about God; or, on the other extreme, they thought that if they
wanted to please God and go to heaven, they would not only have to
behave themselves perfectly but have to reinforce their lives with all
sorts of additional religious observances. So we, too, find our faith
faltering because we are tempted to forget about God, "do what comes
naturally," "live it up"; or because we expect that we have to substitute
for faith by doing things we dream up ourselves in order to please
God. But no wonder we get tired when our faith in God slips! For
God is the Source of our life and power; He has to renew our strength

like the eagle's every day. And when we don't count on Him for it —
and that's what we mean by a faith that falters — of course we weaken
and get flabby.

B. How wonderful, then, to sound to one another this morning *the
prescription of our text for keeping faith strong:* "This is a faithful
saying and worthy of all acceptation, that Christ Jesus came into the
world to save sinners." It reminds us of Jesus' own words when He
met Zacchaeus, the man who had lost faith under temptations of
business: "The Son of Man is come to seek and to save that which is
lost." Here's something that you can set the teeth of your faith into
and hold onto for dear life; but better: here's God Himself renewing
our grip, telling us that He will never back away from His plan to
make us His own, no matter how tired or wayward we get.

C. Here is help for even the gravest sin that plagues us with the
murmur "Forget about God; you can't face His anger." St. Paul said
that God's mercy was great enough to reach him even though he had
persecuted the church. Here is *help for that terrible fatigue of faith*
that we don't even notice at the moment, when we have found everything else in life more important than He is, or when we have started
to persuade ourselves that He doesn't care and really doesn't count
too much in life anyway. As we ponder those moments, we become
hot with shame at our own apathy. The mercy of God is unfailing
and faithful, and right this moment it reaches out to us as we remember His Son dying for us on the cross and rising again from the grave.
There we see the power of God Himself at work to keep us strong in
the faith.

D. In the mercy of God in Jesus Christ we have *help for the lag-
ging in faith* that comes with the murmur "I guess I'll have to get
busy with this church work in order to keep God satisfied." That just
turns the plan of God for us upside down. For then we become
susceptible to every virus of pride and penny pinching; then again
we pull our eyes away from God's help for our task and make out of
church work a strut instead of a service. But the mercy of God can
reach us. St. Paul remembered his own ignorance, as he called it, his
thoughtlessness about what God had done for him in Jesus Christ and
the unbelief that led him to work his own way to God; and he marveled

that God could still have mercy on him. Well, we can marvel too; and we can do better. We can have God's own hand of mercy reach right down into our own hearts as we today and always keep on re-membering God's precious mercy to us in Jesus Christ.

II

St. Paul tried to help Timothy for a second big and wearying job, and that was *to keep on worshiping God.* The Bible calls worship to God a service; we call this hour in this building a church service. Where shall we get the power to keep on serving God with our wor-ship — properly, sincerely, regularly?

A. This is an important question. Our nation is experiencing a sort of revival of interest in religion, and perhaps we hope that we shall be swept along in it when we lose interest ourselves. Yet often pop-ular religion is a sort of *disguised selfishness,* the attempt to find some quick cure for illnesses without paying doctor bills or a scheme to get wealthy without benefit of capital and dividends. We know what happens to that sort of interest in religion and worship: it dies the moment that hard times set in. You probably know many people who love to debate religious questions; down inside us we have some-times been beset by the temptation to think of church as a place to be right because others are wrong. St. Paul warns Timothy in our text against getting involved in bickering about speculations and fables and curious questions. No, steadiness in worship has to lean for help on better props than that.

B. St. Paul breaks out at the end of this text with a wonderful *hymn of praise and adoration to God:* "Now, unto the King eternal, immortal, invisible, the only wise God, be honor and glory forever and ever. Amen." He tried to help Timothy's worship to God by joining him across the miles in a paean of praise to God in which he reminded himself and Timothy what God means to him; and that is exactly what all of our worship together must do. St. Paul had found that God was ruling and governing his heart. Even though he could not see God, he was discovering that God was in control of his life in the wisest and best way possible. So he proclaimed that God is high, that He is King. And he affirmed that God had made His invisible self show in the visible life of himself and that he wanted this to go on always. We are reminded of the leper in this morning's Gospel. To him Jesus said, "Thy faith hath made thee whole" — he glorified God when he had been healed, for he saw not merely sound skin, but he saw God at work in producing it. Our worship is to be not just the routine of churchgoing but the adoring of God and the recognizing of His presence in our lives. Where do you get the power for this?

C. You don't get the will to adore God simply by lucky breaks, fun and hilarity, by having everything your way. You have to acknowledge Him as wise, and this means that you have to know and be sure that your hard days are as right as your easy ones; that God's gift of tears is as important as His gift of smiles. St. Paul tells Timothy how to get the power for it: "The grace of our Lord was exceeding abundant with faith and love which is in Christ Jesus." *Our faith in God and our love for Him, and that means our will to worship Him, must come from God Himself,* from His love to us in Jesus Christ. Remember God's gift of His Son into death for our sins. See the lengths to which God went to love us and make us His and have us be not just physically well and happy but whole, whole in Him. Then you will find it in your heart to keep on thinking about Him, in your heart to lift up your hands and whole self to Him in thankful and sincere praise. As you plan to worship God in your private prayers day by day, in your family circle each evening, in our church week in, week out, turn your eyes to Jesus, lift them to His cross, see there God's mercy for you, and thus keep on telling God that He has bought you wholly and that your whole life belongs to Him forever.

III

One more set of jobs need help. St. Paul wrote to Timothy because he wanted him to be a good pastor. A pastorate, however, simply helps people *be good ministers to one another,* as St. Paul told the Ephesians.

A. That is what it means to be the member of a church and to do church work: help your fellow member remain firm in the faith and rich in love to other people. The moment that I say this, I can imagine you listing *your handicaps for it.* "I don't have the time to come to services and meetings." "I'm not able to talk about the Christian religion to people." "I'm pretty weak in faith and pretty selfish myself; how am I supposed to be able to help other people be better than I am?" "Some of these people in this church are sort of hopeless; and I don't think it's my business to help them." "We don't get to talk much religion in our family."

B. In our text St. Paul reminded himself and Timothy how *God Himself had helped* them for that purpose. "I thank Christ Jesus, our Lord, who hath enabled me, putting me into the ministry." When God sent Jesus Christ into the world and to the cross, He didn't merely produce a story that we read in churches or describe in crucifixes. But He planted power into people, He gave them ability to work for Him. For in Christ God gave Himself back into the hearts of His people so that they might believe in Him and love one another. Paul had been a persecutor of Christians; he became a tool of God to keep many with God forever. That has happened to many millions of Christians since. Petty jealousy and self-interest or plain old weariness can begin to weaken the fabric of a group of Christians anywhere; but the mercy of God in Christ is rich enough to strengthen it again, anywhere, any time — and it can happen here.

C. Thus we have one great lesson to learn for all our faith and worship and church work today: *keep on, and help each other keep on, taking hold of the mercy of God in Jesus Christ.* We have to be wide awake about speaking that mercy of God to one another in our worship and our hymns and prayers of thanksgiving and in this pulpit and our Bible reading and this Sacrament of God's mercy in the body and blood of Jesus. Remember how we prayed in the collect for this morning, and turn to it, and memorize it, and make it a constant plea: "Keep, we beseech Thee, O Lord, Thy church with Thy perpetual mercy; and because the frailty of man without Thee cannot but fall, keep us ever by Thy help from all things hurtful, and lead us to all things profitable to our salvation." In our families parents keep pumping good food and vitamins into the little children. In our motor trips we keep pumping good gasoline and oil into our cars. Very well, in our church life let us be busy keeping at it, pumping the mercy of God into one another through remembering Jesus Christ as Redeemer. As we pray over the vacant pastorate of this congregation, let us remember that it is a system planned by God for keeping the mercy of God at the peak importance that it should have for the life of each one of us. Through that mercy of God to us in Jesus we shall be able to help one another's faith and life in this church, worship God sincerely and purely, keep our faith strong.

"Keep, we beseech Thee, O Lord, Thy church with Thy perpetual mercy." Amen.

APPENDIX II

Service Themes for the Christian Year

The following are possible co-ordinations for each day of the propers for the Common Service as provided in *The Lutheran Hymnal* (St. Louis: Concordia Publishing House, 1941), pp. 54—83. Several are possible for some days; these illustrate syntheses.

1 in Adv. A new year of teaching and fellowship.

2 in Adv. Cultivating the Christian hope.

3 in Adv. Looking to the second coming with faith.

4 in Adv. Our joy in the promise of the incarnation.

Christmas. God has fulfilled His promises.
Our Savior is born.

S. a. Christmas. Life through the atoning Christ.

N. Year, Circumcision. Christ's ministry to us as our Savior.

S. a. N. Year. Trust through Christ for every need.

Epiphany. Christ is the Revelation of God's grace to all.

1 a. Ep. We pursue God's business because Christ pursued- it.

2 a. Ep. Christ's rule in heart and life.

3 a. Ep. Christ's redemption works faith.

4 a. Ep. God supports in every situation, for Christ's sake.

5 a. Ep. Christ gathers and preserves His church.

6 a. Ep. Christ's glory is our glory in this world and that to come.

Sept. Forgiveness and life are by God's grace.

Sex. God sustains against adversities of body and soul.

Quinq. We need to look to Christ for the gifts of faith and love.

Ash W. The purpose of the Lenten vigil for penitence and forgiveness.

1 in Lent. Christ's conquest of Satan and its comfort for us.

2 in Lent. God's mercy in Christ our help for overcoming the flesh.

3 in Lent. Accept the grace of God for every trial.

4 in Lent. God's grace: Its source and supply.

5 in Lent. The atonement of Christ provides power for the new life.

6 in Lent. Christ's determination to undertake the Passion.

M. Thurs. The receiving of the Sacrament to its proper end.

G. Friday. Christ died for us.

Easter.   Christ's resurrection means our life now and in eternity.

1 a. E.   Christ's atonement means Christ's guidance.

2 a. E.   Christ is the Good Shepherd.

3 a. E.   Certainty and power in the atoning Jesus.

4 a. E.   The power of the redemption triumphs over unbelief.

5 a. E.   The completed redemption works joy, faith, prayer.

Ascension.   Our triumph over death through the work of Christ.

S. a. Asc.   Through the Spirit Christ's redemption gives us life.

Whitsunday.   The work of the Spirit in individuals and the church.

Trinity.   How God reveals Himself to us as the Triune God.

Tr.   1.   Use Word to carry out God's purposes for us in Christ.

Tr.   2.   Use Christ in the face of all earthly obstacles.

Tr.   3.   Let us care for the lost and erring as Christ did.

Tr.   4.   Christian witness in the face of earthly suffering.

Tr.   5.   God's blessings on Christian discipleship.

Tr.   6.   Through God's grace we are raised spiritually from the dead.

Tr.   7.   Christ will feed our life that it may grow.

Tr.   8.   Effective obedience to Jesus.

Tr.   9.   God's help in life through the Word against unbelief.

Tr. 10.   Grace to overcome unbelief and to serve God.

Tr. 11.   Forgiveness through Christ the source of every blessing.

Tr. 12.   God's help for the witness to the Gospel.

Tr. 13.   God fits us for abundant life under His covenant.

Tr. 14.   The benefits of the Word and the Spirit.

Tr. 15.   God helps us that we might help others.

Tr. 16.   God's grace our help in every need.

Tr. 17.   Our worship: God's help to and through us for spiritual life.

Tr. 18.   The power of the Spirit for faith and works.

Tr. 19.   Help one another to be well in body and soul.

Tr. 20.   Our service to God comes only through His forgiveness.

Tr. 21.   The life grows because of the help of God in Christ.

Tr. 22.   The fruits of forgiveness: love and further forgiveness.

Tr. 23.   The life in Christ versus fleshly fear and materialism.

Tr. 24.   As the redeemed of Christ our lives are whole.

Tr. 25.   Our need for Christ in view of judgment and eternity.

Tr. 26.   God's help for endurance to the second coming.

Tr. 27.   Faithfulness and vigilance in view of the second coming.

APPENDIX III

Biblical Modes of Depicting the Atonement

Each complex of Law and Gospel is set on one line. Where Law complexes are repeated, the previous line is indicated by its numeral.

Man's Problem *(Law)*	God's Answer *(Gospel)*
Effecting a Change in the Relation of Man to God	
1 Separated from God, Is. 59:2; 53:6	Atonement, KJV, Rom. 5:11
2 State of hostility toward God	Reconciliation, 2 Cor. 5:18 ff.
3 Wrath of God, Eph. 5:6	Peace, John 16:33. Healing, Is. 53:5. Mercy
4 Death, Rom. 6:23; Gen. 2:17	Life, Rom. 6:23; John 3:1-16
5 Sin: rebellion, disobedience, Titus 3:3	Kingdom, Spirit, Matt. 4:17; 2 Cor. 3:17
6 Sin: guilt under judgment, Psalm 130	Forgiveness (like 3); Rom. 3:19 ff.
7 Sin: debt, Matt. 6:12	Redemption (like 26)
8 Sorrow (due to sin), 2 Cor. 7:10	Joy, John 16:20
9 Disquiet (due to unfaith), Psalm 42:5	Hope, faith, Heb. 12:1 ff.
10 Darkness (life away from God)	Light, Luke 1:79; John 3:19; 12:35
11 Unrighteousness, Rom. 1:18	Righteousness of God; Jer. 23:6; Rom. 3:19 ff.
12 Self-righteousness, Luke 18:9 ff.	Righteousness of God; Jer. 23:6; Rom. 3:19 ff.
13 Filth of sinful nature, Rom. 1:21 ff.	Cleansing, John 1:29; Psalm 51
The One Through Whom God Effects the Change	
14 1—13	The Anointed One, Psalm 2:2; Matt.16:16
15 1—13	The Servant, Is. 53:13 ff.; Phil. 2:5-8
16 3—7, its enormity, our helplessness	The Sacrifice; Lamb, John 1:29; Heb. 10:12
17 3—7, its enormity, our helplessness	The Priest, Heb. 4:15; 5; 7; 8; 9:24-28
18 3, 6, 13; 1, 10	The Mercy Seat, Rom. 3:25; 1 John 2:1
19 Malice, wickedness, insincerity, 1 Cor. 5	The Passover, 1 Cor. 5:7
20 God unknown to us, John 1:18	The Word, John 1:1-14
21 Temptation, 1, 9, 6, 7	Intercessor, Paraclete, 1 John 2:1; Rom. 8:34
22 Waywardness, 1, 5, 9, 10	Shepherd, Ezek. 34:23; John 10:2 ff., etc.
23 1, 4, man's total plight	Jesus, Savior, Matt. 1:21
24 1, 2, 9, 10	Immanuel, Is. 7:14; Matt. 1:23

330

The Act by Which God Enables the Change

25 6, 11   Christ's undergoing indictment of Law,
                                               Gal. 4:4; 2 Cor. 5:21

26 Bondage under 4—8, Law   Christ's ransom through death,
                                               Matt. 20:28

27 1—7   Christ's death on the cross, Col. 1:22

28 26   Christ's death and resurrection: victory,
                                               1 Cor. 15:57

29 Enormity of the wrath of God, 3   Christ's Going to the Father (cross),
                                               John 14:2

The Message Which Communicates the Change to Men

30 1, 2   The Word of Reconciliation,
                                               2 Cor. 5:18 ff.

31 1—13   The Preaching of the Cross, 1 Cor. 1:18

32 4—12   The Gospel of Christ, to convert,
                                               1 Peter 1:23

33 Continuing damage of sin,   The Gospel of Christ, to build,
      Rom. 7:18 ff.   1 Peter 2:2

34 4, 12   Baptism, Titus 3:4-7; Rom. 6:4

35 6, 9   Holy Communion, 1 Cor. 11:24-26

APPENDIX IV

A Chart for the Critique of a Recorded Sermon

The user will arrange the chart on a legal-size sheet of paper to allow space for his notations.

Text .... Theme ....

Preached at .... Date .... New .... Repeated ....

Number present .... Recording quality good .... fair .... poor ....

Manuscript in pulpit .... Special circumstances ....

Content
    Introduction and approach
    Goal explicit
    Diagnosis explicit
    Gospel explicit
    Gospel relevant to diagnosis
    Text apparent

Style
    Language direct
    Paragraphs coherent and unified
    Sequence of ideas clear
    Illustrations apt
    Conclusion

Delivery
    Mispronunciations
    Articulation
    Voice and breathing
    Inflection
    Rate
    Thoughtfulness

INDEXES

INDEX OF TOPICS

335

imperative to action 189

Experience; see Growth

Exploring
of maladies 37
of text 81

Exposition of text 70, 76, 81

Expository preaching 70, 71, 159; see also Homily
advantage of 70

Extra-Biblical texts 74, 141, 142

Eye contact with hearers 127

Facts 49
checking of 245, 246
and doctrines 313

Faith xi, 16, 17, 39
barriers for 181, 182
goal for non-Christians 64
goals of 17, 88, 179 to 184
importance of 180, 181
pleading for 183, 184
preaching to goal of 179—184
strengthening of 18, 88
term 136, 183, 185
Word of 182, 183
in yourself 179

Family 177, 198
preaching to goals of 197—202
problems of 198, 199
service 201
special opportunities for preaching to 200, 201
worship 200

Faultfinding 187, 239, 240

Feedback 39, 238

Feelings 9
of insufficiency 6, 7
of sadness over sin 25, 26

Fellowship xi, 192, 284

File 220, 227, 233

Filling out divisions of sermon 96, 97

Finding approach 42

Finding meaning of text 81—86

First draft of sermon 103, 104
checking, against working brief 106
reviewing of 106

Flesh 22, 62
as barrier of faith 181
battle against 18
cravings of, and prayer 211
as obstacle 187, 188
preaching as tool of 281

Foolishness of preaching 3, 6, 7, 29

For the church xii, 13, 59, 65

Force 6; see also Persuasiveness

Forgiveness 17, 30, 181, 183
conveyed in sermon 6, 57
mutual 192
sermon as answer to 59

Free form of worship 58

Free text 69, 81, 219

Freedom 44, 45, 136

Freshness 146, 147

Funerals 207

Gathering material 139 to 144

Gestures 51, 52, 115, 117

Getting attention 33, 36, 37, 41—43, 46
of nonmembers 63

Getting meaning from text 82—85

Giving 1, 188, 189, 194, 195

Goals 15, 16, 19
behavior 36, 88
believing 212
church 191, 194—196, 212

confused with means 36

faith 17, 88, 179—184

family 197—202

hope 203—208

life 88, 185—190

persuasion toward 36

in planning sermon 87, 88

of preaching 15—20, 49, 116

of preaching to church 192—194

writing out of 36

God
agents of, for help in ministry 7
applying thrust of 37
as caller of His people 10
as caller of pastor 9
changing power of 6
concern of, for human beings 8, 24
and faith 180
as giver of message xi, 1
as gift to man 1
goals of, for family 197, 198
goals of, for His people 16, 17
hearer's encounter with 49
judgment of 21, 23, 89, 180
love from 291, 292
people of, sound His call 10, 11
plan of 5, 6
power of 1, 6—8, 28
preacher as co-worker with 51
preacher as tool of 24
preaching and 1—32
preaching as act of 3
preaching to goals of 18—20
and rescue 3, 31
word as work of 35
wrath of 23, 30

INDEX OF REFERENCES TO SCRIPTURE

INDEX OF NAMES